# CONEY ISLAND

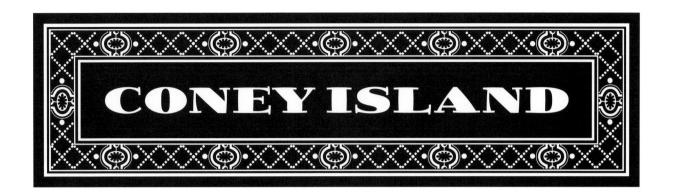

# THE

# PEOPLE'S

# PLAYGROUND

❊

MICHAEL IMMERSO

RUTGERS UNIVERSITY PRESS

*New Brunswick, New Jersey, and London*

LIBRARY OF CONGRESS CATALOGING-IN-PUBLICATION DATA

Immerso, Michael, 1949–

Coney Island : the people's playground / Michael Immerso.

p.cm.

Includes bibliographical references and index.

ISBN 0-8135-3138-1 (cloth : alk. paper)

1. Coney Island (New York, N.Y.)—History.

2. New York (N.Y.)—History.

3. New York (N.Y.)—Social life and customs.

4. Middle class—New York (State)—New York—Social life and customs.

5. Working class—New York (State)—New York—Social life and customs.

6. Amusement parks—New York (State)—New York—History.

7. Resorts—New York (State)—New York—History.

I. Title

F129.C75 I46 2002

974.7′1—dc21      2002020159

British Cataloging-in-Publication information
is available from the British Library.

BOOK DESIGN AND COMPOSITION BY JENNY DOSSIN

Manufactured in the United States of America

# CONTENTS

*Color illustrations appear between pages 56 and 57 and 184 and 185.*

# ACKNOWLEDGMENTS

I WANT TO acknowledge and to express my gratitude to those who encouraged and supported me during the course of this project. I received invaluable assistance from the librarians and staff at several New York City institutions whose collections included much of the primary source material I relied upon in my research. I wish to especially thank the staff at the Brooklyn Collection of the Brooklyn Public Library, the New-York Historical Society, the Museum of the City of New York, and the New York Public Library.

I gained insight from and drew upon the work of a several authors who have explored the history of Coney Island. I owe a special debt to John F. Kasson, whose *Amusing the Million* traces the rise of the amusement park at Coney Island at the turn of the century and examines its impact upon American popular culture; and to Stephen Weinstein, author of "The Nickel Empire: Coney Island and the Creation of Urban Seaside Resorts in the United States," a Columbia University doctoral dissertation. Weinstein's work is particularly thorough in documenting working-class participation at Coney Island at an early date. I gleaned a great deal of information from Edo McCullough's *Good Old Coney Island* and from *Sodom by the Sea: An Affectionate History of Coney Island* by Oliver Pilat and Jo Ranson. Both are well-informed histories of the resort that include substantial anecdotal material. Also helpful were Michael Paul Onorato's oral history of the demise of Steeplechase Park, "Another Time, Another World: Coney Island Memories"; "Coney Island: A Case Study in Popular Culture and Technical Change" by Robert E. Snow and David E. Wright, which appeared in the *Journal of Popular Culture* in 1976; *Cheap Amusements: Working Women and Leisure in Turn-of-the-Century New York* by Kathy Lee Peiss (Philadelphia: Temple University Press, 1986); *Delirious New York: A Retroactive Manifesto for Manhattan* by Rem Koolhas; *The Kid of Coney Island: Fred Thompson and the Rise of American Amusements*, by Woody Register; and Richard Snow's *Coney Island: A Postcard Journey to the City of Fire* (New York: Brightwaters Press, 1984). Snow was also insightful as a collaborator with Ric Burns on the documentary film *Coney Island* (1991). An additional and very helpful source of Coney Island material is Jeffrey Stanton's on-line Coney Island History web-site.

I am also in debt to a number of other authors who have produced insightful works on related topics. On the evolution of the amusement park: *The American Amusement Park Industry: A History of Technology and Thrills* by Judith A. Adams and *The Great American Amusement Parks* by Gary Kyriazi (Secaucus, N.J.: Citadel, 1976). On the history of carousels in America: *A Pictorial History of the Carousel* by Frederick Fried, *The Great American Carousel: A Century of Master Craftsmanship* by Tobin Fraley, Charlotte Dinger's *Art of the Carousel*, and *Fairground Art* by Geoff Weedon and Richard Ward. On the history of roller coasters and the amusement industry in the United States: William Mangels's *The Outdoor Amusement Industry* and *The Incredible Scream Machine: A History of the Roller Coaster* by Robert Cartmell. On the evolution of exposition midways: *Chicago's White City of 1893* by David F. Burg (Lexington: University Press of Kentucky, 1976) and Edo McCullough's *World's Fair Midways* (New York: Arno Press, 1966). On popular culture in America: *Going Out: The Rise and Fall of Public Amusement* by David Nasaw (New York: Basic Books, 1993), *The Unembarrassed Muse: The Popular Arts in America* by Russel B. Nye (New York: Dial Press, 1970), *The Freak Show: Presenting Human Oddities for Amusement and Profit* by Robert Bogdan, *For the Love of Pleasure: Women, Movies, and Culture in Turn-of-the-Century Chicago* by Lauren Rabinovitz (New Brunswick, N.J.: Rutgers University Press, 1998), *Early Motion Pictures: The Print Collection in the Library of Congress, 1894–1912* by Kemp R. Niver (Berkeley: University of California Press, 1967), and *Dancing Till Dawn: A Century of Exhibition Ballroom Dance* by Julie Malnig (New York: Greenwood Press, 1992). On the early history of Brooklyn and its neighborhoods: *Brooklyn! An Illustrated History* by Ellen Snyder-Grenier for the Brooklyn Historical Society (Philadelphia: Temple University Press, 1996) and *The Neighborhoods of Brooklyn*, edited by Kenneth T. Jackson and John Manbeck (New Haven: Yale University Press, 1998).

I am especially appreciative of the support and encouragement I received from the director, editors, and staff at Rutgers University Press, including Marlie Wasserman; Leslie Mitchner, who guided this book from its inception; Marilyn Campbell, who copyedited it; and Jenny Dossin, who designed it. I wish to express my gratitude to Dick Zigun of Coney Island USA for his assistance, and to Patricia Semmel and Rachel Fried for granting me access to materials from Fred Fried's collection. I especially want to thank John Matturri for creating photographs expressly for this book, Linda Lobdell for her assistance with the photographs, and my partner, Elizabeth Ainsley Campbell, whose pursuit of Coney Island artifacts on my behalf both enhanced my collection and prodded me to undertake this book.

# CONEY ISLAND

# INTRODUCTION

CONEY ISLAND at the very beginning of the twentieth century was the uncontested epicenter of America's emerging popular culture. Historian John F. Kasson has called it a laboratory of the new mass culture, where the raw embryonic elements of physical sensation and mechanical invention were tested. Equally important, Coney Island was the prototypical "people's playground" where America's urban workers, those who had heretofore been excluded from the pursuit of leisure, had their day in the sun.

Coney Island was the quintessential American resort: the birthplace of the hot dog, the enclosed amusement park, and the roller coaster. Its history is one of breathtaking transformation and reinvention. Celebrated at its pinnacle for its glittering amusement parks and its enormous crowds of visitors, it was in earlier times a vast seaside pleasure ground with grand hotels, racetracks, beer gardens, gambling dens, concert saloons, and dance halls. It gained notoriety as Sodom by the Sea long before it gave rise to Steeplechase and Luna Park. Its staggering concentration of resources and mechanical devices deployed purely for the purpose of pleasure was unprecedented. Visitors gawked at the Elephant Colossus, at Pain's pyrotechnic spectacles, and at Little Egypt's erotic gyrations. Buffalo Bill's Wild West Show had its premiere season at Brighton Beach and Harry Houdini worked his wonders there. Sigmund Freud paid a visit to Coney Island's Dreamland and is reported to have remarked, "The only thing about America that interests me is Coney Island." Charles Lindbergh ecstatically rode the Cyclone roller coaster and proclaimed it more exhilarating than his solo flight across the Atlantic. Coney's shimmering, incandescent seascape left writers breathlessly straining for adequate words to describe it. Some envisioned a substantial city of brick by the sea. But Coney Island was destined to be a city of lath and of fire, a place of transformation and illusion. A city of transitory wonders.

Coney Island's evolution as an amusement center began during the 1870s and coincided with America's centennial celebration. The world's most popular resort long before its first amusement park appeared, it was hailed as a uniquely American phenomena by José Martí, who called it "that immense valve of pleasure opened to an immense nation." Indeed, to fully understand America, one had first to visit Coney Island. The Old World had not witnessed anything quite like it. By the 1880s it was the center of the mechanical amusement industry and was dubbed the "People's Watering Place." Ready-made for the masses, it glorified speed, motion, and the unfettered human body. It harshest critics decried it as Bedlam by the Sea, but others deemed it a necessary outlet for the masses, a place where the democratic spirit was granted free rein.

Situated at the outer edge of America's metropolis, Coney Island emerged from relative obscurity just as New York was securing its position as America's financial, industrial, and cultural capital. The city was feverishly reinventing itself. In 1882 Thomas Edison installed the first electric street lamps in Lower Manhattan. The Brooklyn Bridge was inaugurated in 1883 and the city's first skyscrapers appeared shortly thereafter. In 1898, the year the United States triumphed in the Spanish American War and emerged as a formidable global power, New York's five boroughs were consolidated, leaving it second only to London among the world's cities. It soon became a magnet for Europe's underclass. By 1900, more than a third of its inhabitants were foreign-born, prompting cultural critic James Huneker to lament that New York had become the "dumping-ground of the cosmos." Arriving at our shores those "huddled masses" caught sight of Coney's fretted towers

before they ever glimpsed Bartholdi's *Liberty*. To Coney Island they came, and Coney gave them a portion of the freedom they yearned for.

Coney Island's early development was financed by railroad men and entrepreneurs who wished to exploit the burgeoning interest in ocean bathing. Austin Corbin, who conceived Manhattan Beach, sought to create an elegant resort in close proximity to New York that would rival Newport, Rhode Island. The creators of Brighton Beach, named after the fashionable English seaside resort, hoped to attract middle-class Brooklynites. At West Brighton, in the very heart of Coney Island, the railroad and hotel men had to contend with a host of small entrepreneurs whose hotels and resorts appealed to the working class. The roots of Coney's West Brighton lay in America's antebellum seaside resorts, in picnic groves such as Jones Woods on Manhattan's East River and Scheutzen Park in New Jersey and, to a lesser extent, in European pleasure grounds such as Vauxhall Gardens in London and the Prater in Vienna. Its amusements mirrored the beer gardens, concert saloons, and dime museums found on New York's Bowery. It had very little in common with Brighton or Newport and is best compared to Blackpool, the English working-class resort on Britain's North Sea that drew its crowds from the laboring classes of Liverpool and Manchester. The result, partly by design, was the division of Coney Island into three separate zones, from east to west, corresponding to social classes. The wealthy summered at Manhattan Beach, the middle class selected Brighton Beach, and the working and poorer classes thronged to

BATHERS AT CONEY, CIRCA 1896.

(MUSEUM OF THE CITY OF NEW YORK, THE BYRON COLLECTION, 93.1.1.1328)

West Brighton. By the 1880s, with more leisure time available to working men and increasing numbers of young working women, more working-class families became consumers of leisure. The era of cheap amusements at West Brighton was in full swing.

Coney Island, and especially West Brighton, thus became a battleground for contending visions of the modern-day resort. Coney confronted "reformers" and "progressives" who sought to impose their idea of wholesome recreation upon the lower classes with a mode of leisure that was emerging from below. The debate sought to determine whether the emerging mass culture would be defined in terms of cultural improvement driven by social intervention, or mass consumption driven by commercial enterprise. Reformers sought to uplift the masses by cleansing Coney and replacing its Bowery with a seaside park, creating a Central Park by the seashore. They envisioned a suitably democratic environment where the classes would mingle together for their mutual benefit. Pitted against them were the entrepreneurs of the emerging amusement industry. The goal of the entrepreneurial classes was quite simply to lure the masses to West Brighton in ever greater numbers. To that end they worked in league with the men who operated the railway and steamship lines that delivered the masses into their hands. The men who ran West Brighton's hotels, bathhouses, and concert halls did not want to improve the masses; they accepted them exactly as they were and catered to their demand for cheap amusement in the form of picnic parties, fraternal gatherings, songfests, and ocean bathing.

The ever-increasing market for suitable amusements for great numbers of formerly marginalized consumers led to the development of the amusement park. A sanitized version of the carnival midway, the amusement park was designed to appeal neither to the elevated rich nor the degraded poor, but was geared toward the middle-class leisure consumer. Its purveyors were pioneers of the mechanical amusement industry. The showmen who created Coney Island's amusement parks drew their inspiration from the expositions held at the century's end. These expositions displayed the avant-garde wonders of technology—the machinery that was remaking the world. It was a world driven by electric dynamos and alternating current, which powered telephones, sewing machines, and incandescent lights—a world of accelerated speed and motion. The amusement entrepreneurs examined the machinery arrayed before them, designed to employ a vast workforce in producing millions of durable goods, and saw instead tools they could employ to create new

forms of play for those vast numbers of bodies. They were particularly inspired by the Midway Plaisance at Chicago's Columbian Exposition of 1893, with its Ferris wheel and beguiling Street of Cairo. The Midway Plaisance institutionalized the carnival midway, incorporating elements of both the exotic and popular culture into a more formal structure. Two years later, in 1895, Paul Boyton unveiled Sea Lion Park at Coney Island. Separated from the hurly-burly of the Bowery, Sea Lion was the first enclosed amusement park. The enclosures surrounding Coney Island's amusement parks enabled the showmen who built them to control the crowds that entered their concessions and to organize them according to a thematic plan. The showmen thus carved out a middle ground between the idealized White City envisioned by the reformers and the less savory aspects of the midway.

By the turn of the century, Coney Island had been transformed into a glittering Eden. Coney's three amusement parks, Steeplechase, Luna Park, and Dreamland, redefined the amusement industry. Fred Thompson's Luna Park was arguably the greatest amusement park ever devised. An entirely original form of environmental sculpture for mass amusement, Luna Park was a dazzling Arcadia of minarets, trellises, spires, promenades, and swirling fountains of electric lights. It established a standard by which all subsequent amusement parks would be measured. Dreamland, the self-proclaimed Gibraltar of the Amusement World, was Coney Island's most opulent amusement park. Although it borrowed many of Luna Park's motifs,

DREAMLAND

(LIBRARY OF CONGRESS)

its creators sought to attract a refined crowd to their park but found that Dreamland's architectural elegance did not impress Coney's masses. George Tilyou's Steeplechase Park employed a master showman's unfailing instinct to delight the audience. The success of Steeplechase lay in its ability to make the crowd a complicit instrument of its own amusement. Tilyou contrived a labyrinth of mechanical amusement devices, slides, and human pool tables to seduce and beguile those who entered his realm. He called his park "the most enchanting and magnetic fun-making resort in the world" and guaranteed "ten hours' fun for ten cents."

The Coney Island of glittering amusement parks seemed to have materialized overnight. This "New Coney" embodied by Luna Park and Dreamland shimmered, even if it did not altogether expunge the Old Coney that sizzled in the Bowery. Twenty million people visited during the summer season of 1909, as compared to 5 million annually who were attracted to

Disneyland when it opened in 1955. The era of the great amusement parks was, however, short-lived. In 1911, Dreamland burned to the ground in a spectacular fire that transformed its 375-foot-high beacon tower into a shaft of flame. Fire was a regenerative element at Coney Island. By periodically burning itself down it was able to re-create itself in a new guise. Combustible in a literal as well as a figurative sense, it was most potent at that point where the illusion of danger ignited into conflagration. The fire that decimated Dreamland began in an attraction called Hell Gate and released lions into the streets. During another of Coney's many fires, seventy thousand people gathered to watch, while just beyond the engulfed area the dancing and concert halls played on.

Elegant Coney Island never entirely rebounded after Dreamland was reduced to ashes. The park was not rebuilt. Sam Gumpertz's Dreamland Circus Sideshow rose in its place and Coney became a house of mirrors populated by Zip the What-Is-It and Joe-Joe the Dog-faced Boy. When the five-cent subway reached Stillwell Avenue in 1920, Coney was resurrected as the Nickel Empire—where the sideshow, the bathhouse, and the wax museum were king. New attractions such as the Wonder Wheel and Cyclone were added to the skyline, and landmarks such as Feltman's Pavilion and the Half Moon Hotel became celebrated icons. Coney had embarked upon its most prosperous era.

Prosperity was cut short when the Depression struck. The Depression cost Coney at least half its attractions, but while its amusement resources were greatly diminished, the crowds were larger than ever. Coney became the resort of last resort for those who could afford little more than the five-cent subway fare and a hot dog at Nathan's. The beach became Coney Island's most enduring attraction and the crowds that swarmed over it gave the resort its signature image. Coney was transformed into an empire of the body, celebrating the human form in all its diversity. Reginald Marsh likened Coney's crowd to the "great compositions of Michelangelo and Rubens." During World War II it became a symbol of the homefront for countless servicemen on leave. Forty-six million people visited Coney Island in 1943.

Coney still drew enormous crowds after the war, but it was now dubbed the "Poor Man's Riviera" and it catered to far fewer middle-class patrons. With greater mobility enabling people to seek recreation elsewhere, Coney Island was soon eclipsed by new theme parks and entertainment resorts such as Disneyland, which recycled some of the very same attractions that had been unveiled by Coney showmen a generation earlier. Luna Park, which for many years had been hobbled by bankruptcy and declining crowds, survived until 1944 when it, like Dreamland, succumbed to fire. At the same time, Coney was waging a protracted battle with Parks Commissioner Robert Moses, who sought to eradicate its amusement zone. As its fortunes declined Moses implemented his redevelopment plans. High-rise housing eventually displaced the neighborhoods that anchored the amusement zone. Beset by crime and urban decay, Coney Island suffered its worst season ever in 1964, when Steeplechase Park closed its doors forever.

CONEY ISLAND BEACH PHOTOGRAPHED BY WEEGEE IN 1940.

(CULVER PICTURES)

Coney Island's landscape was once more transformed. Luna Park's towers and minarets were replaced with a residential complex and Steeplechase Park's Pavilion of Fun was leveled to make room for a housing development that was never built. Through much of the 1970s Coney Island was embattled. Many factors had contributed to Coney Island's decline. It suffered from a debilitating erosion of its amusement resources, crime, the avarice of its landlords, misguided urban renewal, and racial tension. The last two warrant closer examination because they could have been addressed by more careful public policy and planning. Instead, city planners took steps that hastened Coney's decline, exacerbated its racial divisions, and undermined its viability. A campaign to revitalize Coney's amusement zone began with the creation of Coney Island USA in 1980 and continues to the present time. New attractions such as the annual Mermaid Parade and a new baseball stadium have begun to restore some

CONEY ISLAND AMUSEMENT DISTRICT IN THE MID-1950S.

(CITY OF NEW YORK DEPARTMENT OF PARKS AND RECREATION, PHOTO ARCHIVE)

luster to Coney's tarnished image. Old icons such as the Wonder Wheel and the Cyclone roller coaster, after years of neglect, have been awarded landmark status. And a new generation of Americans, including immigrants from the Caribbean and South Asia, has rediscovered Coney Island's beach. New Yorkers have remained loyal to Coney, affectionately embracing it even in its decline as a kind of anti-Disneyland, an unreconstructed Baghdad by the Boardwalk.

Coney Island's name remains a metaphor for the American amusement industry and the hundreds of honky-tonk resorts and amusement parks it has spawned. This Coney Island of song and story, however, tends to obscure and diminish the role that it played in America's cultural evolution. Coney was more than just a laboratory of the nascent amusement industry. Indeed, it is a misnomer to categorize it as an amusement park, although it was home to three great parks. It was, rather, a pleasure resort of a kind that had never before existed, the product of a unique period in American history. Its history is a rich narrative of the way Americans, and particularly immigrants and urban Americans, came to invent their own forms of leisure, and to regard the enjoyment of leisure as part of their national birthright.

# CHAPTER ONE

# CONEY

CONEY ISLAND lies at the southern rim of the Borough of Brooklyn, not quite ten miles from Manhattan. Shaped somewhat like a hammerhead, it has been likened to a "tooth in one jaw of the harbor mouth." It is, in both a literal and a figurative sense, a point of contact, and for millions of immigrants who glimpsed the towers of Dreamland and Luna Park as they passed into New York Harbor, it marked the Atlantic Ocean's outermost edge and the tangible shoreline of America.

The island's western tip, now an exclusive community known as Sea Gate, was once a Native American settlement called Narriockh. It was here that Native American contact with the Europeans first occurred in the New York area. In September 1609, Henry Hudson, who sailed under the aegis of the Dutch East India Company, anchored his ship, the *Half Moon,* in Gravesend Bay and engaged in a brief encounter with the Canarsie inhabitants before going on to explore the river that now bears his name. With the arrival of the Dutch, the marshlands of Coney Island became part of the New Nether-

lands colony. The Dutch renamed it Conyne Eylant after the "conies," or rabbits, that lived among its dunes, and used it as grazing land for their livestock. A sandbar about five miles in length, Coney Island was throughout much of its history really several small islands that were shaped and reshaped by the tides. It ceased being a true island more than a century ago when a portion of the Coney Island Creek separating it from the rest of Brooklyn was filled in.

Although the Dutch drove out the native inhabitants, they did not choose to live there. In 1643 a patent was obtained by Lady Deborah Moody, an English Mennonite, granting her and her fellow colonists title to land held by the Dutch East India Company. The tract, including the grazing land on Coney Island, became the town of Gravesend. The Gravesenders, under Lady Moody's leadership, practiced religious tolerance. The first Quaker meeting in America was held at her house in 1657. The colonists also sought to treat the Native Americans equitably, negotiating a separate agreement with the Canarsie for the island that had already been conveyed to them by the Dutch. However, Coney Island still remained almost entirely uninhabited for almost two centuries and it had few visitors.

The first attempt to exploit the island for use as a summer resort occurred in 1824 when John Terhune, Gravesend town supervisor, proposed the construction of a road linking the town with the island to enhance access to its beach. When the town balked, Terhune and his brother formed the Coney Island Bridge and Road Company and built a causeway across the Coney Island Creek. At the terminus of what became known as the Shell Road, they built a secluded inn called the Coney Island House. The inn provided excellent accommodations, hearty meals, and an unobstructed view of the harbor. Moreover, its guests were advised that those "exposed to the debilitating effects of the hot summer day in New York will find tonic in sea bathing." The success of the Coney Island House led to the creation of a second small inn called the Wyckoff Hotel, erected on the Sand Hills by a Gravesend schoolmaster. Soon several stagecoach lines were providing daily service from the Brooklyn mainland to Coney Island. By the 1840s a sufficient number of excursionists were arriving by carriage to cause some misgivings among the Gravesenders. But, apart from the two hotels, the only other structures on the island at that time were two farmhouses.

In 1844, at the western tip of the island,

THE CONEY ISLAND PAVILION DEPICTED IN AN 1845 TRADE CARD.

(THE BROOKLYN HISTORICAL SOCIETY)

about two miles from the Coney Island House, a small pier was built and daily ferry service was inaugurated. To entice excursionists to their resort the managers of the ferry company built the Coney Island Pavilion. The pavilion was quite modest, a circular open-air enclosure under a large tent with facilities for bathing, dining, and dancing. Rough and a bit rowdy, the pavilion was Coney Island's first organized pleasure grounds. An advertisement promoting it stated: "The natural advantages of this beautiful site upon the western extremity of Coney Island, have received such improvements as to render this an agreeable place of resort. Its facilities for sea bathing in the ocean surf are unsurpassed." Visitors to Coney Island in those early days included Walt Whitman, then an editor at the *Brooklyn Eagle.* Whitman came on one occasion with a party of sixty prominent citizens for an outing to celebrate plans for Brooklyn's new City Hall. The poet and his companions feasted on clams roasted in their own broth in beds covered with brush, drank toasts of champagne, and bathed in the salt surf. It was Coney's seclusion and its rugged and undisturbed vistas, however, that inspired Whitman to revisit time and again the "long bare unfrequented shore . . . where I loved after bathing to race up and down the hard sand, and declaim Homer or Shakespeare to the surf and seagulls by the hour."

The Swedish author Fredrika Bremer, who visited the island at about the same time, was also captivated by its solitary shoreline and its "wild charm." By then, the Coney Island House had gained considerable fame. Its guest list during this period included such notable literary figures as Washington Irving, Herman Melville, and Edgar Allan Poe; statesmen Henry Clay and Daniel Webster; and the showman P. T. Barnum, who visited in 1850 with Swedish songstress Jenny Lind. Meanwhile, at the extreme western end of island, not far from the Coney Island Pavilion, the best-known theatrical figures of the day stopped at the summer house of William Wheatley. Wheatley was an actor of some renown and the stage manager at Niblo's Garden, whose landmark production of *The Black Crook* caused a theatrical sensation in 1866.

The Coney Island House, Wyckoff's Hotel, and a relatively new inn called the Oceanic House sought to attract respectable middle-class businessmen with sufficient means and ample leisure time to justify the long and rather arduous journey to the shore. In contrast, the Pavilion at the island's West End catered to excursionists who came for the day to enjoy an ocean bath or a picnic party. They were a rougher crowd and they mixed easily with the barefooted "coney catchers" and the hunters of fiddler crabs who plied their trade along the beach. The rush of city-dwellers to the seaside prompted diarist George Templeton Strong to decry the encroachment of the metropolis upon the country. "Coney Island," he groused in an entry for 1851, "seems to be nothing more than Church Street transported bodily a few miles out of town." The Pavilion demonstrated that men and women of more modest means could be efficiently delivered to Coney Island, thus establishing it as a bathing resort that could profitably attract all classes. Transportation to the island, however, remained erratic and quite time-consuming. In 1862 the Brooklyn, Bath, and Coney Island Railroad launched the Gunther Line, the first direct rail service from New York to Coney Island, with horse-drawn cars departing every six minutes from Fulton Ferry in Manhattan. Passengers had to change cars at Prospect Park and the entire journey consumed up to two and a half hours. A more appealing trip by steamboat from Peck-Slip or Fulton Ferry required just under an hour to reach the island. There were boats thrice daily. Those who came on the steamboat had the advantage of being able to walk about on the upper or lower deck; they could breathe "a pure atmosphere instead of dust" and could take in the scenery of the Narrows and the Upper Bay. If the boat was not too full there was dancing to music provided by a string band, which performed during the entire trip. By 1864, the Gunther Line had completed the first steam railroad link to Coney Island. The slow-moving line was derided as the Dummy Road by those who complained that it progressed no faster than the horse-drawn cars; however, a fashionable hotel called the Tivoli was built at its terminus. Soon all along the beach in the vicinity of the depot there were signs, flags, and banners indicating small hotels, bathhouses where bathing dresses could be had for twenty-five cents, lager beer bars, and open-air pavilions where one could dine on chops, steak, or chowder and "clams in all styles."

The virtues of the Coney Island clam were celebrated on a par with the charms of its beach. By 1866, ten thousand were consumed daily. Visitors to the island were encouraged to sample the "delicious morsels" drawn from the sea by the "coney catchers" at Ravenhall's and Peter Tilyou's Surf House. Those who hadn't yet sampled them were instructed to "take them one at a time from their blackened shells, that fly open at the lightest touch, and, dipping them in a plate of melted butter suitably seasoned, swallow them before they have ceased to simmer, and follow them quickly with a pickled bean or cauliflower."

At the same time, ocean bathing and its beneficial effects had been gaining increased attention. Saltwater bathing was a relatively new phenomenon in America. It had found favor in England at the very beginning of the eighteenth century when physicians began to prescribe it as a cure for myriad illnesses. Its popularity grew and by the latter half of the century English seaside resorts such as Brighton and Margate were in full swing. It took another fifty years for American resorts such as Cape May and Long Branch at the Jersey shore to develop fully. Americans had to be convinced of the desirability of an ocean bath. Moreover, until about 1850 when it became fashionable at Newport, Rhode Island, beaches, "mixed bathing" was regarded as improper and was frowned upon.

The railroad men and hoteliers of the newer resorts such as Atlantic City and Coney Island were eager to capitalize on the growing popularity of sea bathing in the 1850s and 1860s. They touted Coney's "long, wide, winding, smooth, gently shelving beach," which extended about two and a half miles from the railroad depot to the steamboat landing at the western end. Bathers could wade out a great distance from the shoreline before coming into deep water and there was "ample room for every one to dash about in the foaming surf." The *New York Times* reported that "while thousands of people sweltered in our streets, the Coney Island cars from Brooklyn and the little steamer *Naushon* from the city were carrying hundreds to the island where they enjoyed the luxury of a bath in the surf." A hot July day in 1866 found "more people on the island than were ever known to be there at one time before."

But unlike at Newport, where bathing was viewed solely as a leisurely diversion for the very rich, a bath in the surf at Coney Island was extolled by journalists in Brooklyn and Manhattan as a beneficial tonic for the working man and his family. "There are thousands in this city," the *Times* wrote, who must "through all the 'heated term' of July and August . . . ply their busy tools in almost air-tight shops, where the blasts of the furnaces consume what little air they might have, hammering the red-hot iron upon the anvil, or pouring the molten metal into 'flasks' or working at other callings equally laborious. These men must have their tumble in the surf." The effects of ocean bathing upon the working man were both practical and redemptive, according to the *Brooklyn Eagle*. "A poor, jaded specimen of humanity, encrusted all over with the rust and dust of crowded workshops and confined homes, steps into the beating surf, and before he is aware of it, is like a happy shell fish that has just shed its crustaceous covering, emerging literally born again, and increased in capacity for the endurance of life and hard knocks." Anyone who wished could partake of

this invigorating exercise. A plunge in the surf rendered all men equal, regardless of their station. "Old Ocean is a grand old Democrat," wrote the *Times*. "He buffets the rich and poor alike, who, clad for a bath, present very much the same appearance. It makes little difference when you get under the brine who may be tossing to the right or left of you. If the hue of their filth be ebony, they shall be washed clean without so much as staining the huge waves that sweep over them."

Coney Island's proximity to the city and the easier access to transportation routes made it a magnet for the "rougher class." By 1869 the "upper ten" had abandoned it for beaches more remote, according to *Appleton's* guidebook of that year, leaving Coney uncontested as the "great democratic resort—the ocean bathtub of the great unwashed." Much was written of the disorder that seemed to prevail at the island's West End. The crowds that came on the excursion boats were regularly set upon by a legion of pickpockets, confidence men, swindlers, and "panel-girls." Most odious were the three-card monte players, who plied the beach with their single-legged tables planted in the sand and preyed upon those gullible enough to wager that they could "follow Miss Polly." The king of the monte players was a fellow named Valentine, who gained fame as the "Chow-Chow Man." A newspaper described him as a stout, neatly dressed, mustachioed fellow wearing green-tinted glasses, whose face, nose, and neck were reddened by "the sun beating down under his hat brim, which was somewhat less in width than that of a Quaker."

Despite complaints that the Brooklyn police turned a blind eye to the West End "cappers" and "sports," the crowds at "the point" were greater than at any other part of the island—the bathers who came daily numbered between two and three thousand. The beach was said to be unsurpassed and the view of the ocean and the Narrows was extensive. Around 1874, Michael "Thunderbolt" Norton and his partner, Jim Murray, leased the Coney Island point, site of the old Pavilion. (Norton was a Tammany Hall politician who eventually won appointment as a judge through the patronage of Tammany boss William Marcy Tweed.) Norton and Murray erected the Point Comfort House along with bathing pavilions and facilities for dining and

drinking. Under Norton's sway, the West End, thereafter known as Norton's Point, became even more lawless, serving as a haven for New York gangsters such as Red Leary and "panel-house king" Shang Draper. When Boss Tweed escaped from prison in 1875 he too sought refuge at the point. Norton's Point cast a long shadow across Coney Island and sullied the entire resort's name for many years to come.

At the other end of the island, events were unfolding that would profoundly alter Coney Island's future. Since 1868, William Engeman had been quietly and methodically acquiring land to the east of the railroad depot. Engeman was a colorful figure who amassed a fortune during the Civil War procuring pack animals for

THE CONEY ISLAND BEACH IN 1867.

(HARPER'S WEEKLY)

the Union Army. After the war he was one of the first to recognize the value of Coney Island real estate. The land acquired by Engeman was called Duck Hill. It occupied Coney Island's middle division and was separated from the western half of the island by a creek the Dutch settlers called the Gut. It encompassed several hundred acres of scrubby sand dunes and marshlands. In 1869 Engeman built a small pier to receive steamboats and in 1871 he opened a rather modest inn called the Ocean Hotel. Two years later a wealthy New York banker named Austin Corbin ventured out to Coney Island, heeding the advice of a physician who pre-

scribed a regimen of salt air for his ailing infant. While lodging at the Oceanic House, Corbin had time to explore the land lying to the east of Engeman's property, a desolate swath of sand flats, little hills, and marshlands that the Graves-enders called the Sedge Bank. Its only use was as a hunting stand for shooting sandpipers and snipe. Corbin saw potential and he set out to acquire the entire eastern end of the island. It took several years and a bit of chicanery to complete the task but Corbin eventually assembled more than five hundred acres for his project, which he called Manhattan Beach. There he proposed to build a "resort for the wealthy and

THE "THREE-CARD MONTE" GAME.

*(HARPER'S WEEKLY)*

refined multitude" of New York. Engeman's project, just to the west of Corbin's resort, would in its turn become Brighton Beach.

.　　.　　.

By 1873 Coney Island was attracting crowds numbering twenty-five to thirty thousand visitors on weekends and as many as ten thousand midweek. It was well on its way to becoming the most frequented summer resort in America. Transportation had improved to such a degree that newspapers could now report that "little time is wasted in going to and from the beach." However, the resort still lacked even a medium-sized hotel and had but one railroad line. Few could have foreseen the extraordinary changes that, in just a few short years, would sweep across the island, transforming its landscape and along with it the cultural landscape of America.

# CHAPTER TWO

# THE AMERICAN BRIGHTON

Coney Island's sudden transformation into a popular seaside resort coincided with America's centennial celebration in 1876. In the decade that followed the conclusion of the Civil War, New York City and the neighboring City of Brooklyn grew at a feverish pace, accumulating a reserve of wealth and industrial development matched by a great increase in population. The attraction of a nearby ocean retreat as an outlet for this teeming populace and the benefits to be gained from undertaking its development gave great impetus to Coney Island. "Here," wrote the *New York Times,* "within a stone's throw of some 1,800,000 people, was an island, with a bad name it is true, which only wanted . . . pluck, enterprise, and capital to develop and to render a favorite resort." The most pressing need was an efficient transportation system to deliver great numbers of citizens to the sea. Between 1875 and 1881, four railroad lines, two immense ocean piers, and a highway and ocean concourse were created, enabling vast numbers of people to travel with great speed to and from Coney Island.

Andrew Culver's Prospect Park and Coney Island Railroad was the first to harness Coney Island's potential as a resort for the masses. The Culver Line began service in 1875, transporting passengers from Brooklyn's Park Slope to Coney Island, a distance of five and a half miles, in just fifteen minutes. Culver built a spacious seaside terminal and enlisted New York hotelier Thomas Cable to erect the resort's first true hotel. Cable's Ocean View Hotel measured 575 feet by 158 feet and was surrounded on all sides by piazzas. Culver's railroad soon carried nine thousand passengers daily.

Two years later the Brooklyn Park Commission completed Ocean Parkway. Designed by Fredrick Law Olmsted and Calvert Vaux, this great public road extended five and a half miles from Prospect Park to the ocean. There it intersected a broad roadway called the Concourse, which ran parallel to the sea for more than half a mile. Along the Concourse, twin pavilions were erected, each capable of sheltering 4,500 people, where "safe from the glaring sun or passing squalls . . . the cool, pure air of the ocean can be imbibed." It was, wrote the *Times,* "a grand avenue, which for colossal proportions has scarce an equal in the world," and afforded the metropolis the "breathing spot" it so sorely needed. "When the terrible scourge cholera infantum rages in both New York and Brooklyn it will be to Coney Island that mothers will carry their little ones," the paper wrote. "No better sanitarium in close proximity to a populous centre has ever been imagined."

The New York and Sea Beach Railroad inaugurated service to Coney Island in 1879. The Sea Beach carried passengers from Bay Head to the beach for a reduced fare of twenty cents. Its impressive glass-roofed terminal, the Sea Beach Palace, had formerly served as the United States

Government Building at the Centennial Exposition in Philadelphia before being transported to Coney Island.

That same year the first of Coney Island's two great ocean piers was completed. Built by the Ocean Navigation & Pier Company and supported by 260 tubular iron pilings, it extended 1,200 feet into the sea. Its entire lower level was a bathing pavilion standing directly over the ocean. The floor above served as a promenade lined with iron aquaria, and held a restaurant seating fifteen hundred people, cigar and refreshment kiosks, and a music stand where Grafulla's band played every afternoon and evening. A vast ornamental iron roof covered its galleries and arcades. Draped in bunting and glistening

THE CONEY ISLAND CONCOURSE.

*(HARPER'S WEEKLY)*

in the sunlight, it presented an enchanting sight. "It is an interminable, dainty palace," wrote one astonished visitor, "pinnacled, gabled, arcaded, many-storied, raised on slender columns above the water, like a habitation of some charming lake dwellers." From the vantage point of the great iron pier, the shore seemed gay and ephemeral. At night the pier was illuminated with powerful electric lights. In 1881, a second and equally spectacular pier was completed. Built by the Iron Steamboat Company, it too contained bathing pavilions, arcades, restaurants, and a promenade. At its ocean end was a pavilion rising to a height of two stories. The upper level held a theater, capped by a great

dome illuminated with electric lights, with a seating capacity of twenty-five hundred. The Iron Steamboat Company eventually gained control of both piers. Boats arrived and departed every half-hour. Each boat could transport two thousand passengers, with the capacity to carry forty thousand to the island on peak days.

Culver Plaza lay midway between the two ocean piers. Facing the terminal of Andrew Culver's Prospect Park and Coney Island Railroad, it was landscaped with lawns, flower stands, and plank walkways lined with gas lamps and fountains. Rows of benches lined its plank terrace, providing a splendid view of the ocean. Its most impressive artifact was the 300-

DANCING ABOARD THE IRON STEAMBOAT.

(FRIED COLLECTION)

foot-high Centennial Observatory, an enormous iron tower that once served as a centerpiece at the Philadelphia Centennial Exposition. Culver acquired it at the close of the fair and brought it to Coney Island in 1878. The Iron Tower stood taller than any building in Manhattan. Visitors ascended to its observation deck in steam elevators, each carrying twenty-five people, and could peer into a telescope for views out to a distance of twenty miles. As they climbed the tower's iron frame a band below played "Lurline." Nearby was Professor Janton's Camera Obscura and an unusual refreshment kiosk called the Inexhaustible Cow where, for five cents, one could obtain iced milk drawn by dairymaids from the mechanical udders of a cow, its hide and horns intact and its glass eyes staring out.

All about the plaza in the shadow of the Observatory, hotels, small pavilions, bathhouses, and resorts sprang up. The largest was Paul Bauer's Atlantic Garden, built in 1876. Bauer was an Austrian-born New York hotelier. The Atlantic Garden had one hundred guest rooms, a large dining pavilion that could serve two thousand at one time, and four tower rooms for private banquets and coach parties. The grounds of the hotel were lit with colored globes, electric lights, and a thousand gas jets. Rechristened the West Brighton Beach Hotel a short time after its opening, it was enlarged considerably until Bauer, who styled himself "Mine Host" and sported a handlebar mustache, boasted it had the largest dining hall on Coney Island. It was a popular resort, especially among German American excursionists. Bauer's energetic nature was revealed during an exchange with his wife on their first visit to the island. "This is the worst place I ever saw," she complained. "It can be made the best," Bauer replied. Bauer's hotel stood at the western end of Culver Plaza and faced Cable's Ocean View Hotel, William and Lucy Vanderveer's Ocean Concourse Hotel, and Sleight's dining pavilion. Those who dined at Cable's had their meals served on a balcony overlooking the Observatory where they could enjoy the music of cornetist George Washington Arbuckle. The Vanderveers' hotel, equipped with a spacious carriage house, was a popular destination for those who drove down for the day from Brooklyn. Their expansive Bathing Pavilion housed Doyle & Steubenbord's restaurant. It had an ornamental cupola and a bathing bridge, and space for four hundred bathers. Coney Island's first carousel was erected on the Vanderveers' grounds in 1876.

Just beyond Bauer's hotel lay Charles Feltman's Ocean Pavilion, the largest establishment of its kind at Coney Island. Charles Feltman is celebrated as the inventor of the hot dog. Born in Hanover, Germany, he immigrated to the United States in 1856 at the age of fifteen and settled in Brooklyn. By 1870 he had acquired a bakery shop that supplied pastry and other baked goods to the pavilions and clam houses at Coney Island. Feltman and a wheelwright named Donovan conceived the idea of installing an oven in Feltman's pie wagon, which enabled him to sell boiled sausages wrapped in pastry rolls up and down the beach. Feltman then leased a small pavilion near the Brooklyn, Bath, and Coney Island Railroad depot. When he lost his lease he erected the Ocean Pavilion on a site near

Culver's new terminal. Feltman's pavilion, reminiscent of a German beer garden, included a spacious dining hall and an open-air Deutscher Garden set amid three hundred evergreens and trellisses with overhanging bowers. He hired waiters in white coats, employed a troupe of Tyrolean singers, and served Bavarian lager beer. Feltman was constantly expanding his grounds. Indeed, it was his good fortune to have his property considerably enlarged when the ocean added several acres of sand to his beach. By 1880 he had added a ballroom large enough to ac-

commodate three thousand dancers, a theater, and a carousel. When the Ocean Navigation Company's pier and the Sea Beach Palace terminal opened, they practically delivered their passengers to Feltman's door.

By 1876 Austin Corbin's New York and Manhattan Beach Railroad was ready to proceed with its ambitious plans to develop a fashionable resort at the eastern end of Coney Island. The imposing Manhattan Beach Hotel opened in July 1877. Designed by the architect J. Pickering Putnam in the Queen Anne style, the hotel

CONEY ISLAND BATHING PAVILION.

(PHOTO BY RICHARD HOE LAWRENCE. COLLECTION OF THE NEW-YORK HISTORICAL SOCIETY, 32411)

BATHERS NEAR THE IRON PIER. HEEDING THE ADVICE OF NOTED PHYSICIANS SUCH AS JOHN H. PACKARD, BATHERS WORE WOOLEN OR FLANNEL SUITS AND BROAD-BRIMMED HATS. WOMEN'S BATHING DRESSES WERE OF TWO PARTS: A BLOUSE WITH LOOSE-FITTING SLEEVES AND PANTALOONS CUFFED AT THE KNEES AND UPHELD BY SUSPENDERS. SUITS WERE OFTEN MAROON OR BLUE, COLORS THAT WERE DEEMED LESS LIKELY TO BE BLEACHED BY THE SALT WATER.                    (LIBRARY OF CONGRESS)

had a length of 660 feet with 360 guestrooms, and was alternately three and four stories high, crowned with towers, turrets, and dormers. Painted a pleasant shade of ocher, it was surrounded by a spacious verandah eighteen feet wide. Meals were served in a grand dining hall in the west wing that seated over one thousand. There were additional dining areas throughout the hotel, as well as a piazza that served four thousand guests at one time. The hotel was sur-

rounded on all sides by a broad esplanade with manicured lawns extending to the sea, lined with floral stands of heliotrope, lobelia, coleus, and geranium. The grounds included a large picnic pavilion, housed in a structure that formerly served as the Brazilian building at the Philadelphia Centennial Exhibition, and a bathing pavilion. The bathing pavilion stood two stories high and was 520 feet in length with space for twenty-two hundred bathers. It held an amphitheater with a bandstand shaped like a scallop shell where bands played in the afternoons and evenings. The amphitheater was enclosed on three sides and afforded guests "a sheltered and luxurious resting-place from which to watch the amusing antics or petty mishaps of the bathers." The entire grounds were protected by a sea-wall extending a half-mile, atop which was a boardwalk. Former president Ulysses S. Grant was present at the opening of the hotel and an enormous fireworks display marked the occasion. The prestigious Union Club, the Union League, and the University Club soon took up summer residence there.

The Manhattan Beach Hotel provided accommodations for excursionists and short-term guests; however, Corbin also wished to attract wealthy New York families who might desire to encamp at his resort for the entire season. To entice them he built the lavish Oriental Hotel. Standing a little more than a quarter mile east of the Manhattan Beach Hotel, the Oriental abandoned the Queen Anne style in favor of Eastern and Moorish flourishes. Its length was 477 feet and it rose six stories to a height of 100 feet. It had eight round towers, 12 feet in diameter, capped with minarets that rose to a height of 118 feet. There were also forty-three smaller minarets, making a total of fifty-one. Its sixth floor had a promenade at a height of 72 feet surrounding a central pavilion with views in every direction. The exterior was painted green. The hotel had 346 rooms of various sizes furnished in the Eastlake style and could entertain nine hundred guests. The Oriental opened its doors in 1880 with President Rutherford B. Hayes in atten-

PROMENADING NEAR THE ORIENTAL HOTEL AT MANHATTAN BEACH.

(COLLECTION OF THE NEW-YORK HISTORICAL SOCIETY, GEO. P. HALL COLLECTION, 66786)

dance. It quickly became summer headquarters of Thomas Platt, a Republican Party boss. When the Oriental opened, the *Times* wrote approvingly:

> What changes, what great improvements have been and are being made at Manhattan. Chief among them is, of course, the new hotel. It is called the Oriental, and reminds one of the story of the great Alladin. Two months ago the site of the immense structure was a sandy waste; now it is covered by probably the most complete hotel that adorns any seaside resort on this continent. Mr. Corbin has rubbed his wonderful lamp, and a building, a marvel of architectural beauty, has sprung into the air.

Corbin's grounds extended two and a half miles from neighboring Brighton Beach to the eastern tip of the island. A tiny Marine Railroad ran from Brighton Beach Bath House to the Marine Terminal at Manhattan Beach, with its terminus at the Point Breeze Pavilion at land's end where guests came for Rhode Island clam bakes and a view toward Rockaway. To control access to his resort, Corbin built a fence around it and hired Pinkerton detectives to patrol the grounds and ensure that it was "free from plebian intrusion." Corbin went further, however. In 1879 he excluded Jews from Manhattan Beach, decrying them as offensive to the "class of people who are beginning to make Coney Island the most fashionable and magnificent watering place."

The development of Manhattan Beach gave further impetus to William Engeman, who re-tained the land just west of Corbin's resort. Engeman gained a great advantage with the opening of Ocean Parkway and the Concourse, which brought carriage traffic almost to the door of his Ocean Hotel. In 1878 he erected the two-story Brighton Bathing Pavilion with accommodations for twelve hundred bathers. A unique feature was the pavilion's arched "bathing bridge" thrust out from the changing rooms on the second story and extending some 213 feet over the sand to the ocean's edge. The footbridge allowed bathers to visit the surf without crossing the beach. At the foot of the bridge an electric lamp was installed to permit evening sea baths. The nightly sport of "electric bathing" became quite popular, as bathers gathered around an illuminated maypole and plunged into the surf. A year later Engeman created the Brighton Beach Racing Association and built the first of Coney Island's three racetracks.

By then a Brooklyn consortium had created the Brooklyn, Flatbush, and Coney Island Railroad. The railroad's board of directors included many of the city's most influential figures, who wished to create a resort to rival Manhattan Beach. Its president, former mayor Henry C. Murphy, was instrumental in the building of the Brooklyn Bridge. The railroad acquired half of Engeman's property and in 1878 built the three-story, 174-room Brighton Hotel. Built in the Gothic cottage style, and comparable in size to the Manhattan Beach Hotel, the Brighton rose alternately from three to five stories high. Its length was 525 feet with a wide verandah on the first floor and a piazza on the second extending the entire length of the building. Like those of its rival at Manhattan Beach, its rooms had Axminster carpets and Eastlake furnishings. Its exterior grounds, which included a music pavilion, were laid out in greensward, with serpentine paths and flower parterres. The hotel, said one admirer, "rises out of the sea all quaint corners and gables and hooded sun-shades and piazzas . . . a fairy-like piece of architecture." The New York Club and the Bullion Club soon took up residence at the Brighton. From its inception, however, the Brighton was less pretentious than its neighbors to the east and appealed more broadly to the Brooklyn's middle class.

*Leslie's Illustrated Newspaper* called it a "golden promise to those who toil and spin when the mercury is coquetting with the nineties, and who long, with a thirst of fever, for the fresh gladsome caresses of the healthy-giving breeze from the sea." Among the early visitors to Brighton Beach was African American abolitionist leader Frederick Douglass.

The astonishing pace of these developments left contemporary journalists breathless. Practically overnight Coney Island had achieved a national reputation comparable to that of Niagara Falls or Long Branch, New Jersey, "the sum-

THE BRIGHTON BEACH HOTEL. A DECADE AFTER ITS COMPLETION, SEVERE BEACH EROSION THREATENED THE HOTEL. IN 1888, THE ENTIRE 5,000-TON STRUCTURE WAS JACKED UP AND PLACED ON 112 RAILROAD FLATCARS ATTACHED TO 6 STEAM ENGINES AND MOVED 600 FEET INLAND.

(COLLECTION OF THE NEW-YORK HISTORICAL SOCIETY, GEO. P. HALL COLLECTION, 66787)

mer White House," and had secured its position as "the people's watering place." About twenty million dollars had poured into the resort in a space of less than seven years, producing its marvelous grid of railroad lines and steamship piers, hotels and pavilions, its Ocean Parkway and its Concourse. "Probably no great business enterprise," the *New York Times* observed, "combining in so large a degree public benefit and private profit has ever been conducted in a more liberal spirit or with greater intelligence than the transformation of Coney Island from a dreary waste to a Summer city by the sea." Those who came to visit after a short absence were stunned at what they discovered. Coney was no longer the resort of the "capper" and the "thimble rigger." "The famous 'Chow-Chow' man," wrote the *Times,* "will have to seek other pastures." Indeed, as early as 1877 the *Times* was questioning whether Coney was still the "people's resort" or whether it had become something else entirely. The paper pronounced it "about half and half." Mechanics and small tradesmen made up fully half the crowd; clerks, salesmen, merchants, politicians, brokers, and persons of independent means supplied the other half. However, all classes of people found something to their liking there. By 1879 estimates of the number of visitors on the Fourth of July for the first time exceeded one hundred thousand.

.     .     .

What Coney Island became after 1875 was something entirely original and quite distinctly American. Prior to that date its progress had been stalled, mostly out of concern over its proximity to the metropolis. But rather than descend into a "saturnalia of vulgarity," as some had feared, the crowds drawn to Coney Island were orderly and well behaved. William H. Bishop, writing in *Scribner's Magazine,* compared it to the Centennial Exhibition. "It is a Centennial of pleasure, pure and simple, without any tiresome ulterior commercial purpose, held amid refreshing breezes by the sea. There is the same gay architecture, the same waving flags, the same delightful, distracting whirl, the same enormous masses of staring, good-natured, perpetually marching and counter-marching human beings." Coney Island's "essential character," wrote Bishop, "is bound up with the crowd." José Martí, who visited Coney Island in 1881, wrote about it with equal amazement. What most astonished Martí wasn't the "murmurings of lovers, the bathhouses, and the operas sung from atop tables in the cafes," or even the "majestic beach and the soft still sunlight," but rather its prodigious nature.

> The amazing thing there is the size, the quantity, the sudden tangible outcropping of human activity, that immense valve of pleasure opened to an immense nation, those dining rooms which, at a distance, seem the pitched camp of an army, those promenades that for a distance of two miles seem like carpets of heads, that daily overflow of a prodigious nation onto a prodigious beach, that mobility, that quality of advance, that purposefulness, constant change, feverish rivalry of wealth, that

monumental aspect of the whole that makes this land of amusement worthy of measuring itself against the majesty of the nation which supports it, the ocean that caresses it and the sky that crowns it; that flowing tide, that overwhelming and irresistible expansiveness and the taking for granted of the marvelous: these are the things that amaze.

An Englishman who visited at about the same time was somewhat less impressed. "Coney Island," he wrote, "is a reproduction in miniature of the United States, an epitome in fact of the great country—as active, as pushing, as materialistic, as unartistic. To New York one goes for business, to Coney Island for pleasure." Its crowds reminded him of "Margate in the summer months, with an admixture of coloured folk."

It was the ingenious nature of Coney Island that it lent itself to all classes and tastes. With the completion of its three great hotels, the island was efficiently subdivided into four zones that mirrored to a remarkable degree the class divisions of the metropolis. Manhattan Beach, segregated to an extent from the rest of the island, was a bastion of the very rich; Brighton Beach, the creation of Brooklyn merchants and entrepreneurs, was patronized by the middle classes of the two cities; the island's middle zone, now called West Brighton, enjoyed very wide appeal and attracted chiefly middle-class and working-class daily excursionists; while Norton's Point at the island's west end solidified its unsavory reputation as a resort of

AFRICAN AMERICAN FAMILY AT CONEY ISLAND BEACH, CIRCA 1880, PHOTOGRAPHED BY GEORGE B. BRAINERD.

(BROOKLYN MUSEUM OF ART/BROOKLYN PUBLIC LIBRARY–BROOKLYN COLLECTION)

the underclasses. This natural and apparently seamless division of the resort did not pass unnoticed. "Along that stretch of sandy beach," the *Times* observed, "thoughtful provision has been made for the multifarious wants of the pleasure-seeker, and due regard has been made for the greatest diversity of taste. Between turtle and champagne at the Oriental Hotel and roast clams and lager at Norton's Point there is a regular gradation." The result, the paper noted, was a "natural classification of the visitors," which was "mutually agreeable from either the democratic or aristocratic point of view."

The diversity of tastes at Coney Island gave rise to a steady proliferation of "diversions not ordinarily attainable at the seashore." Although peddlers and catchpenny amusements were excluded from Manhattan Beach, they were everywhere present from Brighton to Norton's Point. Between those opposite poles a thousand and one amusements could be had such as were found at any country fair, carnival midway, or minstrel show, some occupying permanent structures, some under tents fronted by garishly painted valentines, some offered by hawkers strolling the beach. The strolling peddlers and outdoor amusements gave Coney Island an air of a perpetual feast. Weight-guessers, test-your-strength and test-your-lung machines, and shooting galleries were in abundance, as were archery, ring-the-cane, Aunt Sally, and ball toss games. There were scales upon which to weigh oneself, tintype stands and itinerant photographers, and a silhouette artist who cut portraits from bits of black paper. There were jugglers who breathed fire, acrobats performing "feats of

ground and lofty tumbling," a lovely Circassian girl who charmed snakes, and an escape artist who presented himself bound with rope from head to foot. The peanut and popcorn peddlers all did a fine business as did those who sold goggles of smoked or colored glass. Peddlers offered all manner of goods, everything from a salve for wooden legs to exotic flowers fashioned from the skins of fish. Straw-hatted, bare-footed clam, crab, and lobster peddlers sold their wares from canopied boats on the beach. Vendors in wagons sold peaches, apples, and watermelons. A band of Negro bone-guitar and banjo players whose leader sang and acted out "Mulligan's Guards" and other Irish airs reaped a harvest of nickels, as did the fortuneteller with her little glass demons that danced and jumped in long tubes. She charged ten cents and was, by one account, "a damsel whose transcendent beauty is enhanced by a small patch of court-plaster on her chin."

The Seaside Aquarium, which opened in 1877 after the completion of Ocean Parkway, was one of Coney Island's earliest attractions. Part aquatic menagerie, zoological garden, and aviary and part music hall, its collection of marine curiosities included a man-fish, a woman-fish, and an assortment of sea creatures and marine mammals displayed in tanks. It also exhibited performing horses, bears, giraffes, ostriches, trained birds, and a conjoined pair of human twins. Professor Hutchings gave instructive lectures, and there were song-and-dance acts, a Punch-and-Judy show, a magician, a slack-wire juggler, a "Chinese impersonator," and an "imitator of animals." A steam orchestrion played in the cupola of the two-story building that also served as a Gravesend police substation.

The Aquarium stood at the west end of the Concourse, alive with handsome carriages and gay couples promenading. Strolling to the east, at the Brighton Beach Bathing Pavilion one could visit the Midget's Palace, where the Lilliputian Opera Company performed in a hall that held about seven hundred people. Around 1883, G. B. Bunnell established a dime museum there. Bunnell's Brighton Museum, styled after his New York concession, presented a Convention of Curiosities that included eleven-foot-tall Colonel Routh Goshen, whom Barnum had exhibited as the Palestine Giant; Dahoma the Giant from Jacksonville; Major Tot, who weighed ten and a half pounds; Richard James the fat boy, "nine feet around the waist"; and Miss Nellie Walker the albino lady, who asserted, "I'm not a Madagascar or a Moorish lady. I was born in Paterson, New Jersey." There was also a bearded lady, an armless boy who wrote with his toes, a Hindoo lady, and a marionette show.

The greatest number of amusements was concentrated on the grounds of the Centennial Observatory at what was now called the West Brighton Terrace. Here were Forrester's Patented Steam Swings, Looff's carousel, and Vandeveer's pavilion with Morris & Hickman's Museum. Here the Spanish students and mermaids gave their exhibitions flanked by Bohemian glassblowers and William Lord's Egyptian donkeys that no amount of beating could coax along. Here were velocipedes and flying horses, and "machines of great size capable of riding fifty to a hundred people at one time." Here also were countless tent shows with minstrels and marionettes, a serpent's den advertising a boa "a hundred feet in length" but actually about one-fifth that long, and Colonel Green's Megalaloscopic Ponti Venezia Privilegiato and Polemiscope housed in a box-sized enclosure where one could glimpse "life-like moving wonders" for a nominal fee. A small octagonal building near the Observatory sheltered Henry Janton's Camera Obscura. When its doors were closed and the chamber was in darkness, moving images from without, captured by a magnifying lens and reflecting mirror, were projected onto a revolving disk. A guidebook issued in 1880 observed that "the miniatures are so distinct that the movements of the eyes and lips of persons half a mile away can be observed distinctly." Admission was ten cents and dozen people could enter at a time. Janton also exhibited a device called a Georama, displaying the "finest revolving views true from nature ever placed before the public," and claimed it was the only one of its kind in the country. At Feltman's theater Professor Seeman employed an "electro-motor" and other devices to produce wondrous "dissolving views" and fountains that spouted jets of color while his daughter floated through the air. The program included a pair of blind musicians who performed piano and violin duets. The nearby Brighton Theater at the ocean end of the New Iron Pier proclaimed itself "the only theater in the world located a quarter of a mile out in the ocean." It presented operatic works and variety shows every afternoon and evening "in the style of the famous summer gardens of Europe."

Although catchpenny diversions and peddlers were banished from Manhattan Beach, that resort did not lack amusements. Manhattan Beach Hotel had daily balloon ascensions in Professor King's captive air balloon, the *Pioneer*. An intrepid aeronaut, Professor King had first unveiled his balloon at the Philadelphia Centennial Exhibition. A crowd of thirty thousand was on hand as he embarked on a long westward journey, but an uncooperative wind set him down a few hours later in New Jersey. He came to Coney Island in advance of a proposed flight across the Atlantic Ocean. His handsomely painted balloon was sixty-five feet in diameter and resembled a "circular circus poster" with its name inscribed in big letters. It was housed in a mysterious-looking enclosure that held the gasworks used to inflate it, scores of sandbags, and a steam engine that helped steer it back to earth. The balloon was tethered to a 1,200-foot-long cable and could accommodate ten people at a time in a wickerwork car suspended beneath it. There was an amphitheater for those who chose to observe but not ascend.

The Alexandra Exhibition Company was housed in a quadrangular arena not far from

ESPLANADE NEAR THE NEW IRON PIER.

(PHOTO BY RICHARD HOE LAWRENCE. COLLECTION OF THE NEW-YORK HISTORICAL SOCIETY, 32356)

JAPANESE FIREWORKS DISPLAY AT MANHATTAN BEACH.

(*LESLIE'S ILLUSTRATED NEWSPAPER*)

nightly tableau of magnesium balloons, asteroid rockets, silvery fire-wheels, floating stars, glittering blossoms, spiraling serpents, and fiery fountains. In the afternoons there were equally fantastic aerial displays of Japanese pyrotechnics, with canisters fired high into the air discharging brightly limned paper figures of dragons and birds and "strange animals peculiar to Japanese zoology," which, sometimes held aloft by kite strings, floated over the heads of the spectators below. Not wanting to be outdone, Brighton Beach enlisted the services of Messrs. Warden and McMahon from London's Crystal Palace for their own nightly displays, while West Brighton staged exhibitions of American fireworks.

In 1883 Pain introduced a grand pyropageant called "The Bombardment of Alexandria." Described as "a magnificent naval and military spectacle, prepared in England at great expense," it employed 350 actors dressed as Arabs, soldiers, and seamen. It was presented in tandem with a "Fairy Land and Feast of Lanterns," which illuminated Manhattan Beach with ten thousand prismatic lamps and Chinese lanterns. That Fourth of July, the Observatory enjoyed its biggest day's business ever and Lucy Vandeveer's bathing pavilion had long lines all day. "The Bombardment of Alexandria" was a great success and for that special occasion included a portrait of General Washington, the Falls of Niagara, Aladdin's Jeweled Tree, Fiery Phoenix, and innumerable rockets. There was a grand concert at the Brighton Theater and afterward the Iron Steamboat Company presented aquatic fireworks on the ocean between the two piers.

King's enclosure. It was under the direction of James Pain, self-proclaimed "pyrotechnist of Her Majesty the Queen," who had come to Coney Island from London to inaugurate Manhattan Beach with a spectacular display of English fireworks. He remained in residence there for the next twenty-five years. Pain staged pyrotechnic spectacles and panoramas, re-creating historical events such as "The Defeat of the Spanish Armada" and "The Destruction of Pompeii" with extravagant effects, rapid changes of scenery, and hundreds of costumed actors. Professor King sometimes assisted by dropping fireworks from his balloon. Pain's pyrotechnic exhibitions turned Manhattan Beach into a

That same year, Coney Island witnessed the appearance of an entirely new and undeniably American form of amusement. "Buffalo Bill's Wild West Show was born in Brooklyn in 1882," according to Dexter Fellows, a publicist for William Cody. Cody and future partner Nate Salisbury were performing at Brooklyn theaters when the two men first outlined plans for a combination show. Cody inaugurated his "Wild West, Rocky Mountain, and Prairie Exhibition" the following year in Omaha, Nebraska, and concluded the season with a five-week run at Coney Island in August 1883. After initially being set up at the Prospect Park Fair Grounds, the show was transferred to Brighton Beach, where an amphitheater was constructed, equipped with calcium and electric lights for evening performances. Two shows were given daily before crowds that sometimes exceeded five thousand people. The elaborately staged panorama of the American West included buffalo herding, roping, trick riding, a re-creation of the Pony Express, exhibitions of marksmanship by Doc Carver (who shared top billing with Cody), a dramatic reenactment of an attack upon the Deadwood stage, and the burning of a settler's cabin and "capture and torture of the inmates by the Indians." The *Brooklyn Eagle* proclaimed, "No form of amusement that has been offered to the public is at once so unique, so replete with life and color, inspiriting, entertaining, and instructive as the 'Wild West.'" Cody, who had enjoyed an earlier stint as a performer at the Coney Island Aquarium, took up residence at the Brighton Hotel and, in a letter to his sister, noted that "the papers say I am the coming Barnum."

.    .    .

The air of perpetual spectacle and revelry at Coney Island encouraged those stopping at its hotels and dining places to consume vast amounts of food and drink. The crowd dining at the Manhattan Beach Hotel on the Fourth of July in 1883 required the services of 26 cooks, 7 bakers and pastry chefs, and 306 waiters, and no less than 7,000 pounds of beef, 1,800 pounds of lobster, 1,200 pounds of rack of lamb and mutton, 1,500 pounds of bluefish, 20,000 clams, and vast quantities of wine and other beverages to wash it down. Those of lesser means patronized the sausage roasters and sandwich pavilion, such as Doyle & Steubenbord's near the Iron Pier. Many brought their own picnic baskets to the dining pavilions, where they were welcomed, and could quench their thirst with beer, cider, or tall glasses of mineral water. Coney was dubbed the "great national chowder pot" and clams were available in countless forms. One could dine on chowder at the Hotel de Clam or enjoy a "genuine old style Coney Island clam roast" while taking in the show at the Louisiana Serenaders.

.    .    .

Musical entertainment was a constant presence at Coney Island. At Culver Plaza the celebrated cornetist George Washington Arbuckle gave concerts with Downing's 9th Regiment Band. Graffula's 7th Regiment Band performed at the Iron Pier, and Carlberg's Ochestra gave afternoon and evening concerts from a gallery overlooking the grand concourse of the Sea Beach Palace under its hundred-foot-high dome. At Manhattan Beach, Patrick Gilmore's 22d Regiment Band featured Jules Levy, the dashing "king of cornetists." Gilmore, a consummate showman, would occasionally perform the Anvil Chorus from *Il Trovatore* with fifty men pounding on anvils, and sometimes concluded concerts with artillery fire. At Brighton Beach, Admiral Neuendorf's Naval Band was in residence, while Conterno's 23d Regiment Band performed Wagner's "To Thee This Flower I Send" and Donizetti's "La Favorita" at Bauer's West Brighton Hotel, which also claimed the only band composed entirely of women, the Vienna Female Orchestra. Bands performed at the smaller hotels as well and everywhere present were the brass bands that "neither the authority of man nor the awful powers of nature can stop or control." They were "Bedlam and Pandemonium combined," a critic complained.

Choral societies and fraternal organizations staged summer gatherings and songfests at Coney Island. Feltman's Ocean Pavilion and the Sea Beach Palace played host to the Harmonia Maenerchoir and the Leiderkranz, with thousands in attendance. The Arion Society's festival at Paul Bauer's West Brighton Hotel in 1879 was described by one witness as "the most remarkable affair of its kind which has ever been attempted in this country." The hotel and its grounds were extravagantly decorated. Over its main entrance an enormous transparency depicted Arion in a shell chariot drawn by sea monsters, while on its roof and towers were fantastic life-sized silhouettes of dancers, fat men, lean men, cats, and "all the fancy forms the Arion mind could conjure up." The piazzas surrounding the hotel were afire with Chinese and Japanese lanterns strung between the gas candelabra posts and atop the roof, rising in double rows that climbed to the flagstaffs crowning its towers. The piazza facing the shoreline was decorated with papier-mâché models of imaginary sea monsters, huge snails, lobsters, and creatures of the deep, while along the beach "Neptune's three fiery steeds stood rampant" and Arion's dolphin "sat on his fins with a fiery expression in his eyes and his red tongue lolling out as if he wanted a drink." The galleries and ballroom were festooned with flags of every nation, Chinese lanterns, bunting of blue, red, and gold, and heraldic and armorial shields adorning the facades, columns, and rafters. There were afternoon concerts by the Red Hussars Band and the Arion Society chorus with an eighty-piece orchestra. However, it was at nightfall that the amusements began. With blue and red lights casting their reflections over the waves and skyrockets cascading through the air, Arion emerged, mounted his dolphin, and put out to sea to greet Neptune astride his horses. Arion, shaped like a firkin of butter, laughed heartily while Neptune, a stalactite crown resting upon gray locks surrounding a jocund face, saluted with his trident. The entire party, including a court of Tritons and Nereids, came ashore on a catamaran bearing an enormous sea serpent, which, when cut open at the hotel, was found to contain choice items such as champagne, tongue sandwiches, bonbons, and a cornucopia of other treats. A fireworks display followed, with Bengal lights, revolving wheels, and fire balloons. Dancing, feasting, and promenading went on well past midnight, and the last steamer did not depart until 3:00 A.M. About fifteen thousand people were on hand.

Indeed, it was at night that the island reached a crescendo of spectacle and revelry, when the bands sounded their gayest and loudest and garlands of colored lights illuminated and transformed the darkness, turning the Observatory into a fiery cobweb, etching the Iron Pier with lanterns of yellow, red, and green, with electric lights "suspended from high like celestial orbs." "Were such spectacles arranged for a day and night only, on the occasion of some important fete, they would pass into history," observed William H. Bishop, "but here they are for every day and every night the whole summer long." José Martí, describing the same scene, wrote, "It seems that all the stars that populate the sky have fallen suddenly into the ocean in four colossal clusters." It was night when the island was "thronged with the toilers of the great city," the common people who "enjoy their liberty the more because of the recent confinement of the day," when the Concourse was crowded with the carriages of those who came to gaze at the weird play of the light upon the waves inscribed by the fireworks and countless gas jets that left the beach almost as light as day from the great twin piers to Manhattan Beach. "What beauty at night!" Martí exclaimed.

# CHAPTER THREE

# THE ELEPHANT COLOSSUS

DURING THE winter of 1884 an extraordinary structure began to acquire shape on the sands immediately west of the esplanade of the Sea Beach Palace. It was an immense wooden carcass shaped like an elephant that bore on its back a howdah crowned with a gilded crescent. Gazing out over the ocean from Surf Avenue, it rose to a height of 150 feet. Dubbed the Elephantine Colossus, this massive creature was the most astounding edifice yet contrived on the island and stood apart from the cavernous hotels and railroad terminals that had preceded it. Its length from the hind legs to the tip of the trough in which its enormous trunk rested was 150 feet. Its legs alone were 18 feet in diameter and its tusks were 40 feet long. The forelegs contained a cigar store and diorama and the hind legs held circular stairways leading to the rooms contained above. Its entire body was sheathed in a skin of blue tin. Although initially conceived as a hotel, the Elephant served primarily as a concert hall and amusement bazaar and the canopied howdah atop its back functioned as an observatory. Within it were thirty-one rooms that varied in shape and size, including a grand hall, a gallery, various amusement and novelty stalls, and a museum where the creature's left lung would have been. Telescopes enabled visitors to peer out through the Elephant's glass eyes. It was set amid restaurants, saloons, shooting galleries, and photography booths. The Elephant opened for inspection in August 1884, although one of its immense ears still lay unattached on the ground. It was completed in May 1885. A brass band played under its stomach, flanking a star-shaped flower garden. Visitors were awestruck. "The work is really an architectural wonder," one writer exclaimed. "It bursts upon the astonished gaze of passengers on the in-coming European steamers, it gives them their first idea of the bigness of some things in this country." Others were less convinced of the artistic merit of the structure for, despite its imposing scale, it was essentially a commercial enterprise. A writer for *Scientific American* observed:

The Colossal Elephant at Coney Island has

not been favored with much serious public attention, owing to the fact principally that it is not an artistic work, and secondly, because it is the project and property of a stock company, whose unexalted aim was to rear a structure that would serve, not so much to elevate the public mind artistically, nor to stand as a monument to some of our noted forefathers, but rather to abstract the unwary dime from the inquisitive sightseer.

Nevertheless the article's author provided an architectural tour of the innards of the beast. The Elephant became one of West Brighton's premier attractions and the phrase "seeing the elephant" became synonymous with a trip to Coney Island to view the Colossus and explore the body of the immense pachyderm.

That season of 1884 indeed proved a watershed at Coney Island. That spring La Marcus Thompson introduced an amusement invention called the Switchback Gravity Railway. Thompson's device, installed at the corner of West Tenth Street, was the first roller coaster ever built in the United States and the first device of its kind constructed solely for the purpose of amusement. The Switchback was primitive. Passengers climbed a 50-foot-high flag-draped loading station and boarded a train. The cars, propelled by gravity, coursed downward along a 600-foot-long undulating wooden track at a speed of about six miles an hour until gradually coasting to a stop near the crest at the other end of the track. There the passengers disembarked and waited briefly at a second loading station while the train was switched to the opposing track. They then reboarded for the return trip. An early account of the coaster described it as a sort of "summer coasting hill," which whirled riders along a "frightful rate of speed." The *New York Herald* observed that it was "the prevailing impression among the onlookers that it was a question of but a very short time when somebody would be killed on the new-fangled arrangement." But the ride was an immediate success upon its inauguration in June 1884. Admission was five cents and lines formed early in the morning as riders waited up to three hours for a chance to board it. It grossed as much as seven hundred dollars in a single day.

The immense popularity of Thompson's coaster prompted others to enter the field. A second coaster was installed that same summer by Charles Alcoke near the New Iron Pier. Alcoke's gravity ride, called the Serpentine Railway, had sideways-facing seats. It improved upon Thompson's design by linking the two tracks together, forming a continuous oval. The following year Philip Hinkle, who had filed a patent for a coaster a year earlier than Thompson, erected a gravity device at Coney Island with several unique features. Hinkle's coaster was elliptical in design, with a track more steeply graded. It had forward-facing seats and was the first coaster in America equipped with a mechanical conveyer to lift the cars to the top. It was arguably the first true roller coaster.

.   .   .

The architectural audacity of the Elephant Colossus and astounding success of the Switch-

THE ELEPHANT COLOSSUS AND SEA BEACH PALACE VIEWED FROM THE OBSERVATORY TOWER. ALTHOUGH IT REMAINED A POPULAR LANDMARK, THE ELEPHANT NEVER PROVED A FINANCIAL SUCCESS. IT WAS ABANDONED AND IN 1896 IT BURNED TO THE GROUND IN A SPECTACULAR FIRE VISIBLE AS FAR AWAY AS SANDY HOOK. (PHOTO BY J.S. JOHNSON, MUSEUM OF THE CITY OF NEW YORK)

back Railway transformed West Brighton's amusement zone and subsequently reshaped the topography of leisure in America. Oversized and fantastic architecture and speed and motion became the central motifs as competitors began to create faster, bigger, and more exciting rides that encouraged casual contact between the opposite sexes. Charles Feltman installed a spectacular double-decker, Greco-Roman carousel on the grounds of his ever-expanding Ocean Pavilion in 1885. The steam-powered carousel was housed in a pagoda "where people traveled on animals that never found a likeness among beasts of the earth or fowls of the air during any period of evolution." A short-lived balloon carousel hoisted riders aloft in gondolas suspended from small balloons affixed to mechanical arms resembling the tentacles of a devilfish. A forerunner of the Circle Swing, it enabled "adventurous youths and maidens" to embark upon "dizzy aerial voyages for the insignificant sum of ten cents."

But nothing could compete with the coasters in terms of popularity and the degree of conflicting opinions they inspired. *Leslie's Illustrated Newspaper* observed:

> The Coney Island roller coaster is a contrivance designed to give passengers, for the significant expenditure of five cents, all the sensations of being carried away by a cyclone, without the attendant sacrifice of life or limb. Like the traditional boomerang, the roller coaster makes a complete circuit and returns to its starting point in something less than a minute. The first second which elapses after the start gives the novice time to think that he had made a fatal mistake in trusting his vertebrae to such a machine. The next, off goes his hat. The ladies scream and the novice shuts his eyes to await the terrific crash which seems inevitable, for the car is shooting and zigzagging through space like a misdirected rocket. Suddenly its mountings and divings lose their frenetic energy, and before the bewildered passenger can catch his breath, the round trip is ended. We never knew of an instance when a visitor asks for a second one on the grounds of not having received the worth of his money.

Scenic railways, toboggan rides, Russian slides, and other coaster variants soon appeared. The Double Whirl, installed in 1889, gave riders the thrill of a near-collision on a figure-eight track. A coaster eventually encircled the Colossal Elephant, giving riders a thrice-around glimpse at its enormous bulk.

The development of mechanical rides coincided with the Saturday "half-holiday" movement initiated in 1885, when the vast labor force employed in America's industry, including increasing numbers of young women, began to win a measure of leisure time. This created an ever greater demand for cheap, mass entertainment and at the same time provided an unprecedented market for the revolutionary new leisure devices, which were transforming the machinery of work into the machinery of play. This transition was well under way at Coney Island by the 1880s and it gave currency to forms of recreation that were less structured and less regulated. It expressed itself in less restrained forms of ocean bathing, in a more casual mingling of the sexes, and in the sensory thrills provided by the mechanical rides. This newly minted code of leisure prioritized and glorified motion and movement of the human body. It was available to practically everyone, regardless of gender and race, and was inherently democratic. In a short span of time inexpensive mechanical rides brought about a transformation of West Brighton's amusement district, turning it into a populist pleasure zone. *Harper's Weekly* gave this description of a visit in 1889:

> Here are the multitude—a motley throng. Here are the catch-penny devices, each curious enough to merit a story itself. Here are

the economical provisions for the feeding and for the amusement of the people who have little to spend. And here are the quaint and strange and picturesque scenes that make Coney Island a ground for the philosopher's speculation and the student's careful thought. The great mass of the toilers of the city—not the poorest, but the struggling many—here find their only summer outing, and for their pleasure there are queer things done.

Fortunately for the mass of toilers who chose to spend a day at Coney Island during the 1880s, a nickel was the standard fare for practically all of the myriad forms of diversion the resort had on hand. "To him who may be studying the investment of a nickel, there is offered a variety of temptations, sufficient to bewilder the calmest judgement," *Harper's* reported. "You may mount a veritable griffin, a camel, an ox, a stag, a horse or a lion in a merry-go-round, and canter violently around a strident orchestrion that will drown the tones of ordinary conversation," or for the same trifling sum, "ride on a spurious toboggan slide of mammoth proportions on which little cars serve for toboggans, and rails for the ice and snow."

Foremost among Coney Island's five-cent pleasures was the hot dog. Considerable attention was given to those "weird-looking sausages" cooked on a fiery gridiron and served up muffled between the twin halves of a roll. By the 1880s, Coney "red hots" had surpassed the ubiquitous clam in popularity. Although much maligned, the hot dog contributed greatly—in

tandem with the West Brighton's mechanical amusements and its outsized architecture—in securing Coney Island's position as a populist pleasure ground. A visitor counted "over a dozen sausage stands . . . within twenty paces" where the "freckled and sun-burned" delicacy was served up for the sum of five cents. Five cents was also the price of the frothy glass of lager that was consumed to wash it down. At West Brighton, beer was drunk in gargantuan quantities. "Beer is sold everywhere, drunk by everybody and all the time, and is the mainspring and motive power of the excitement," a journalist observed. "If instead of pouring it all out in glasses, all the beersellers there should take one day's store of beer to the top of the iron elevator and let it pour down upon the sand, Niagara would that day rank as a second class cataract. As it is, not the Ganges nor the Nile has as many cataracts as the beer at Coney Island."

Into West Brighton's whirl and din were drawn all classes and castes. Immigrant laborers in ever increasing numbers flocked to Coney in search of cheap pleasures as well as the chance of employment. Germans especially, but also Greeks, Jews, Italians, and African Americans entered the workforce at West Brighton. Venues such as Bauer's Casino hosted labor outings, including a conclave of twenty thousand Knights of Labor in 1887. The Sea Beach Railroad, in particular, became a magnet for working-class patrons, who took advantage of its reduced fares.

The cars of the Sea Beach line delivered their passengers to the most crowded and congested part of the island. All about the Sea Beach

Palace, sheds, shanties, booths, hotels, pavilions, and platforms were thrown together in a chaotic jumble. With the exception of museums and show houses, every one of these establishments was without doors and to get to half of them it was necessary to pass through the others. Each had its own method of attracting a crowd and many employed musicians to cajole passersby. Many of the dining establishments had live acts such as one-legged dancers and female minstrel shows, while at others, the standard fare was eleven items for half a dollar. The din was tremendous. "Step this way," called out a red-nosed youth in checked trousers, "see a troupe of minstrels and tumblers direct from London." "Right this way," cried another with twice as much volume, "two hundred pounds of fun to the square inch—the longest roller coaster on the island." A hundred couples whirled above the heads of a troupe of Tyrolean singers, while a door or two away a painted canvas advertised the "beautiful Mexican girl who murdered her father and mother." Close by, a fat woman in calico sold roasted sausages in competition with

SURF AVENUE, 1896.

(MUSEUM OF THE CITY OF NEW YORK, THE BYRON COLLECTION)

an African selling hot wheat cakes. "The space thus occupied is a big as Washington square," observed the *Sun,* "and the noises, queer sights, and bustling masses of people form a bewildering combination. It reminds New Yorkers of the Bowery, but it embraces twice as many shows. The Bowery is really dignified by comparison." Just beyond the grounds of the Sea Beach terminal lay Surf Avenue, crowded with vehicles of every description, from stagecoach to Irish jaunting car, parading up and down. On either side were more coasters, dime museums, carousels, and the Colossal Elephant, where a band of

"imported Italians" played the music of their native land. West Brighton had by then become "the home of all amusements which are actually insane or nearly so," wrote the *Brooklyn Eagle.* "The further west you get the more dementia increases and the wilder and more lunatic the sport becomes."

The noise and hurly-burly, the clanking and jangle of amusement devices, and the sound of brass bands surrounding the Sea Beach Palace and Elephant Colossus sharply contrasted with the ideals of reformers such as Frederick Law Olmsted, who designed Brooklyn's Prospect

WEST BRIGHTON MUSEUM, CIRCA 1890.

(PHOTO BY RICHARD HOE LAWRENCE. COLLECTION OF THE NEW-YORK HISTORICAL SOCIETY, 32347)

Park and Coney Island's Concourse. "Modern civilized men," Olmsted wrote, "find more refreshment and more lasting pleasure in . . . natural landscape." It was disconcerting, therefore, for reformers who espoused ocean bathing as a tonic for the downtrodden working class to witness the encroachment of commercial amusements upon the beach. "The beach and water are not what people go to enjoy," wrote a commentator who noted that barely one in twenty visitors to Coney Island set foot in the sea. Those who did plunge in, bathers of both sexes, did so with a sort of wild abandon that was itself cause for alarm.

Far greater numbers were seduced by West Brighton's concert halls, mechanical amusements, and catchpenny attractions. Reformers, and especially those drawn from the classes that had the least degree of interaction with the new machinery of industry, found the mechanical amusements and the hubbub of West Brighton jarring and unappealing. The class of workmen who came face to face with machines on a daily basis in the workplace, however, rather than shunning the noise, clamor, and whirring effects of West Brighton's rides, lights, odors, and intentional disorders, found them appealing and stimulating. Reformers argued that workingmen whose lives were daily devalued by machinery were too easily ensnared by the mechanical rides during their brief few hours of respite. They should be pried loose, to flee to the uplifting arms of nature. Yet those who visited Coney Island found its mechanical pleasures refreshing, and no doubt part of the reason for this lay in the conversion of the familiar machinery of the factory into monumental playthings, thus making the humblest workman the master of the machine, empowering and exhilarating him at one and the same time. The mechanic rode the coaster the way a rider might mount a horse in order to tame it and bend it to his will. A coaster ride parodied his daily, workaday life, providing the kind of liberating inversion that in times past had been reserved for festivals when normal behavior was mocked by grotesque caricatures. In contrast with the contemplative recreation of the picnic grove or public park, West Brighton offered the liberating leisure of the coaster, the ocean surf, and cascading electric lights. It was more immediate, more sensual and sexually charged, and thus immensely more seductive.

.    .    .

Both Manhattan and Brighton Beaches staged ever more spectacular programs so as not to be eclipsed by West Brighton. John Philip Sousa replaced Patrick Gilmore as music director at Manhattan Beach, where he introduced the "Manhattan Beach March." Edward J. Rice staged his comic opera *Evangeline* at the Manhattan Beach Theater and presented equestrian and aerial acts in an arena adjoining Pain's fireworks enclosure. Lew Dockstader's minstrel company eventually took up residence at Manhattan Beach's seaside theater and Sousa was succeeded by Victor Herbert. Pain, meanwhile, produced an array of pyrotechnic spectacles, including "The Storming of Pekin," "The Siege of Sebastapol," and "The Burning of Moscow," which depicted Napoleon's assault on the Russian capital.

Diamond Jim Brady, who watched the fireworks from the broad verandahs of the Manhattan Beach Hotel in the company of Lillian Russell, was moved on one such occasion to cry out, "God, Nell, ain't it grand!" Brighton Beach staged its own pyrotechnic spectacles, including "The Taking of New Orleans" with a cast of one thousand, and presented the Metropolitan Opera Orchestra under the direction of Anton Seidl, who favored Wagnerian operatic scores.

While the mechanical amusement craze swept across the western half of the island, horse racing became the passion at Brighton and Manhattan Beaches. William Engeman established the first of the resort's three racetracks at Brighton Beach in 1879. The track was a spectacular success. A year later the Coney Island Jockey Club launched the Sheepshead Bay Race Track. The Jockey Club, headed by Leonard Jerome, enlisted some of New York's most prestigious figures, including J.G.K. Lawrence, William K. Vanderbilt, A. J. Cassatt, August Belmont, and Pierre Lorillard. The track occupied 112 acres along Ocean Parkway across the bay from Manhattan Beach and its grounds included an elegant grandstand and a music pavilion. It became the premier racetrack in America. In 1888, Philip and Michael Dwyer formed the Brooklyn Jockey Club and launched the Gravesend Race Track on the former site of the Prospect Park Fair Grounds.

By 1890, with three competing racetracks, Coney Island was the horse racing capital of America. The Futurity Stakes, first held at Sheepshead Bay in 1888, was the richest event of its time, with August Belmont once collecting a purse of $67,675. The Suburban, held at the same track, was the first of the great handicaps. The Sheephead Bay track also staged the Lawrence Realization Stakes, the Century Stakes, and the Annual Champion Stakes. Gravesend hosted the Brooklyn Handicap, the Preakness, the Brooklyn Derby, and the Tremont Stakes, while Engeman's track had the Brighton Handicap and Brighton Derby. The finest horses of the era, including Henry of Navarre, Domino, Roseben, Colin, and Synosby, competed at Coney Island's racetracks. They were mounted by such legendary jockeys as Tod Sloan, Edward "Snapper" Garrison, Isaac Murphey, Fred Taral, Jimmy McLaughlin, and Walter Miller. Crowds at the Futurity and Suburban sometimes swelled to thirty-five thousand and the betting-ring on Derby Day attracted gambling luminaries such as Riley Grannon, "Bet-a-Million" Gates, and "Pittsburgh Phil." The racing crowd helped transform Sheepshead Bay's north shore into a tony playground. Gilded Age doyens such as Clarence MacKay, Harry K. Thaw, and Lillie Langtry dined at Big Jim Villepigue's and Tappan's with Vanderbilts and Whitneys. It was at Villepigue's that Diamond Jim Brady once consumed eight lobsters in a single sitting and in the process lost a diamond cufflink.

.    .    .

The pleasures of Manhattan Beach and Sheephead Bay reflected the tastes of what one writer called "our fledgling but ambitious aristocracy of commerce." West Brighton, in contrast, mirrored the forceful personality of a

# "THE GREATEST MATCH AMERICA EVER SAW"

Coney Island's racetracks were the scene of many classic contests. Among the fabled races were Domino's victory over Dobbins in the Futurity in 1893 and the match race between Domino and Henry of Navarre at Gravesend in 1895 that ended in a dead heat. The intense rivalry between James R. Keene and William C. Whitney came to a head at the 1900 running of the Futurity when Whitney's Ballyhoo Bey outpaced several horses fielded by Keene. Ballyhoo Bey was guided by Tod Sloan, the most flamboyant jockey of his era, who rode in a crouch known as the "monkey-on-a stick" style. Sloan, who inspired George M. Cohan's "Yankee Doodle Dandy," had gone to race in England in 1899 but was summoned back to ride for Whitney.

The most storied race of the era was the match between Salvator and Tenny. Salvator competed in the inaugural running of the Futurity at Sheepshead Bay in 1888 but lost to Proctor Knott. When Salvator defeated Tenny by a head to win the Suburban in 1890, Tenny's owner issued a challenge for a match race. The race took place at Sheepshead Bay on June 24, 1890. Salvator was ridden by the great African American jockey

Isaac Murphy, winner of three Kentucky Derbies. Tenny was ridden by "Snapper" Garrison, whose fame lay in his ability to charge to victory in the waning moments of a race. Salvator prevailed in what the *New York Tribune* hailed as "The greatest match America ever saw." The race was immortalized by Ella Wheeler Wilcox, whose poem, "How Salvator Won," appeared in the *Spirit of the Times.* It included the lines:

*One more mighty plunge, and with knee, limb and*
*    hand*
*I lift my horse by a nose past the stand.*
*We are under the string now—the great race is done —*
*And Salvator, Salvator, Salvator won!*

"It was a race," the *Spirit of the Times* observed, "few if any of us had seen before and none of us may ever see again."

GRAVESEND RACE TRACK.
(CULVER PICTURES)

single individual, John McKane. McKane was born in Ireland in 1841 and was fifteen months old when his family settled in Gravesend. He first achieved prominence as a contractor for many of West Brighton's hotels and bathing pavilions. After serving as a constable, McKane won election as Gravesend town supervisor in 1879 and subsequently assumed the post of police chief. The Chief, as he was henceforth known, became Coney Island's undisputed political czar and was dubbed the King of Coney Island by the city's newspapers. McKane lorded over West Brighton, sporting a gold-handled cane and diamond-studded police badge presented to him by his admirers. He laid out Surf Avenue, Coney Island's principal thoroughfare, organized its police force, and made many other improvements. McKane once predicted that Coney would some day become a seaside city built of brick. "Such a city is not going to be found anywhere else in the world," he insisted. "The sea calls it. There lies the charm of its growth. The salt water is good for everybody. It saves infants over the summer. It prolongs life in older persons ten years. It fattens lean women and plumps them like partridges. They are all coming this way, sir, yes, all of them."

He was able to shape West Brighton by controlling the leases and licenses of hundreds of small businesses, many of them immigrant-owned, that appealed to the urban working class now flocking to Coney Island. At the same time he sought to diminish the influence of railroad barons such as Austin Corbin and Andrew Culver. His was a self-indulgent populism, however, and sausage vendors who failed to pay his licensing fees risked arrest. McKane's reign gained notoriety for election-rigging and for its tolerance of gambling and prostitution in West Brighton. He did little to interfere with the faro tables and roulette wheels at the Jumbo Hotel on Surf Avenue and at Gary Katen's pavilion, and once remarked that "houses of prostitution are a necessity on Coney Island." The notorious Princess Zaza and the antics at Mme. Korn's and Mother Mary Weyman's that tarnished West Brighton's reputation provoked reformers who denounced McKane's "Sodom by the Sea."

The bane of West Brighton was the district known as the Gut. The Gut was Coney Island's Tenderloin, a degraded area bordered by Ocean Parkway and the elevated railway that linked West Brighton and Brighton Beach. "This seamy side of Coney Island," wrote the *New York Times*, "is entirely hidden behind the colossal elephant, which hides a multitude of sins." The Gut housed a transient population of stablehands and grooms from the racetracks, German and "Hebrew" shopkeepers, laundrywomen, waiters, and boarders residing in a nest of wooden shanties and cottages. It gained notoriety when concert saloons and gambling dens began to sprout there. Notorious outposts such as the Buckingham operated within sight of the Seaside Home for Children. Even McKane conceded, "I don't suppose that there was a wickeder place on the globe than the Gut in its palmy days." He was obliged to conduct periodic raids of the gambling pits and brothels, but the zeal of the reformers such as Anthony Comstock and the imposition of blue laws at Coney Island cut against his grain. "If we carried out the law literally," he complained, "we would have to stop the sale of liquor on Sundays, close all the booths and bathing houses and photograph galleries and switchback railways and merry-go-rounds and museums. How do you think the community would like that? I think they would lynch the Puritans."

During McKane's tenure prizefighting became the rage at West Brighton. Prizefighting was illegal in New York State but several bouts, including matches that featured middleweight champion Nonpareil Jack Dempsey, were staged at Norton's Point. McKane had initially opposed prizefighting on Coney Island and personally halted a championship match between Dempsey and Fulljames. McKane reversed course when Dick Newton, a political ally, suggested that bouts could be sanctioned if they were promoted as "boxing exhibitions." The matches were held in Paul Bauer's old Casino, where Gilbert and Sullivan light operas were once staged. Police Justice Newton served as matchmaker and McKane, who now controlled the Casino, received a fee. Renamed the Coney Island Athletic Club, it became a premier boxing venue. Numerous matches, including a

## GENTLEMAN JIM, THE SAILOR, AND THE CALIFORNIA GIANT

The Coney Island Athletic Club was the scene of several classic championship bouts staged by the showman William A. Brady. The bouts were grand affairs. A crowd of several thousand boxing enthusiasts greeted the champion, Robert Fitzsimmons, in June 1899 with cheers and hats tossed skyward as he emerged from his hotel, the throng swelling to even greater numbers as it accompanied him to the boxing pavilion. Fitzsimmons was dethroned that night by challenger Jim Jeffries in the first world heavyweight cham-

pionship bout held in New York State. The crowd in the cavernous barn let loose a great roar with every blow that landed.

Jeffries defeated "Sailor Tom" Sharkey in November of that year in a twenty-five-round affray that the New York Herald called "the greatest championship contest of their time." The match was the first championship bout recorded on film using electric lights for illumination. Over 350 arc lamps were suspended above the ring and the intense heat was said to have hampered

both the fighters. It was filmed by the Biograph company by arrangement with Brady, and a great controversy ensued with the discovery that a camera crew from the Edison-Vitagraph Company was on hand and had produced a pirated film of the bout.

Jeffries overcame former champion Gentleman Jim Corbett in a twenty-three-round contest in May 1900. Three months later the Horton Act was repealed and prizefighting in New York State was outlawed.

dozen championship bouts, were staged there and every boxer of note including Gentleman Jim Corbett, Bob Fitzsimmons, Jim Jeffries, "colored champ" George Godfrey, George Dixon, Kid Lavigne, Terry McGovern, Young Griffo, and Tommy Ryan stepped into its ring.

McKane's sole challenge came from Peter Tilyou and his son George C. Tilyou. Peter Tilyou was a well-respected Coney Island entrepreneur—the proprietor of the once-prosperous Surf House—who attributed his declining fortunes to the debased conditions in West Brighton. His outspoken advocacy of reform alarmed McKane and eventually cost Tilyou his lease. George C. Tilyou was more resilient. Born in New York City in 1862, he had helped his father establish West Brighton's first theater and laid the planks for Coney Island's Bowery. A showman by nature, he once devised a scheme to sell vials of sand and salt water from the Atlantic Ocean to tourists as authentic Coney Island souvenirs. Later he ventured into the real estate business and in 1886 he published the sole edition of *Tilyou's Real Estate Telephone,* which touted the glory of Coney Island. "If Paris is France," he declared, "then Coney Island, between June and September, is the world. English dukes and earls, French viscomtes, German barons, senators and even presidents and vice presidents, railroad kings, merchant princes, society queens—every human being of eminence or note in the American Continent can be found promenading the enormous hotel corridors, dining in the vast saloons or wandering on the beach." Tilyou prospered as an inventor and promoter of mechanical amusement de-

vices, but his ambitions inevitably led to another confrontation with McKane. Tilyou believed that the gambling dens, concert saloons, and brothels that lined Surf Avenue and the Bowery discouraged many who might otherwise have visited the resort. In 1887 he testified before the Bacon Commission, convened to investigate West Brighton's excesses. When McKane was absolved by the Commission, the Tilyou family's fortune sank even further.

McKane's reign reached its peak in 1893. That August, the Volunteer Firemen's Convention was held at Coney Island and huge crowds descended upon West Brighton. McKane and Governor Rosewell Pettibone Flowers reviewed the marchers as they strode with their engines under an arch erected on Surf Avenue. McKane told the firemen: "All we ask of you is that when you have finished with it . . . let us have the town back in as good order as you got it." His foes, however, complained that McKane's policies brought disgrace to the resort. A championship bout between Jim Corbett and Charles Mitchell slated for that December became the focus of a bitter campaign by reformers. The bout was canceled and one month later, the controversy surrounding McKane's election-rigging came to a head when he defied an order from the State Supreme Court to open the election rolls for inspection. McKane had once boasted that he personally secured the margin of victory for President Benjamin Harrison in 1888. His Election Day retort, "Injunctions don't go here," galvanized his opponents and sealed his fate. He was prosecuted for election-rigging, convicted, and hauled off to Sing Sing prison in 1894.

Gravesend was subsequently annexed to Brooklyn by the State Legislature with the intention of cleansing Coney Island.

.    .    .

McKane's downfall gave new impetus to the career of George C. Tilyou. Tilyou, along with every other showman in America, was profoundly impressed by the World's Columbian Exposition held in Chicago in 1893. The heart of the Chicago fair was the Court of Honor and the elegant exhibition halls that surrounded it. However, its greatest attraction was the Midway Plaisance, the fair's mile-long amusement zone. Its far-flung attractions included a Javanese village, a Chinese market, a Japanese bazaar, Hagenbeck's Animal Show, and the photographic motion studies of Eadweard Muybridge. "A sideshow, pure and simple," said one guidebook. Its most popular attraction was the Street of Cairo, populated by 180 North Africans, including Algerian, Syrian, Egyptian, and Sudanese dancers whose performance of the "danse du ventre" caused a sensation, scandalizing many visitors.

Towering over the Midway Plaisance was the Ferris wheel, the exposition's most imposing mechanical device. Created by George W. G. Ferris, it rose to a height of 250 feet and gave a commanding view of the fairgrounds and the adjoining city. After the fair closed, Tilyou immediately sought to acquire the Ferris wheel. Having failed to do so, he decided to build one. He returned to Coney Island where he planted a sign that read: "On This Site Will Be Erected the World's Largest Ferris Wheel." Tilyou's Ferris wheel, when completed and installed at the east end of the Bowery, was about half as high—a hundred feet in diameter. It had twelve cars, each carrying eighteen passengers, and was lighted with 460 incandescent lamps. It was visible from thirty-eight miles at sea.

West Brighton's landscape was continuously transformed during the 1890s by new mechanical devices and attractions. New coasters and toboggan rides were unveiled, including the short-lived Snow and Ice Railway imported from the Chicago fair. A more successful attraction was George Tilyou's Aerial Slide, on which riders glided along a slack-wire a distance of a hundred yards into the arms of an attendant. Among the most innovative diversions was the Aqua Aerial Shuttle. Its riders enjoyed "a trip through the breakers" in a boat suspended like a trolley car from a cable. It carried its passengers 825 feet out over sea, just above the crests of the waves. A reporter for the *Brooklyn Eagle,* after viewing one of the new devices, observed:

> The tendency of the West End amusements has been of late years towards greater extravagance in sea sickness breeding swings, merry go rounds, toboggan slides and razzle dazzles. The greatest novelty this year is a giant swing that goes by steam and plays automatic music. . . . It is shaped like a water wheel and will hold close upon one hundred people in little boats, seating four each. In twirling round the boats rise to a height of fifty feet. No matter how frightened they get, the girls have to stay there

CONEY ISLAND BEACH NEAR BALMER'S BATHING PAVILION (TWO VIEWS), CIRCA 1895.

(AUTHOR'S COLLECTION)

once the machine is started, and that gives glorious opportunities to rescue them with both arms. Hence the thing has made a hit.

The area once occupied by Culver Plaza became a warren of arcades and amusements. They lined the plank walkways leading to the New Iron Pier, crowded the Observatory, and pressed up against Balmer's Bathing Pavilion. Fires in 1893 and 1895 decimated many old concessions including Bauer's West Brighton Hotel, but they were quickly replaced by new attractions such as Jackman's Shooting the Rapids. By 1896, the crowd on the Fourth of July, numbering 150,000 pleasure seekers, jammed the Bowery, the Midway Plaisance, and the Streets of Cairo and filled the beach and every pavilion. An even larger number was on hand a week later. So great was the crowd that for five hours the bathing establishments had to turn people away. Coney Island, wrote Julian Ralph, had become New York's "homeopathic sanitarium,

our sun-bath and ice-box combined, our extra lung, our private, gigantic fan."

An obstacle still remained for showman such as George Tilyou, whose concessions, including an Intramural Bicycle Railway and a Double Dip Chutes, were dispersed throughout West Brighton. To reach them one had to run a gantlet of some three hundred concert saloons and dance halls frequented by racetrack touts and plungers. The Streets of Cairo had also found its way to Coney Island. The concession, with its sword dancers, camel rides, and candle dancers, was re-created at the corner of West Tenth Street within sight of Tilyou's Ferris wheel. The Streets of Cairo and other relics from the Chicago fair, such as the Algerian Theater and the Turkish Theater, brought the "danse du ventre" to Coney Island and introduced Little Egypt and countless other "cooch" dancers to the resort. Many of these attractions were clustered around Maiden Lane, an extension of the Bowery just east of Feltman's Pavilion, in what was now called the Midway Plaisance. Mayor Charles A. Schieren, who visited Coney Island shortly after McKane's departure, had emphatically declared: "The Bowery must go. We will clean the whole place out and shut up every dive and concert hall there." Reformers, in particular, railed against the "fake Oriental dance-houses" that "engage their stars from among the low and degraded creatures of all nationalities to represent the Egyptian, Turkish, and Moorish licentious degradation, expressed in so-called muscle dances." The police raided the Turkish Theater and the Congress of Nations and arrested "couchee-couchee" dancers Fatima and Saida, while revoking the licenses of the Maiden's Dream and the Museum of Anatomy, where "indecent exhibitions" were allegedly given. The cleansing efforts also netted fortunetellers and palmists, who were charged with giving "fake shows." But despite repeated attempts to reform it, the Bowery invariably reverted to its old ways.

A practical solution to the problem was provided by Captain Paul Boyton. Boyton, a

STREETS OF CAIRO PAVILION.

(PHOTO BY ROBERT BRACKLOW. COLLECTION OF THE NEW-YORK HISTORICAL SOCIETY, 75055)

TILYOU'S FERRIS WHEEL VIEWED FROM CONEY ISLAND'S MIDWAY PLAISANCE, CIRCA 1896.

former Atlantic City lifeguard, was a nautical adventurer and an inventor celebrated for his long-distance swimming feats, having traversed the English Channel, the Irish Sea, and the Straits of Gibraltar in a pneumatic swimsuit. After performing with a troupe assembled by P. T. Barnum, Boyton launched his own aquatic circus, which he presented at the Earl's Court Exhibition in London in 1892. At Earl's Court and at the Antwerp World's Exposition of 1894, Boyton introduced the first successful large-scale water amusement ride, the Shoot the Chutes. In 1895, he brought his aquatic show to Coney Island and built an enclosed fairground directly behind the colossal Elephant to serve as

its permanent home. Boyton's Sea Lion Park opened its gates on July 4, 1895, becoming the first enclosed amusement park ever built. It featured aquatic acrobats, water sports and exhibitions, an old mill sluice ride, cages of live wolves, and the troupe of trained sea lions that inspired the park's name. A ballroom and other amusements were later added, including an experimental centrifugal railroad called the Flip-Flap coaster. The coaster's twenty-five-foot-high circular loop jolted and jostled riders and left many complaining of sore bones. "You could send a bucket of water around the loop in one of our cars and not a drop will spill," Boyton countered. "Centrifugal force never fails to

FEEDING THE ELEPHANT AT THE STREETS OF CAIRO PAVILION.

(AUTHOR'S COLLECTION)

work." The park's centerpiece was the Shoot the Chutes, which Boyton billed as the "King of All Amusements" and which he successfully marketed to amusement resorts all over the world.

Boyton's enclosed park offered a solution to the problem confronting George Tilyou. Tilyou seized upon the idea. Following Boyton's lead, he gathered his widely scattered rides and inventions into a single amusement concession. At the same time, he cast about for a signature attraction, on a par with Boyton's Chutes, to anchor his park. The device he settled upon

was a mechanical racetrack called the Gravity Steeplechase Race Course. The ride was modeled after a British gravity ride invented by William Cawdery. Tilyou secured a patent for the ride, redesigned it, and made it the mainstay of his Steeplechase Park. The ride's motto, "Half a mile in half a minute, and fun all the time," expressed, quite succinctly, the operating principal that propelled Tilyou's enterprise.

Steeplechase Park opened in the spring of 1897. The enclosed park covered about fifteen acres and charged a single admission for its vari-

ORIGINAL TURKISH HAREM, CIRCA 1896.

(MUSEUM OF THE CITY OF NEW YORK, THE BYRON COLLECTION)

# A CONEY ISLAND ALBUM

CABINET CARD PROMOTING THE ELEPHANTINE COLOSSUS. UPON ITS COMPLETION IN 1885 A *NEW YORK TIMES* REPORTER DESCRIBED A TOUR OF THE COLOSSUS CONDUCTED BY ITS MANAGER. "AFTER FORTIFYING HIS GUESTS WITH A BIG DINNER IN HIS RESTAURANT MR. BRANDENBURGH LED THEM UP THROUGH THE ELE-PHANT'S LEFT HIND LEG INTO HIS STOMACH. . . . FROM THE STOMACH ROOM THE EXPLORERS WALKED THROUGH THE ELEPHANT'S DIAPHRAGM AND ALONG HIS LIVER UP INTO HIS LEFT LUNG, WHERE A MUSEUM IS TO BE SITUATED DURING THE SUMMER . . . THEN UP TO THE CHEEK ROOM, WHERE THEY LOOKED THROUGH THE ELEPHANT'S RIGHT EYE OUT ON THE OCEAN AND PEERED DOWN INTO HIS TRUNK. . . . FROM THIS GALLERY THE GUESTS WERE TAKEN UP TO THE BACK OF THE ELEPHANT, A DISTANCE OF 175 FEET FROM THE GROUND, WHERE A VAST PANORAMA WAS SPREAD BEFORE THEM ON EVERY HAND. 'YOU SEE THAT LITTLE PUFF OF FOAM OFF A LITTLE TO THE NORTH OF WEST, THERE?' SAID MR. BRANDENBURGH. 'THAT IS THE SPRAY ABOVE NIAGARA FALLS. . . . THAT TINY SILVER THREAD FURTHER TO THE WEST IS THE MISSISSIPPI RIVER. OVER TO THE EAST YOU CAN CATCH SIGHT OF QUEENSTOWN AND OF THE LITTLE VILLAGES ALONG THE BAY OF BISCAY, AND EVEN OF THE STEEPLES OF LONDON AND PARIS—IF YOUR EYESIGHT IS CLEAR ENOUGH. REMARKABLE, ISN'T IT. ALL FOR TEN CENTS, TOO.'" (*NEW YORK TIMES*, MAY 30, 1885).                    (AUTHOR'S COLLECTION)

TRADE CARD ILLUSTRATION OF THE IRON PIER.
(AUTHOR'S COLLECTION)

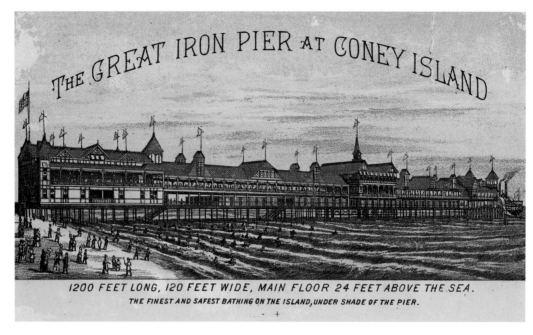

CONEY ISLAND JOCKEY CLUB RACING PROGRAM.
(THE BROOKLYN HISTORICAL SOCIETY)

BILL OF FARE FROM

THE WEST BRIGHTON BEACH HOTEL.

(AUTHOR'S COLLECTION)

CYCLING WAS IN FASHION WHEN

E. T. PAULL COMPOSED THE "NEW YORK AND

CONEY ISLAND CYCLE MARCH" IN 1896.

(AUTHOR'S COLLECTION)

MANHATTAN BEACH AMUSEMENT

PROGRAM FROM JULY 1896.

(AUTHOR'S COLLECTION)

PROGRAM FROM PAIN'S FIREWORKS SHOW
AT CONEY ISLAND IN 1897. PAIN STAGED
PYRO-SPECTACLES IN AN ARENA AT MANHATTAN
BEACH THAT HELD 12,000 SPECTATORS.
THE PERFORMANCES REQUIRED HUNDREDS OF
COSTUMED ACTORS AND COMPLEX SCENERY
ON A VAST STAGE AND MANMADE LAGOON WHERE
SEA BATTLES WERE ENACTED. AFTER 1909,
PAIN'S ARENA WAS AT BRIGHTON PARK.

(AUTHOR'S COLLECTION)

LUNA PARK SOUVENIR
PROGRAM FROM THE
INAUGURAL SEASON
IN 1903.
(AUTHOR'S COLLECTION)

TICKET STUB FROM
THE DREAMLAND'S
CIRCLE SWING.
(AUTHOR'S COLLECTION)

CONEY ISLAND SOUVENIR GUIDEBOOK

ISSUED IN 1904.

(THE BROOKLYN HISTORICAL SOCIETY)

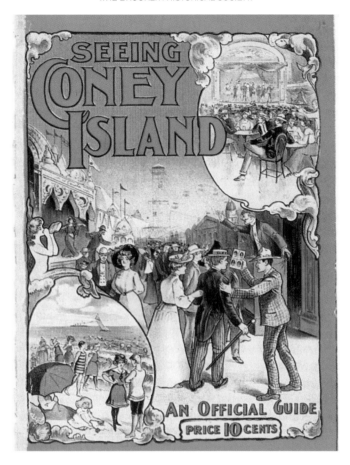

PROGRAM FROM

THE NEW BRIGHTON THEATRE,

CIRCA 1910.

(THE BROOKLYN HISTORICAL SOCIETY)

CONEY ISLAND POSTCARDS. BEGINNING IN 1898 WHEN POSTAGE FOR COMMERCIALLY PRINTED CARDS WAS REDUCED TO A PENNY, THOUSANDS OF IMAGES OF CONEY ISLAND WERE CREATED. THE RESORT'S POST OFFICE OFTEN HANDLED AS MANY AS A QUARTER OF A MILLION CARDS ON WEEKENDS AND SET A RECORD WITH TWO HUNDRED THOUSAND ON A SINGLE DAY. (AUTHOR'S COLLECTION)

POSTCARD DEPICTING THE GLOBE TOWER. THE TOWER'S ASCENDING AMUSEMENT ZONES ARE EXPOSED IN THE CUTAWAYS OF THE ILLUSTRATION. ARCHITECT REM KOOLHAAS DESCRIBED IT IN *DELIRIOUS NEW YORK, A RETROACTIVE MANIFESTO OF MANHATTAN* AS A "GIGANTIC STEEL PLANET THAT HAS CRASHED ONTO A REPLICA OF THE EIFFEL TOWER." INVESTORS CRIED "FRAUD" WHEN PLANS FOR THE TOWER COLLAPSED. (AUTHOR'S COLLECTION)

ous attractions. On its midway, called the Grand Promenade, were fifty amusements, including the Earthquake Floor, the Electric Fountain, Razzle Dazzle, the Electric Seat, the Revolving Seat, and the Eccentric Fountain. Scattered about the pavilion grounds were novelties such as the Aerial Slide, a centrifugal amusement called the Barrel of Love, the Uoylitscope, and the Funny Stairway, which, Tilyou asserted, "caused laughter enough to cure all the dyspepsia in the world." The park's signature attraction, the Steeplechase Gravity Ride, was by far its most popular and profitable concession. A promotional pamphlet declared: "A ride on the horses is a healthful stimulant that stirs the heart and clears the brain. It straightens out wrinkles and irons out puckers. . . . The old folks like it because it makes them young again. Everybody likes it because it's cheap fun, real fun, lively fun." In 1899, the park attracted over a million visitors.

Tilyou's Steeplechase compressed all of the amusement resources found on a carnival midway and wove them together into a seamless, self-contained pleasure ground. He presented

FLIP-FLAP COASTER AT SEA LION PARK, CIRCA 1901.
(MILSTEIN DIVISION OF UNITED STATES HISTORY, LOCAL HISTORY AND GENEALOGY,
THE NEW YORK PUBLIC LIBRARY, ASTOR, LENOX AND TILDEN FOUNDATIONS)

"clean fun," but without sacrificing the festive, free-spirited, and sensual contours of the carnival that sought to turn normal everyday life on its head. By enclosing his park he was able to exert a greater degree of control, barring those who might disrupt or abuse the environment he had carefully sculpted, while at the same time guaranteeing a manic, topsy-turvy, sanity-splitting experience to those respectable folk who paid their way into his park. Tilyou's concession brought together all the elements that have come to be associated with the American amusement park: the roller coaster and scenic railroad, carousel and Ferris wheel, arcades, funhouse, food concessions, dancing pavilion, water rides, and bathing pavilion. Within three years he was able to create Steeplechase amusements in San Francisco, St. Louis, and Atlantic City, and at the Paris Exposition of 1900.

.    .    .

West Brighton's transformation in the waning decades of the nineteenth century had

THE SHOOT THE CHUTES AT SEA LION PARK, TOUTED BY BOYTON AS "CONEY ISLAND'S GREATEST ATTRACTION"—"A RIDE DOWN WATER AT 70 MILES AN HOUR."

unleashed a tidal wave of democratic leisure. Steeplechase, and to a lesser degree Sea Lion Park, advanced this democratizing process by institutionalizing the amusement industry in ways that the world's fair midways and expositions had not sought to, creating a self-enclosed, easily replicable commercial enterprise that could deliver cheap amusement to the masses in a manner that was enormously profitable. Outside the park, with its arcades that hinted at Chicago's White City and entranceway resembling the Brandenburg Gate, the hurly-burly of the Bowery was in full swing. Coney Island never entirely shook off the broad, earthy appeal it acquired during the heady days of John McKane. The old Coney Island lingered on side by side with Steeplechase for decades to come. But, with the advent of Sea Lion Park and George Tilyou's Steeplechase, the template of the American amusement industry was unmistakably created.

# CHAPTER FOUR

# BAGHDAD BY THE SEA

THE CROWD that gathered on Surf Avenue on the evening of May 16, 1903, froze in its tracks, gazed upward, and seemed to rub its eyes in disbelief. At precisely 8:00 P.M., two hundred thousand electric lights shown forth from the towers, fretted domes, and minarets rising above the new amusement concession touted as New York's World's Fair. "It seemed that a huge mantle of light had been let down from the sky to disclose the domain of an unknown world," a reporter observed. When the gates of Luna Park were thrown open five minutes later, the crowd entered a realm of electric fountains, cascading lights, and winding pathways converging upon a spectacular Court of Honor. The overall effect defied human comprehension. "When Coleridge, in an esthetic revel of opium-inspired imagination, wrote that marvel of word music and painting, 'Kubla-Khan,'" the reporter asserted, "it might have been the scenery of Luna Park as it stood revealed last night that stood before his vision. The brilliance and beauty and weirdness of it all beggars description." By 10:00 P.M. there were sixty thousand people in the park.

The fiery apparition that transformed Coney Island was the handiwork of Luna Park's creator, Frederic Thompson. Thompson was born in Irontown, Ohio, in 1873. He began his professional life as an architectural draftsman. After managing a concession at the World's Colombian Exposition in Chicago, Thompson embarked upon a career designing and operating amusement concessions. He was active at the Tennessee Centennial Exposition of 1897 and at the Omaha Trans-Mississippi Exposition the following year, when he introduced a cyclorama called "Darkness and Dawn." At the Omaha fair, Thompson faced competition from the man who was to become his future business partner, Elmer "Skip" Dundy. The two men joined forces at the Buffalo Pan-American Exposition of 1900.

The Buffalo fair was a glittering event. Its exposition halls were illuminated nightly by an unprecedented number of electric lights powered by a generating facility at nearby Niagara Falls. Its centerpiece was a four-hundred-foot-high Electric Tower. Thompson and Dundy dominated the fair's amusement midway with concessions that included the "Darkness and Dawn" cyclorama and a 235-foot-high Aerial Cycle. The most successful show on the midway was Thompson's innovative illusion "A Trip to the Moon," conceived during the previous winter while he was enrolled at the Art Student's League in New York. The ride used motion and scenic devices to simulate a trip in an airship from the exposition grounds to the moon. Thirty passengers at a time boarded a cigar-shaped craft, with propellers and flapping wings, which was tethered to a tower and housed in an aerodrome. As it rocked and swayed, simulating the ship's movement through space, passengers peered out at revolving screens, images projected onto the walls, and intricate lighting effects, and saw the fairgrounds, the Falls, the North American continent, and the earth recede into the distance. After encountering an electrical storm, the airship *Luna* emerged from the darkness and below it loomed the crusty surface of the moon. The ship landed and the passengers disembarked to explore the moon's subterranean region, represented as an eerie papier-mâché underworld of grottos, icy stalactites, and dark caverns where midgets with spiked backs and moon giants greeted them. They crossed a moat, arriving at the Palace of the Man on the Moon, where moon maidens danced about, then exited through the mouth of a mechanical moon-calf.

"A Trip to the Moon" was a creative and a financial success and at the close of the fair Thompson and Dundy struck an agreement with George C. Tilyou to transfer the ride to Steeplechase Park and operate it as an inde-

pendent concession. The Aerial Cycle was also brought to Steeplechase, where it was rechristened the Giant See-Saw. The following season, however, was a disastrous one for Coney Island showmen when businesses suffered from unrelenting rain. At the end of the season, Tilyou

LUNA PARK AT NIGHT. "THE VIEW OF LUNA PARK FROM SHEEPSHEAD SUGGESTS A CEMETERY OF FIRE, THE TOMBS, TURRETS, AND TOWERS ILLUMINATED, AND MORTUARY SHAFTS OF FLAME," WROTE JAMES GIBBONS HUNEKER. "EVERYTHING IS FRETTED WITH FIRE. FIRE DELICATELY ETCHES SOME FAIRY STRUCTURE; FIRE OUTLINES AN ORIENTAL GATEWAY; FIRE RUNS LIKE A MUSICAL SCALE THROUGH MANY OCTAVES, THE DARKNESS CROWDING IT, THE MIST BLURRING IT."

(LIBRARY OF CONGRESS, GOTTSCHO-SCHLEISNER COLLECTION)

sought to renegotiate his agreement with Thompson and Dundy. The partners instead chose to branch out on their own. They left behind the Giant See-Saw, having wagered its fate on the toss of a coin.

Paul Boyton's Sea Lion Park was in a precarious state after the disastrous 1902 season. Thompson and Dundy leased the park from Boyton, along with the adjacent property where the Colossal Elephant once stood. On the site of the old park they planned to erect an entirely new amusement concession anchored by Thompson's "Trip to the Moon." Boyton's water chute was left standing but the rest of the park's attractions were cleared away. Thompson wanted to work from the ground up. He had in mind an ambitious plan that borrowed freely from the fanciful motifs of the Arabian Nights and his own experiments on exposition midways. Dundy had the task of securing the capital for the project he described as "Fred Thompson's Coney Island sideshow." He raised half from speculators such as "Bet-a-Million" Gates and the rest from Wall Street bankers. The partners poured every cent into the venture. Dundy spent the evening prior to its opening scraping together twenty-two dollars in change for the park's ticket-sellers. It was Dundy who first suggested naming the park after his sister, Luna, whose name echoed "A Trip to the Moon."

The press notices heralding Luna's Park's opening proclaimed it a "Realm of Fairy Romance," but Thompson and Dundy's "colossal electric carnival" outstripped even the most inflated expectations of those who came to visit

PROMENADING AT LUNA PARK.
(BROOKLYN MUSEUM OF ART/BROOKLYN PUBLIC LIBRARY—
BROOKLYN COLLECTION)

it. Luna Park covered about twenty-two acres and was illuminated by a quarter of a million electric lights. Architecturally it was a wonderland, blending the visual elements of many lands, both real and imagined, into a single "delirium of something doing" outlined in orange, white, and gold. Luna's entrance gate was a gigantic arch covering half a city block. The court beneath the arch was a solid mass of electric lights, and rising high above it were "four monster monoliths, traced in electric lights

LUNA PARK, CIRCA 1905.

(PHOTO BY ADOLPH WITTEMANN. MUSEUM OF THE CITY OF NEW YORK, THE LEONARD HASSAM BOGART COLLECTION)

and surmounted by great balls of fire, which shed light over the island." At the entrance gate stood five Roman chariots, ticket kiosks occupied by young women dressed in evening attire and Merry Widow straw hats emblazoned with red feathers. Beyond the gates, manned by helmeted, scarlet-coated Cerberi, were fifty-three buildings arrayed along a Court of Honor. At one side was a reproduction of the Piazza San Marco, with a campanile, an ornate loggia, and a grand canal plied by gondoliers coursing under an illuminated bridge. It faced the sculpted facades of three immense buildings where Thompson's "electro-scenic" illusion spectacles were staged.

The first building housed a revamped "Trip to the Moon." The airship *Luna III* now carried sixty passengers aloft as it ascended high above the fretted towers of Coney Island. A patriotic spectacle called "War of the Worlds" was presented in an amphitheater shaped like a battleship and touted as Thompson and Dundy's

Great Naval Spectatorium. An attack upon New York Harbor by the European powers was depicted, culminating in a great victory by Admiral George Dewey. The park's most massive building housed a new illusion called "Twenty Thousand Leagues Under the Sea." Equipped with its own ice-manufacturing facility to enhance its effects, it simulated a journey in a submarine from Luna Park to the North Pole. Along the way the undersea voyagers encountered mermaids and strange sea creatures, glided beneath icebergs, visited an Eskimo village, and emerged at the North Pole greeted by a luminous, varicolored aurora borealis.

Lining the Court of Honor were other buildings that housed Hagenbeck's Wild Animals, Wormwood's Dog and Monkey Circus, the Infant Incubators from the Buffalo exposition, a Chinese Theater, and various native villages. There was also a Helter Skelter bamboo slide, an Old Mill sluiceway, and a Grand Casino.

At the center of the park was a lagoon flanked at one end by Boyton's Shoot the Chutes, now traced with lights, and at the other end by a tower. The tower recalled the Pan-American Exposition's breathtaking Electric Tower, which was studded with twenty thousand incandescent lamps. Luna Park's two-hundred-foot-high tower was only half as tall; however, with its lights that changed color every second it was a visual confection. Twin circus rings flanked the tower and an electric fountain at its base sent up a spray of alternating colors. Acrobats, jugglers, and equestrian acts gave continuous performances on the twin

stages, and an aerial circus high overhead featured a slack-wire artist performing in evening dress and a bicyclist on trapeze. To top it all, Thompson enlisted Cameroni the Great to duplicate a feat he had performed at the Buffalo fair by descending from the top of the tower on a two-thousand-foot-long cable, with his hands tied behind his back, hanging by a leather strap held between his teeth. Admission to the park was ten cents. A twenty-five-cent surcharge was required for attractions such as "A Trip to the Moon." There were free concerts by Scinta's Luna Park band and nightly fireworks displays.

Thompson's creation was a joyous hymn to pleasure and play that outshown everything that came before it, including George Tilyou's Steeplechase Park. Tilyou, who practically invented the modern amusement park, had not devised it according to an architectural plan. Thompson, on the other hand, started from a very concrete notion of what the ideal pleasure park ought to be like and sought, by every visual trick and device he could summon, to transport visitors to a land of carnival pleasures and to hold them fast once they had surrendered themselves to it. To achieve its aim, Luna Park needed to be architecturally unified in its construction. Thompson's point of departure was the Pan-American Exposition, held two years earlier, which Thompson had singlehandedly rescued from financial disaster through a promotional event called Midway Day. Thompson appropriated the exposition's most enchanting elements, its graceful curves, colonnades, elongated loggias, trellised porticos, rounded domes, and minarets, and above all the exposition's cor-

THE TOWER AT LUNA PARK. A SOUVENIR PROGRAM BOASTED: "BESIDE THE MILLION INCANDESCENT LAMPS WHICH MAKE THE ENCLOSURE AT NIGHTTIME THE BRIGHTEST SPOT ON THE WHOLE TERRESTRIAL SPHERE, THERE IS THE KALEIDOSCOPE TOWER, WHERE 80,000 ELECTRIC LIGHTS GO THROUGH AS MANY CHANGES EVERY SECOND. THESE LIGHTS TAKE THE FORM OF FIFTY DIFFERENT GEOMETRICAL EFFECTS, WHICH IN TURN GO THROUGH 1,100 CHANGES BEFORE THEY REPEAT. THE TOWER IS THE ONLY THING OF ITS KIND IN EXISTENCE, AND IS IN MANY WAYS THE MOST EXTRAORDINARY ELECTRICAL DISPLAY EVER MADE."

(LIBRARY OF CONGRESS)

uscating illuminations, and reconfigured them. At Luna Park, these architectural elements became the carefully orchestrated backdrop of a stupendous carnival where, for a modest sum, one could voyage to the moon or under the sea, encounter elephants and other exotic creatures, or be amused by Singhalese "stitch dancers" or Hassan Ben Ali's Troupe of Hindoos. Thompson spared no expense. If the Pan-American fair had two hundred thousand incandescent lamps

RIDING THE ELEPHANTS AT LUNA PARK. ELEPHANTS WERE A CONSTANT ATTRACTION AT THE PARK WHETHER AT THE HEAD OF THE DURBAR PROCESSION OR SLIDING DOWN THE CHUTES. THE MOST CELEBRATED LUNA ELEPHANT WAS THE ILL-FATED TOPSY, WHO WAS ELECTROCUTED AT THE PARK IN 1903 AFTER KILLING SEVERAL OF HER TRAINERS. THE SAD SPECTACLE WAS RECORDED IN AN EARLY FILM BY THOMAS EDISON, WHO ALSO CONDUCTED THE ELECTROCUTION. (BROOKLYN PUBLIC LIBRARY–BROOKLYN COLLECTION)

for its 366 acres of exposition grounds, Luna must have an equal or greater number to decorate its 22 acres.

In executing the design of Luna Park, Thompson put to test a theory of amusement architecture he had first explored at the Tennessee Centennial Exposition of 1897, where his Moorish palace won an architectural prize. "I have built Luna Park on a definite architectural plan," he explained. "I have eliminated all classic, conventional forms in its structure, and taken a sort of free Renaissance and Oriental type for my model, using spires and minarets whenever I could. . . . It is marvelous what you can do in the way of arousing human emotions by the use that you make, architecturally, of simple lines! Luna Park is built on that theory, and the result has proved the theory's truth." All of Thompson's energy and resources were poured into this single purpose, to instill the carnivalesque spirit into every feature of his park. Everything that contributed to the air of gaiety, spontaneity, and otherworldliness was permitted on his architectural palette; anything that might diminish the effect was dispensed with. "Straight lines have no right in the place of honor of a great outdoor show," he wrote. The architecture "must be in keeping with the spirit of carnival. It must be active, mobile, free, graceful, and attractive." The fact that Thompson succeeded so completely in his purpose set Luna Park apart from anything yet created by the nascent American amusement industry. It was, as its promoters had promised, a "fairy realm." It enchanted all who entered its precincts and sent them reeling into a zone of carnival transformation, albeit of short duration, and of simple pleasures. Luna Park was the handiwork of a midway magician who had wielded a "scintillant wand of fire." His park

THE TEASER AT LUNA PARK.
(FRIED COLLECTION)

was a spectacular success both as an Everyman's World's Fair and a luminous Baghdad by the Sea. In less than three months' time, Thompson and Dundy had recouped 90 percent of their investment.

.    .    .

Luna Park's success inspired the construction of an even grander amusement park at Coney Island. Dreamland, conceived by former senator William H. Reynolds and a consortium of politically connected investors, was built during the winter and spring of 1904 on fifteen acres of land extending from Surf Avenue to the ocean, a site once occupied by Bauer's Casino. Reynolds, who had first planned to name the park Wonderland, touted is as the "Gibraltar of the Amusement World." It cost $3.5 million and every effort was made to surpass Luna Park. Its chief advantage was its ocean frontage with a pier that enabled visitors to enter the park by sea. In its overall plan, Dreamland resembled a horseshoe facing out toward the ocean. At its center was a lagoon with a massive tower and a sunken garden, surrounded by a balustrade and crossed by footbridges. A track on which chariot races were staged encircled the lagoon, and wide boardwalks surrounded the entire center court around which the various buildings of every style of architecture were arrayed. Dreamland's Beacon Tower dwarfed Luna Park's Kaleidoscope Tower, rising to a height of 370 feet, capped with a ball and eagle. It was white and gold in the French Renaissance style with wide arches supporting a fifty-foot-square base, deco-

rated with bas-reliefs by Perry Hinton. In size and general appearance it resembled John Galen Howard's tower at the Pan-American Exhibition. It was studded with one hundred thousand incandescent lamps to produce the effect of "an ocean of electric fire."

Dreamland reproduced many of Luna Park's attractions, but on a greatly enlarged scale. Its double-tracked Shoot the Chutes extended three hundred feet out into the ocean on its own steel pier and was equipped with a "moving stairway" that ferried seven thousand passengers an hour to the top. Its boats carried twenty people at a time careening downward into the lagoon. Dreamland matched Luna Park's Venetian City with its own re-creation of the Doge's Palace and a half-mile-long gondola ride. Its fire-fighting spectacle "Fighting the Flames" was more spectacular than a similar attraction at Luna Park. The park had a submarine ride called "Under and Over the Sea" to rival the Thompson and Dundy attraction, and it more than matched Hagenbeck's Wild Animals with Bostock's menagerie of wild beasts in an arena that anchored the north end of the park. Dreamland also secured attractions directly from its rival, including Wormwood's Dog and Monkey Circus and Dr. Martin Couney's Infant Incubators. Billed as a scientific exhibition of the care of premature infants, the incubator building was, in fact, a small hospital in the style of a German farmhouse, the lower half in brick, the upper part in half-timber, with a tiled roof. A stork guarding a basket of terra-cotta babies decorated its front gable.

Dreamland introduced several novel attrac-

DREAMLAND.
(THE BROOKLYN HISTORICAL SOCIETY)

tions. Midget City was a re-creation of fifteenth-century Nuremberg built to half scale and inhabited by three hundred little people. Residing there were shopkeepers, policemen, wagon drivers, and musicians, all of them dwarfs. There was a Lilliputian theater for tiny folk, a circus under a miniature tent, a livery stable, a midget Chinese laundryman, and even a midget fire department with a small steam fire engine hauled by two fat ponies that responded each hour to a false alarm in the town square. The

*New York Times* noted that "grown folks who visit it can see into third-story windows of the houses without standing on tiptoe." The park's most innovative mechanical attraction was a switchback called the Leap-Frog Railway. It was built on a pier extending about five hundred feet out into the ocean and, as its name suggests, it hurled two electric cars, each carrying up to forty passengers and traveling at a speed of about eight miles an hour, headlong at each other on a single track. At the last moment, one of the cars mounted the curved rails rigged to the roof of the other car and passed over it onto the track beyond. The park's numerous other attractions included a Haunted Swing, a giant human bagatelle board called Chilkoot Pass, and Alberto Santos-Dumont's experimental airship, housed in a Japanese pagoda, which conducted daily ascents over the ocean. Countless small concessions lined Dreamland's Bowery, occupying the lower portion of its pier. Its upper story held an immense ballroom where three thousand couples were accommodated at a time. The park engaged well-known stage performers such as comic singer Andrew Mack and Peter Dailey to act as concessionaires. Marie Dressler, who popularized the song "Heaven Will Protect the Working Girl," had charge of a corps of young boys who staffed the park's popcorn stands.

DREAMLAND'S MIDGET CITY. A WRITER DESCRIBED IT AS A "GIANT COLLECTION OF VARIEGATED DOLLHOUSES, COMPLETE IN EVERY TINY DETAIL," WITH MINIATURE LIVING QUARTERS, SHOPS AND WORKPLACES, AND A MIDGET POLICE FORCE. MIDGET CITY'S MOST CELEBRATED CITIZENS WERE COUNT MAGRI AND HIS WIFE, MERCY LAVINIA WARREN BUMP, WIDOW OF GENERAL TOM THUMB. WHEN "THE ORIENT" REPLACED MIDGET CITY THEY TOOK UP RESIDENCE AT THE MIDGET OPERA HOUSE ON THE BRIGHTON PIKE.   (MILSTEIN DIVISION OF UNITED STATES HISTORY, LOCAL HISTORY AND GENEALOGY, THE NEW YORK PUBLIC LIBRARY, ASTOR, LENOX, AND TILDEN FOUNDATIONS)

Dreamland's architectural achievement won considerable praise. "Verily this is Dreamland, and one rubs one's eyes and pinches one's arms to see if one be really awake," wrote Barr Ferree in *Architects' and Builders' Magazine.* "Such splendor was never before seen at Coney Island." The architects of Dreamland had with great skill restored the straight lines that Fred Thompson had brazenly discarded. Its Beaux-Arts motifs and white facades mimicked the White City of Chicago's World's Colombian Exposition. The park's entrance along Surf Avenue was a monumental foyer, seventy-five feet wide and a hundred feet deep, rendered in Ionic architecture with statue of Education surmounting it. The facades of its various buildings were uniformly white, noteworthy for the architectural use of mural decorations applied with subtle effect to relieve the "brilliancy of whiteness" at attractions such as "The Fall of Pompeii" and "Coasting through Switzerland." The former was a cyclorama enhanced by mechanical and electrical effects depicting the eruption of Mount Vesuvius and destruction of Pompeii. The latter was a scenic railway in which passengers rode in red sleighs through a miniature Swiss valley and ascended, by means of a lengthy funicular tunnel, to an artificially chilled summit of snow-capped peaks. By day, Dreamland was a fairyland of "mystic palaces." By night it was made even more enchanting by a million incandescent lamps with "as many colors as Joseph's coat." Its Beacon Tower alone was etched with a hundred thousand electric lights, all of them a "dazzling sempiternal white." A blanket of heavy fog that cloaked the park the night of its opening con-

tributed to the overall effect. "Dreamland, when it had once passed at dusk into the realm of the electric king was made mysteriously weird, and very, very beautiful," the *Brooklyn Eagle* reported. "The tower that rose by day, a white shaft to a glorious conquest of Good Taste, by night became a beacon against the blackness of the heavens. It rose above the show, radiant beyond belief, a living, glowing thing that excited the admiration and praise of the most prosaic sort of folk."

Dreamland's managers touted the educational and scientific nature of their shows. And yet, as a citadel of refined amusement, it was a bit out of place at Coney Island. Perhaps the sheer size of the buildings cowed the crowds that came to visit, for it was never quite as successful as Luna Park. Thompson, in the meantime, had not sat idly by. He had acquired an additional sixteen acres, increasing his park's size to thirty-eight acres in time for the opening of its second season in 1904. By then Thompson had practically redesigned the park. He dismantled the Venetian City and lined Luna's Court of Honor and lagoon with a double-decked promenade of Japanese tea gardens and flower banks, increasing by seventy thousand the number of visitors the park could accommodate. Thompson's most spectacular new attraction was the Durbar of Delhi pageant, which occupied most of the newly acquired acreage. The Vice Royal Palace was reproduced in miniature and the Durbar procession included a hundred horsemen, five hundred foot soldiers, some sixty elephants, and an "astonishing number of real Eastern people." To complete the illusion,

THE HELTER-SKELTER AT LUNA PARK.

Thompson constructed a miniature Himalayan mountain out of scantling and old tin, rising above the shore of the Coney Island Creek.

.    .    .

Luna Park and Dreamland heralded a "new Coney Island," arisen, so it seemed, from the ashes of the raucous old Bowery recently reduced by fire. "Coney is regenerated," crowed the *New York Times,* "and almost every trace of Old Coney has been wiped out. Frankfurters, peanuts, and popcorn were among the few things left to represent the place as it was in the old days." The two parks were now locked in a spectacular competition. One thousand people, including sixty firemen with engines and extension ladders, took part in Luna Park's production of "Fire and Flame," in which an entire city block was set ablaze. A factory building collapsed nightly, bit by bit, in a glare of fire and pyrotechnic smoke, while all about it was the clamor of horsecars, wagons, and pushcarts with which the firemen had to contend. In Dreamland's near-identical production, twice that number took part with engines and wagons. Both parks added spectacular new attractions. Dreamland installed Hiram Maxim's Airships in its forecourt, equipped with gondolas that revolved around a 150-foot-high tower. The park's scenic railways and water rides included Over the Great Divide, a scenic rail trip through the Rocky Mountains, which wound its way in and out of tunnels, through canyons, and over a seventy-foot-wide trestle; and Hell Gate, a boat ride into a whirlpool. Luna's coast-

ers and water rides included the Dragon's Gorge, Mountain Torrent, and Buzzard's Roost. The Dragon's Gorge was an enclosed coaster with a 4,000-foot-long track and steep curves and grades. Its enclosure had a proscenium arch thirty feet high exposing a waterfall under which the cars passed at great speed. The arch was flanked on either side by enormous dragons. Mountain Torrent was Fred Thompson's attempt to combine the best elements of a water slide and a scenic railroad. It had an eighty-foot-high mountain with cliffs and cascades that carried boats down a sluice-way and under a great cataract into a lake at the bottom. Luna Park possessed a wider assortment of mechanical attractions such as the Double Whirl, the Tickler, Witching Waves, and Virginia Reel, while Dreamland introduced novel attractions such as the Haunted Swing and A Trip in an Airship.

The parks found other ways to distinguish themselves. Dreamland placed greater emphasis on shows that were "morally instructive," drawing upon biblical subjects and making use of dramatic effects and complex stagecraft. To inaugurate its second season, Dreamland added Henry Roltair's "Creation," a spectacular attraction presented with great success at the St. Louis exposition in 1904. "Creation" was staged under an enormous blue dome. It depicted the six days of the Creation as described in the Book of Genesis and concluded with an allegorical tableau representing the creation of man. The arched portal of "Creation" was supported by the outspread wings of an angel, sculpted in the form of a female figure with breasts bared, standing thirty feet tall. Its facade dominated the park's perimeter along Surf Avenue. Roltair also presented "Arabian Nights Up to Date," which recast the Arabian Nights tales, and "Pharaoh's Daughter," in which a statue came to life. A trio of productions by William Ellis—"The End of the World," "The Orient," and "The Here-after"—occupied a prominent place in Dream-land. "The End of the World" was a retelling of Dante's Divine Comedy as depicted by Gustave Doré. "The Orient" encompassed several exotic attractions, including the Hanging Gardens, Herod's Temple, and Salome's Dance of the Seven Veils, and concluded with a spectacular reenactment of the Feast of Belshazzar and the destruction of Babylon. "The Orient" featured La Belle Sultana performing the Dance of the Wicked. A barker enticed the crowd with the words: "This way to the Feast of Belshazzar! One hundred and fifty Oriental beauties! The warmest spectacle on earth! Anywhere else but at Dreamland it would be consumed by its own fire!"

Luna Park countered with Fred Thompson's "Night and Morning." Audiences attending this complex illusion, described as a "wondrous journey through the Stygian chambers," were first entombed in a coffin-shaped room before visiting the River Styx where the souls of the damned endured hellish torments. Thompson took full advantage of Luna Park's size. The Durbar pageant was followed by other "dramatic spectacles," including "The Great Train Robbery," "Days of '49," "The Burning of *Prairie Belle*," and "Crack of Doom." Presented on a 700-foot-wide stage, the shows employed hundreds of actors and required elaborate effects. A full-size

locomotive crossed the stage during "The Great Train Robbery," in which at outlaw gang held up a train, fled to a mining town, and was pursued to a mountain hideout. "The Burning of the *Prairie Belle*," a reenactment of life along the Mississippi, concluded with the burning of a river steamer. "Crack of Doom" depicted a mining town engulfed by floodwaters produced by a tank that held 65,000 gallons of water. Thompson first replaced "A Trip to the Moon" with a cyclorama of "The Battle of the *Merrimac* and the *Monitor*" and later introduced a retooled version called "A Trip to Mars by Aeroplane." He was continually at work transforming the park's appearance. "A stationary Luna Park would be an anomaly," he explained. By 1907 the park had 1,326 towers, domes, and minarets and 1,300,000 electric lights; employed 1,700 people; and housed hundreds of exotic animals, including twenty-five elephants. "The very name 'Luna' and the weird and fantastic charms of the moon and the crescent have been preempted by Fred Thompson in the layout and character of this park," wrote the *Brooklyn Eagle*. "About the court of Luna are corralled all those feats of warriors bold, highway robbers, knights and other adventurers, together with the gruesome and ecstatic imagination of nether worlds and the tom-tom pageant, romp and tinsel display of the present world."

The success of Luna Park, Dreamland, and Steeplechase led to the creation a yet another amusement park, erected between the Brighton Beach Hotel and Manhattan Beach. The Brighton Beach Development Corporation enlisted New York showman William A. Brady to manage the new park. The idea, according to Brady, was to develop a "big amusement layout to compete with Luna Park." The park was a re-creation of the Pike, the amusement midway at the recent Louisiana Purchase Exhibition in St. Louis. To launch the project, Brady secured one of the Pike's big attractions, "The Great Boer War Spectacle," for its opening season. An arena with a grandstand seating twenty thousand people was hastily built and incidents from the South African campaign were reenacted on a battlefield spread over fourteen acres. A thousand British and Boer veterans including General Piet Conje took part, along with Zulus, Kaffirs, mounted lancers, and artillery. Inaugu-rated in 1905, Brighton Beach Park covered seventy-five acres with a mile-long boardwalk extending to Manhattan Beach. Most of its attractions lined an unenclosed midway called the Brighton Pike. More attractions were added for the park's second season, including Ferrari's Wild Animal Arena, a scenic railway, a carousel, an Irish fairground called Donnybrook Fair, and a pavilion called Happyland. "Pawnee Bill's Wild West Show and Great Far East Show" replaced the Boer War in the park's arena. Major Gordon Lillie, dubbed Pawnee Bill, was at various times a competitor and partner of Buffalo Bill and was an heir to the Wild West Show. His show combined Wild West and Far East set-

FERRARI'S WILD ANIMAL ARENA AT BRIGHTON PARK.

(MILSTEIN DIVISION OF UNITED STATES HISTORY, LOCAL HISTORY AND GENEALOGY,

THE NEW YORK PUBLIC LIBRARY, ASTOR, LENOX AND TILDEN FOUNDATIONS)

pieces replete with elephants, camels, Russian Cossacks, South Sea Islanders, Chinese, and Turks. The following year the "Miller Brothers' 101 Ranch," whose cowboy performers included Will Rogers, occupied the arena. After 1907, Pain's fireworks took up residence there, presenting elaborate productions such as "The Destruction of Jerusalem," "Sheridan's Ride," and "Battle in the Clouds," a pyrotechnic spectacle that featured balloon flights and airships. The managers of Brighton Park promoted it as a family playground and sought to strike a middle ground between Coney Island proper and the "sporty" attractions of Manhattan Beach. Although it covered twice as much ground as Luna Park with attractions that included the mile-long Chase Through the Clouds coaster, it was never as popular as its rival, nor did it draw comparable crowds.

Coney Island's amusement attractions were by no means confined to its amusement parks. Countless independent concessions, arcades, carousels, and amusement venues occupied every bit of space along Surf Avenue and the Bowery and every cramped plank boardwalk and alley extending all the way to the ocean. Albert Bigelow Paine was mesmerized by this "horizon of towers, domes, spidery elevations and huge revolving wheels." Coney Island's skyline, which two decades earlier had bewitched José Martí, was so completely transformed as to be almost unrecognizable. Increasingly it was dominated by larger, more daring roller coasters and toboggan rides. Attractions such the Loop the Loop, Cannon Coaster, and Drop the Dip marked the fast-paced evolution of the roller

coaster. By 1907 there were more than twenty coasters and scenic railways at Coney Island, most of them independently operated. In competition with the scenic railways, three massive auditoriums on Surf Avenue produced elaborate "scenographic reproduction" of cataclysmic disasters. Complex stage effects and miniature buildings were used to simulate the eruption of Mount Pelée on the island of Martinique, the deadly Galveston Flood, and the Johnstown Flood. From the westward limits of the amusement zone a bewildering array of shapes were thrust skyward: the Ferris wheel, giant See-Saw, and airship tower at Tilyou's Steeplechase; the undulating tracks of the Drop the Dip, Red Devil, and Rough Rider coasters; Luna Park's Kaleidoscope Tower and its thousand lesser spires and minarets; Dreamland's Beacon Tower, double chutes, and steel pier; the ancient Centennial Observatory; and the lofty campanile of the auditorium housing the Mount Pelée attraction. To the east lay Brighton Park with its great steel coaster, which at night traced a giant illuminated serpent, and farther eastward the stately hotels of Manhattan Beach. Describing this dazzling firmament, Maxim Gorki wrote: "With the advent of night a fantastic city of fire suddenly rises from the ocean into the sky. Thousands of ruddy sparks glimmer in the darkness, limning in fine, sensitive outline on the black background of the sky, shapely towers of miraculous castles, palaces, and temples. Golden gossamer threads tremble in the air. They intertwine in transparent, flaming patterns, which flutter and melt away, in love with their own beauty mirrored in the waters. Fabulous and beyond conceiving, ineffably beautiful, is this fiery scintillation."

. . .

Coney Island's renaissance owed a great debt to George C. Tilyou and the early success of Steeplechase Park. Tilyou continued to introduce novel attractions such as the Human Roulette Wheel and the Human Niagara and was constantly adding to his sprawling pleasure grounds. He acquired a Venetian gondola ride, a giant revolving airship, a circle swing, the Dew-Drop spiral slide, Roltair's House Upside Down, a "French Voyage" panorama, and a figure-eight coaster. He also introduced the Steeplechase combination ticket. When Fred Thompson departed with "A Trip to the Moon," Tilyou had replaced it with another attraction from the Pan-American Exhibition, Cummins's "Indian Congress and Life on the Plains." A Wild West show sanctioned by the United States government, the "Indian Congress" depicted the domestic life of the "red nomads" as well as their combat skills. Forty-three tribes and five hundred aboriginal Americans took part, including Geronimo. Disaster struck the park midway through the season of 1907, however. A fire that ignited in the Cave of Winds leveled most of the park and consumed thirty-five acres of the amusement district along the Bowery, destroying the Drop the Dip roller coaster and everything in its wake. A few Steeplechase attractions, including the Ferris wheel and House Upside Down, survived the conflagration. The fire engines had barely completed their task when

Tilyou planted a sign on the smoldering ruins bearing the park's trademark grinning face and the message: "A little worse for wear, but still in the ring." The next day he replaced it with one that read:

> To Inquiring Friends. I have trouble today that I did not have yesterday.
> I had troubles yesterday that I have not today.
> On this site will be erected shortly a better, bigger, greater Steeplechase Park.
> Admission to the Burning Ruins—10 cents.

Within a week, Steeplechase was open for business again. The park's surviving attractions, rescued from the ashes, were exhibited in a much-reduced enclosure. "We are scorched," said Tilyou, "but we still have twenty-five attractions for twenty-five cents." Tilyou rebuilt the park in time for the season of 1908. The centerpiece of the new park was a glass-and-steel-enclosed Pavilion of Fun covering five acres and housing many of the rides Tilyou had invented or adapted over the years, including the Whirlpool, Barrel of Love, and Human Pool Table. A new and larger Steeplechase race course was built encircling the pavilion. "An Effulgence of Amusement," Tilyou called it.

The success of Steeplechase was built upon Tilyou's insight into human nature and his ability to induce laughter by the most direct and straightforward methods. "Laughter," he once said, "made me a million dollars." Tilyou turned everything on its head. He called his park "Refinement's Pleasure Ground," yet its trademark

Funny Face was a leering libidinous carnival mask. His genius lay in juxtaposing the two. At Steeplechase the carnival spirit without vulgarity was distilled for middle-class Americans. Indeed, Steeplechase's appeal can be attributed to the spirited, liberated, physical play at its core. Everything in the park revolved around the human body and no holds were barred. "We Americans," said Tilyou, "want either to be thrilled or amused, and we are ready to pay well for either sensation." Like Fred Thompson, Tilyou understood that "people are just boys and girls grown tall." But while Thompson added an imaginative, architectural dimension to Luna Park, Tilyou simply built an enormous glass lid over his. Beneath it, much as in Alice's looking glass, things that were small grew large, and those that once were large suddenly lost all proportion.

Thompson and Tilyou were clear about the kind of crowd they wanted to attract to their parks. Both promoted "clean fun." Thompson advertised Luna as "the place for your mother, your sister, and your sweetheart." Tilyou barred intoxicating beverages and posted notices in his theater prohibiting vulgarity and slang and insisted upon "polite vaudeville." Other showmen soon discovered that it was profitable to combine many forms of popular entertainment in enclosed amusement parks that excluded

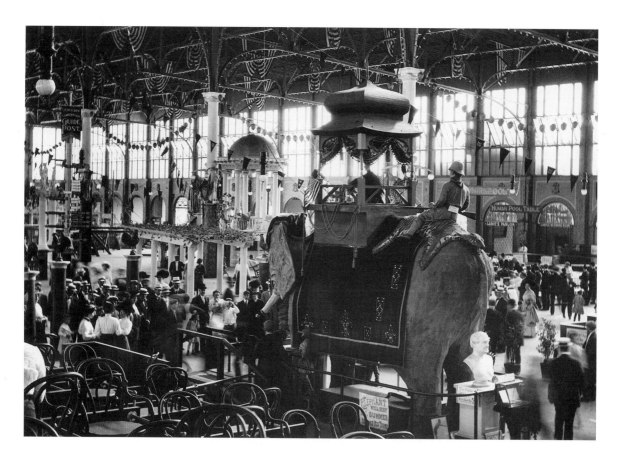

INTERIOR VIEW OF THE PAVILION OF FUN AT STEEPLECHASE PARK.

"fraudulent and offensive features." By 1907, a hundred million dollars had been invested in amusement parks across the United States.

These pasteboard replicas of the exposition midways combined the Parisian fête, the Mardi Gras carnival, the circus, and the dime museum with the "jubilant terrors" of Coney Island. Some likened the new amusement parks to a medieval street fair, a twentieth-century Corso with "illuminated palaces of staff." Rollin Lynde Hartt decried their feeble imitation of John Burnham's great fair in Chicago in the guise of amusement park midways where "a hot boardwalk replaces the delicious lawns and shrubbery, tinsel architecture the exquisite facades, a few plastic fol-de-rols the lavish sculpture-groups." Still, he was forced to concede that its "barbaric ensemble" achieved its main purpose. "It expresses joyousness," he wrote. "In cupolas and minarets, in domes and flaunting finials, in myriads of gay bannerets, in the jocund motion of merry-go-rounds, circle swings, and wondrous sliding follies, in laughter and in shrieks, in the blare of brazen music and in the throbbing tom-toms, it speaks its various language—joyous ever." The eminent critic James Gibbons Huneker was frankly appalled at what he discovered at Coney Island. "Coney Island is a glorified city of flame," he wrote. "But don't go to near it; your wings will easily singe on the broad avenue where beer, sausage, fruit, popcorn, candy, flapjacks, green corn, and again beer, rule the appetites of the multitude." He disdained the architecture of Luna Park and Dreamland where "every angle reveals some new horror" and where everything was but a reflection in a "cracked mirror held in

the hand of a clever showman." "Coney Island," he concluded, "is only another name for topsy-turvydom." Other writers struggling to account for the mass appeal of the new parks were forced to confront the inescapable fact that mankind seemed preternaturally drawn to Coney Island's loop-the-loops and mechanical revolving wheels while shunning nature's ready-made wonders. America, Richard Le Gallienne observed, built itself a Palace of Illusions filled with "every misbegotten fancy of the frenzied nerves, every fantastic marvel of the moonstruck brain—and she has called it Coney Island." Rollin Lynde Hartt was disheartened by the sad spectacle of hordes of city folk "rushing to the ocean-side, to escape the city's din, and crowds and nervous strain, and, once within sight and sound of the waves, courting worse din, denser crowds, and infinitely more devastating nervous strain inside an enclosure whence the ocean cannot possibly be seen." Robert Wilson Neal, who sought to provide an explanation, wrote: "A seething mixing-bowl is Coney in which humanity, without regard to character or station, is kneaded into more compact democracy; and the emollient that makes the combination possible is the spirit of the carnival."

Maxim Gorki stood apart as Coney Island's most unrelenting critic. In an essay entitled "Boredom," the Russian unleashed a withering denunciation of the island that appeared so enchanting when first glimpsed from the sea.

The City, magic and fantastic from afar, now appears an absurd jungle of straight lines of wood, a cheap hastily constructed

DREAMLAND AT NIGHT.

(LIBRARY OF CONGRESS)

toyhouse for the amusement of children. Dozens of white buildings, monstrously diverse, not one with even the suggestion of beauty. They are built of wood, and smeared over with peeling white paint, which gives them the appearance of suffering with the same skin disease. The high turrets and low colonnades extend in two dead-even lines insipidly pressing upon each other. Everything is stripped naked by the dispassionate glare. . . . Everything round about glitters insolently and reveals its own dismal ugliness.

Gorki described a landscape of pasteboard illusions where dispirited souls "swarm into the cages like black flies" or wander about in the "dazzling cobwebs of the amusement halls" where everything "whirls and dazzles, and blends into a tempestuous ferment of fiery foam." Gorki's Coney Island was a "slimy marsh of boredom" that had but one purpose: "to crush the spirit of . . . the working people" and extract their earnings from their pockets. Gorki's ideology permitted little latitude for play that had the capacity to liberate the human spirit. Coney Island capitalists such as Fred Thompson and George Tilyou were showmen first and foremost who promulgated a new ideology of leisure, one that manufactured its diversions out of pasteboard and tinsel, and all things transitory. "Speed," Fred Thompson proclaimed, is "an inborn American trait."

.    .    .

As the first decade of the new century drew to a close, Coney Island was at its pinnacle. America's rapidly evolving mass culture had firmly taken root there. The crowds coming to the resort reached unprecedented numbers, far exceeding those in attendance at any other sport or pastime. Those who visited Coney were participants in a process that was reshaping American popular culture, transforming it into a commodity that could be mass-produced and exported. "Amusement for the masses," roared the advertisements for Luna Park, which collected an astounding 31 million admissions during its first five years in operation. The season of 1909 was perhaps the most spectacularly successful one in the history of the resort. Twenty million visitors came that year, including Carl Jung and Sigmund Freud, who called Coney Island a "magnified Prater." They spent about 45 million dollars and consumed 10 million hot dogs. The "marvelous city of lath and burlap" to which they came was fed with enough electrical power to illuminate a city of five hundred thousand souls. It was, the *New York Times* wrote, "one of the greatest sights of the modern world."

It is Earl's Court, Olympia, Scheveningen, and a good part of Boulogne rolled into one, with some of the attractions of Brighton and Trouville. Its fame is worldwide. It seems to represent, in its entirety, the nearest approach to festival making of which the conglomerate American people are capable. Its growth to a variegated, perpetually crowded, noisy, bustling city by the sea, from its beginning at old Norton's Pier, forms a characteristic chapter of our history.

Coney Island had achieved unparalleled stature as an amusement center; nevertheless, there were signs suggesting that its amusement resources had limits. A scheme to build an amusement park at Manhattan Beach with a reproduction of Niagara Falls cascading into the Atlantic Ocean never materialized; however, a Japanese pavilion with a giant Buddha was erected there. An ambitious plan for a two-mile-long "over-sea" promenade 300 feet out over the ocean also came to naught. Then, in 1906, Samuel Friede unveiled plans for a 700-foot-tall amusement sphere called the Globe Tower. The tower would cost 1.5 million dollars to build and was to occupy a 300-square-foot tract at the northwest corner of Steeplechase Park leased from George Tilyou. The tower was to include a Pedestal Roof Garden with a vaudeville theater, restaurant, and skating rink, 150 feet above the ground; an Aerial Hippodrome at a height of 250 feet with a continuous four-ring circus and a miniature railroad; a ballroom, exposition hall, and revolving cafe at the 300-foot level; an Aerial Palm Garden with a restaurant, promenade, and scenic railroad 350 feet above the ground; an observation deck at an elevation of 500 feet; and a weather observatory and wireless telegraph station 600 feet above the ground. It was to be surmounted by the largest revolving searchlight in the world. The Globe Tower would have dwarfed every other structure at Coney Island, rising three times as high as New York's Flatiron Building. With a circumference of 900 feet, it would have been comparable in size to Madison Square Garden with the capacity to hold 50,000 people at one time. "Thousands of electric lights will make the building a gigantic tower of fire by night," its promoters wrote. A band concert and fireworks marked the laying of the tower's cornerstone in May 1906. It was scheduled to open a year later. Work on its foundation was repeatedly delayed, however, and by 1908, plans for the sphere were abandoned.

Dreamland also faced setbacks. Although artistically successful, the park never gained public favor on an equal footing with Luna Park. Moreover, it had daunting operating expenses to shoulder. During the 1908 season it instituted free admission on weekdays to bolster attendance. The following year Samuel W. Gumpertz was hired as park manager. Gumpertz possessed solid credentials as a showman. He had managed several Midwestern amusement parks and had ventured to the remote corners of the globe in search of novel attractions for his shows. Gumpertz had created Dreamland's Midget City and had also provided two hundred Igorot "headhunters" from the Philippine Islands for the park's Bontoc Village. His task as manager was to add variety to Dreamland's attractions. He organized a sideshow called the Congress of Curious People and added other acts, including an aquatic show called the Diving Venuses and a vaudeville theater. He left undisturbed attractions such as "Creation" and Bostock's Wild Animals that were still popular. Bostock's roster included Little Hip, the world's smallest performing elephant, and Captain Jack

Bonavita, the dashing lion tamer who had lost an arm after being mauled by one of his lions.

Disaster struck Dreamland while preparations were under way for the start of its eighth season. A fire erupted at 1:45 A.M. on the morning of May 27, 1911, in an attraction called Hell Gate, as workmen were completing last-minute repairs. Sparks ignited a sheet of tar that burst into flame. The fire spread through the park. It soon consumed the Infant Incubator building, sparking rumors that the incubator babies had perished when, in fact, they had been carried to safety. There was great alarm as the fire approached the Wild Animal Arena where a hundred animals were sheltered. Captain Bonavita and Colonel Joseph Ferrari worked frantically to control the lions and other beasts that leapt at the bars of their cages. Some of them were bundled into small, movable cages and dragged to safety. Attendants armed with rifles stood guard with orders to shoot any beast that got loose.

Crowds gathered along Surf Avenue to watch the progress of the fire. By 2:30 A.M. the flames, fanned by a strong breeze, had spread to the base of Dreamland's Beacon Tower, which was quickly engulfed. The flames shot up its walls, licking its outer coating of white paint, writhing and twisting through the lattice that formed its decoration, so that it glowed like a great bonfire against the night sky. The sheet of flames quickly mounted beyond the reach of the firemen, who were unable to rest their ladders against the walls of the tower, which threatened to topple over at any moment. In the end it simply collapsed upon itself "like a disabled elevator."

By then, Gumpertz had given orders to shoot the remaining animals. Many either perished in the flames or were shot by their trainers. A few bolted from their cages. A lion named Sultan escaped onto Surf Avenue. When it emerged through the entrance gate of "Creation" with its thick mane resembling "a collar of fire" and sparks trailing "like torrents from its tail," panic overcame the crowd. The animal cut across Surf Avenue and sought refuge in the darkened entrance of a scenic railroad called Rocky Road to Dublin. Pursued by its trainers, it mounted the tracks of the coaster and crouched on a parapet overlooking the street below. The police fired sixty bullets at it before the lion toppled over, still showing signs of life. A policeman struck it dead with an axe. Among the animals that perished in the flames was Little Hip, who was scheduled to board a ship the following day bound for London to take part in King George V's coronation parade.

By 3:00 A.M., trains from Manhattan were unloading thousands of onlookers attracted by rumors that all of Coney Island was ablaze. Police from every precinct were called upon to hold back the crowds. By then the fire had spread beyond Dreamland, taking hold of Pike's Peak scenic railway on Surf Avenue. The flames also swept oceanward, engulfing Dreamland's pier until all that remained of it were twisted iron pilings. Both ends of the park were ablaze and a long line of flame extended to the ocean. The heat grew so intense that fireboats could not get close enough to assist. With no hope of saving Dreamland, firefighters concentrated on containing the flames, but were undermined by

THIS PANORAMIC VIEW TAKEN JUST DAYS AFTER DREAMLAND'S FIERY DESTRUCTION SHOWS NO TRACE OF THE PARK'S BEACON TOWER. ITS FINAL MOMENTS PROVIDED CONEY ISLAND'S MOST SPECTACULAR PYROTECHNIC DISPLAY. "FROM MANHATTAN AND FAR OUT TO SEA," WROTE THE NEW YORK TIMES, "ITS GREAT COLUMN APPEARED FOR FIVE OR TEN MINUTES AS A SPLENDID TORCH, STANDING OUT WITH STARTLING DISTINCTNESS AMID THE SMOKE THAT CURLED UP FROM THE FURNACE BELOW. WHILE IT STOOD IT ATTRACTED ALL EYES, BUT SUDDENLY IT WAS SEEN TO WAVER AND THE ENTIRE STRUCTURE SEEMED TO COLLAPSE ON ITS FOUNDATIONS." THE GIANT RACING COASTER, SHOWN AT THE RIGHT, SURVIVED THE INFERNO. THE COASTER ACTED AS A FIRE-WALL AT THE WESTERN EDGE OF THE PARK, ALTHOUGH ITS WOODEN FRAME IGNITED AND MOST OF THE SMALL STRUCTURES BENEATH IT, INCLUDING A GYPSY ENCAMPMENT, WERE BURNED TO THE GROUND.

BY NIGHTFALL THE WORK OF CLEARING AWAY THE RUINS WAS UNDER WAY. SHOWMEN SET UP MAKESHIFT STALLS ALONG SURF AVENUE EVEN AS TUFTS OF SMOKE OCCASIONALLY ROSE FROM BURNT TIMBERS.

a failure of the high-pressure system that was overtaxed by the number of fire units attempting to draw water for their hoses. By 3:30 A.M., Dreamland was entirely consumed. By 4:00 A.M., the fire had advanced eastward, eating its way through the shacks and amusement stalls near the Iron Pier and engulfing the Observatory Tower. The tower had withstood several previous fires but the intense heat melted its steel frame and it too collapsed.

A few brick buildings to the east of the tower checked the fire's progress at that point. By 5:00 A.M. the blaze was under control. A five-block area had been destroyed. All of Dreamland including "Creation," the double chutes, the Infant Incubators, and the Glacier scenic railroad had disappeared. Many concessions outside the park were also destroyed, including the Iron Pier, Pike's Peak scenic railway, Jackman's Whirlwind coaster, and Balmer's Bathing Pavilion. Quite remarkably, the El Dorado carousel, recently arrived at Coney Island, survived with

Coney Island, N.Y. 1911

COLONEL FERRARI SPRINKLED SAWDUST OVER THE RUINS OF HIS ARENA. THE NEXT DAY HE EXHIBITED HIS MENAGERIE UNDER A CANVAS TENT. NOT FAR FROM FERRARI'S ENCLOSURE, A TENT DISPLAYED THE STUFFED CARCASS OF THE LION SULTAN FOR THE PRICE OF A DIME. ANOTHER CONCESSIONAIRE HAWKED HALF-BURNED PHOTOGRAPHS OF LITTLE HIP AS AUTHENTIC RELICS OF THE FIRE. THE PHOTOGRAPHS WERE AUTHENTIC BUT THE FIRE DAMAGE WAS THE WORK OF THE SHOWMAN'S ASSISTANT, WHO SINGED THE EDGES WITH A CANDLE. OTHER TENTS AND IMPROVISED STRUCTURES WERE QUICKLY ERECTED. A "SEVEN-IN-ONE" FREAK SHOW OCCU-PIED ONE OF THEM. "THE CANVASSES DISPLAYING THE FAT LADY AND THE ELASTIC-SKINNED MAN WERE HUNG OUT IN REGULAR COUNTRY FAIR STYLE," NOTED THE *TIMES*, "AND THE SPIELERS TOOK THEIR PLACES ON THE PLATFORM AND URGED THE PASSERS-BY TO COME IN. 'ALL THAT'S LEFT OF DREAMLAND, BEAUTIFUL DREAM-LAND,' WAS THE BURDEN OF THEIR CRY." A CROWD OF 350,000 PEOPLE CAME TO VIEW THE RUINS.

(LIBRARY OF CONGRESS)

little damage. Property loss was estimated at 5 million dollars; however, not a single human life was lost. "Dreamland is gone," Gumpertz con-ceded, "but I am certain a new amusement park will be built." George Dobson, one of Dream-land's directors, offered a more sober assess-ment. "I think it is safe to say that Dreamland will not be rebuilt," he stated. Recalling that pro-moters of the park had endeavored to appeal to a "highly developed sense of the artistic," he observed: "It did not take them long to discover

that Coney Island was scarcely the place for that sort of thing." Senator Reynolds, the park's principal owner, was even more blunt. "The city should not permit us to rebuild," he said. "There is too much risk." Instead, he urged the city to take over the land and convert it into a public park.

The Dreamland conflagration brought to a close the era of amusement spectacles at Coney Island. As the fire swept through the park, the crowds that gathered to watch could have easily imagined they were viewing one of Pain's pyrotechnic displays. However, when the flames engulfed the animal arena the crowd ceased being a detached audience in the face of the real danger posed by an escaped lion. A thin line of tinsel separated the manufactured spectacles and illusions that were the mainstay of Coney's showmen from the horrors and conflagrations of everyday life. In a way, Coney Island had overstepped those limits. It had glowed white-hot, had momentarily flickered, and burned all the more spectacularly as a result. The great blaze, it turned out, was a fiery exclamation point. "There will be reared on the still hot ruins of last night's fire new and finer structures," the *Brooklyn Eagle* told its readers, "and Coney Island will continue on its way." But it was not to be so. Dreamland was not rebuilt and Coney Island would never again gain such acclaim. The second decade of the century ushered in wonders and horrors that outstripped and outpaced Coney Island's prodigious resources, and were of a kind its showmen could neither compete with nor replicate. And yet, Sam Gumpertz and others like him knew how to take the pulse of the crowd. They promised "old time Coney Island shows" and had their tents up before the embers were cold.

# CHAPTER FIVE

# SEASIDE BAROQUE

THE RAPID development of the amusement industry at Coney Island encouraged an extravagant architectural style and decorative motifs that soon embellished amusement parks worldwide. At various times described as "seaside baroque" and "amusement park baroque," it is perhaps best characterized by a blending together of fanciful decorative effects of European origin with the radical, sometimes daunting machinery of Coney Island's coasters and thrill rides. This melding of ornamentation and centrifugal force gave the Coney Island amusement park its extraordinary dynamism.

In the period that preceded the appearance of its enclosed amusement parks, Coney Island's architecture was rather primitive. It was described by one visitor as a "Chinatown of little frame buildings set about helter-skelter, like a cityful of houses in a panic." Another likened it to a Western mining camp. To bring a measure of coherence to this disharmonious setting, Coney Island drew upon the genius and energies of many protean figures of the amusement industry. Among the showmen were George C.

Tilyou, Fred Thompson, and Frank Bostock. Among the makers of carousels and mechanical rides were Charles Looff, Marcus Illions, William Mangels, and Charles Carmel. Among the creators and innovators of roller coasters and scenic railways were La Marcus Thompson, Stephan Jackman, John Miller, and Christopher Feucht. Among the creators of scenic spectacles and illusion shows were Henry Roltair and William Ellis. These men relied upon the skills of countless craftsmen and artisans, scenic designers, painters, muralists, mechanics, electricians, and engineers to realize their visions. Fred Thompson required a 700-man labor force to build Luna Park. Many of those employed were European immigrants who brought to America skills from the Old World that the domestic labor force lacked, talents they were able to apply to the new requirements of the amusement industry.

Thompson stood head and shoulders above the others as a theorist of amusement park architecture. "An architect who engages in the business of providing temples of amusement for a pleasure-loving, midsummer populace should depart from all set rules of architecture," he wrote. "The schemes of such a man must be fantastical. . . . He must dare to decorate a minaret with Renaissance detail or to jumble Romanesque with l'art nouveau, always with the idea of keeping his line constantly varied, broken, and moving." George C. Tilyou, although he followed a very different plan, also embraced the architectural motifs of the European fairgrounds. Tilyou added baroque embellishments and carved cherubs from Leipzig to his steel-buttressed, glass-enclosed Pavilion of Fun, which was built like a conservatory or a nineteenth-century train shed.

.    .    .

The earliest form of decorative art at Coney Island accompanied the development of the carousel. Carousels were a popular amusement device at European country fairs and pleasure grounds such as Vauxhall and Tivoli Gardens, and primitive carousels were present in the United States as early as the first half of the nineteenth century. Around 1870 an Englishman named Fredrick Savage devised a steam-powered roundabout with a center-truck system. This permitted the production of much larger four-abreast carousels. British, German, and French carousel manufacturers embellished them with gaudy rounding boards and facades carved in a style sometimes called "music hall baroque." Their American counterparts, almost entirely of European stock, eventually developed their own distinct styles of carving, which

were dubbed "Philadelphia style," "Country Fair style," and "Coney Island style."

The first carousel company in the United States was established by Gustav Dentzel in Philadelphia in 1867. Dentzel's horses and menagerie animals were realistically carved and elegantly posed. The carousels he produced were dubbed "Philadelphia style." His company manufactured the first steam-powered carousels in America, and his success inspired other carvers to try their hand in the carousel business. One of these was Charles Looff, who had come to the United States from Schleswig-Holstein in 1870. In 1876, while employed full-time as a woodworker, Looff created Coney Island's first carousel and installed it at Lucy Vandeveer's Bathing Pavilion. He carved all the figures by hand, built the frame and platform, and painted the trim. In 1880 he produced a second and far superior carousel for Feltman's Ocean Pavilion, which enabled him to open his own carousel factory. Looff's animals were more fanciful than those created by Dentzel. He produced well-proportioned horses, especially jumpers, with wild manes and muscular bodies that lunged forward, then embellished them with jewels and beveled mirrors. The carousel figures Looff produced were dubbed "Coney Island style" and his Brooklyn factory soon employed forty carvers and craftsmen. While Looff was creating large, stationary carousels, a Brooklyn competitor named Charles Dare began to produce small, transportable roundabouts called Swinging Platforms and Galloping Horses, which eventually became staples at carnivals and country fairs. The small, plump horses with large marble eyes created at Dare's New York Carousel Company became known as "Country Fair style."

Brooklyn was now a center of the carousel and amusement industry with carousel makers such as Bungarz Steam Wagon and Carousel Works producing portable roundabouts and William F. Mangels establishing a factory there. By 1885 more than a dozen carousels were in operation at Coney Island. They were no longer the hobbyhorses of old on revolving platforms powered by a wooden lever. Housed in beautiful pavilions with groined roofs and stained-glass panels, they were steam-driven, with animals carved according to the "highest German conception of naturalness" and "glittering with looking-glass diamonds." A newspaper observed that "solid country merchants and foreigners of fourscore years are often seen astride the members of these wooden menageries with eyes aflame under the consciousness that he or she who gets a brass ring by spearing among the iron ones with a huge bodkin will enjoy the next ride free." It was estimated that between $75,000 and $100,000 was invested in the construction of carousels during this period. A reporter visiting Charles Looff's factory encountered a "menagerie of the wildest description," including camels and sea serpents and "animals possessing forms that mince pie at midnight could hardly conjure up in a subsequent dream."

The winter of 1888 witnessed the arrival at Coney Island of two more amusement industry innovators. One was English showman Frank Bostock, who arrived with a menagerie of wild animals and show wagons built by Frederick Savage. The other was a Lithuanian carver named Marcus Charles Illions who had been employed by Savage and recently hired by Bostock. In 1893, Bostock had sent to England for a four-abreast Galloping Horse carousel with an overhead crank system devised by Savage, which he planned to operate at the World's Columbian Exposition in Chicago. The overhead crank enabled the horses to move upward and downward in a "galloping" motion. This modification gave the carousel mechanism its present form. When the carousel was late arriving for the exposition, Bostock installed it at Coney Island instead. The following year Bostock added amusement rides to his menagerie of show animals at Coney Island and assembled the first traveling carnival in America. Bostock engaged William Mangels to provide small, portable rides for his new venture.

By then, M. C. Illions had established his own shop in Brooklyn and was producing carousel horses, rounding boards, show fronts, and chariots for various carousel makers. At first his carved horses resembled those created by Looff, but he soon developed his own distinct style. His horses acquired more dramatic poses with expressive manes, mouths wide agape, and glistening bodies, white with trappings that grew ever more resplendent. When Feltman's carousel with horses by Looff was damaged by fire, Illions and Mangels were hired to restore it. The Looff figures that survived the fire had unique features. The outside horses were studded with glass jewels set in embossed escutcheons, with porcelain light fixtures inserted inside the figures so they could be illuminated from within.

Illions restored these figures and also created others in the new style he had developed. The result was the Fabulous Feltman, one of the most spectacular carousels ever created. Illions was subsequently hired by Fred Thompson to create embellishments for Luna Park. He produced decorative scrollwork as well as the carved chariots that served as the park's ticket kiosks. He also produced chariots for La Marcus Thompson's scenic railways. Illions and Mangels formed a partnership and produced other Coney Island carousels. When the partnership dissolved, Illions established M. C. Illions and Sons Carousel Works, producing six separate kinds of carousels, including a four-abreast with seventy-four horses. He also carved chariots, rounding boards, circus wagons, organ fronts, and steeplechase horses in a rococo style that influenced practically every carver that followed him.

Marcus Illions was not the only carver employed at Mangels Carousel Works who produced carousel horses of exceptional quality. Solomon Stein and Harry Goldstein were Russian immigrants who met at the Mangels factory in 1905. They formed a partnership and eventually established their own carousel business in Brooklyn called the Artistic Carousel Manufacturing Company. The horses they created were

FRANK BOSTOCK'S "FOUR-ABREAST BANTAMS" AT CONEY ISLAND IN 1896.

(BARBARA FAHS CHARLES COLLECTION)

MARCUS ILLIONS (AT RIGHT, FACING CAMERA) FLANKED BY HIS SONS AT M. C. ILLIONS CAROUSEL WORKS IN CONEY ISLAND, CIRCA 1922. (COURTESY OF RUTH ILLIONS PEASE)

large and muscular with elongated bodies aggressively posed, often with teeth bared. These massive war horses were given a less fierce appearance by the use of fanciful trappings such as fish-scale blankets and cabbage roses. Stein and Goldstein created five- and six-abreast carousels with sixty-foot platforms, each with a king's horse or armored charger and a pair of chariots and a capacity to seat up to a hundred riders. They were some of the largest carousels ever created.

Among the many carvers active at Coney Island during this period, Charles Carmel was perhaps the most representative of the Coney Island style. The Russia-born Carmel was employed by Looff before opening his own shop in Brooklyn in 1905. Carmel's style displayed the influence of Illions and Looff and other master carvers, but he achieved an expressive quality that was unsurpassed. His horses were exquisitely proportioned, posed in mid-gallop, their manes windswept and often combed forward, their trappings bejeweled and embellished with fish-scales and feathers in a manner that recalled Stein and Goldstein. Carmel worked exclusively as a carver, supplying horses to carousel makers such as Mangels and the Philadelphia Toboggan Company. His work is often associated with Fred Dolle and M. D. Borelli, who built carousel frames. Borelli decorated many of Carmel's horses, often embellishing them with hundreds of glass jewels. The carousel horses created by Carmel are considered among the most perfectly executed examples of carving in the Coney Island style.

The popularity of the carousel led to the invention of other mechanical amusements constructed along the lines of a roundabout but with innovative new elements. William Sassack introduced a balloon carousel at Coney Island in 1888, and steam-powered bicycle carousels and velocipedes also appeared. Hiram Maxim's

THE KISTER CAROUSEL CREATED BY MANGELS AND ILLIONS WAS THE FASTEST AT CONEY ISLAND. THE STYLE OF EACH CONEY ISLAND CARVER WAS DISTINCTIVE. CHARLES LOOFF'S FIGURES WERE DISTINGUISHED BY SCOOPED CANTLES BEHIND THE SADDLES INTO WHICH GARGOYLES, CHERUBS' HEADS, AND ARRANGEMENTS OF FLOWERS AND FRUIT WERE CARVED. ILLIONS'S CREATIONS WERE ORNATE, BEJEWELED CREATURES WITH WILD MANES. STEIN AND GOLDSTEIN'S HORSES WERE AGGRESSIVELY POSED, THEIR FIERCE DEMEANOR OFFSET BY TRAPPINGS DECORATED WITH TASSELS AND FEATHERS AND SADDLES WITH BIG BUCKLES. CHARLES CARMEL'S BEAUTIFULLY PROPORTIONED HORSES WITH MANES SWEPT FORWARD WERE OFTEN STUDDED WITH HUNDREDS OF GLASS JEWELS. (FRIED COLLECTION)

Captive Flying Machine whirled riders about in small airships, as did the Circle Swing devised by Harry Traver around 1903. In 1906, Frank Bostock introduced the first Venetian Gondola in America at Coney Island, while the Double Whirl, combining elements of a carousel and Ferris wheel, was introduced in 1910. At the same time, not all carousel manufacturers limited their production to carousel frames. Charles Dare's company manufactured cane boards, swings,

A CHARIOT ON THE EL DORADO CAROUSEL. CREATED BY HUGO HASSE OF LEIPZIG, GERMANY, THE EL DORADO WAS PERHAPS THE FINEST CAROUSEL EVER DISPLAYED IN THE UNITED STATES. BROUGHT TO CONEY ISLAND IN 1910, THE CAROUSEL STOOD FORTY-TWO FEET HIGH AND WAS SIXTY-TWO FEET IN DIAMETER WITH THREE TIERS OF REVOLVING PLATFORMS, INCLUDING A ROW OF MAGNIFICENT CHARIOTS, EACH ROTATING AT DIFFERENT SPEEDS. IT COULD SEAT 140 RIDERS AT A TIME. THE ENTIRE STRUCTURE WAS EMBELLISHED WITH HAND-CARVED EAGLES, DOLPHINS, BIRDS, AND AMORETTI, AND WITH ART NOUVEAU CEILING PAINTINGS, MIRRORED POSTS, AND ELECTRIC GLOBES. AT ITS CENTER WAS A THRONE ROOM DECORATED WITH OWLS AND LIFE-SIZE FEMALE TRUMPETERS. THE CAROUSEL SURVIVED THE DREAMLAND FIRE AND WAS THEN TRANSFERRED TO STEEPLECHASE PARK'S PAVILION OF FUN. ITS FOUR-TON ORGAN WAS PLACED IN THE PAVILION'S BALCONY, AND ITS FACADE SERVED AS AN ENTRANCE TO THE PARK ON SURF AVENUE. A HALF MILLION PEOPLE RODE THE CAROUSEL IN 1919. RIDERS INCLUDED THEODORE ROOSEVELT, GEORGE M. COHAN, AND ENRICO CARUSO.

(BROOKLYN PUBLIC LIBRARY—BROOKLYN COLLECTION)

shooting galleries, and an early version of the Ferris wheel. Bungarz Carousel Works produced an early, not entirely successful version of a circle swing in 1894. William Mangels was both a manufacturer of amusement equipment and an inventor of popular rides such as the Tickler and the Whip. In 1907 he patented a modified version of Savage's overhead crank system that became the standard for all galloping-horse

carousels. As mechanical rides became more common, other innovators abandoned the carousel's circular track in favor of more daring configurations that relied upon undulating tracks, steep inclines, centrifugal force, and caster wheels. Devices such as Herbert Bradwell's Scrambler, Theophilus Van Kannel's Witching Waves, and Henry Riehl's Virginia Reel were intentionally designed to jostle and jar riders.

. . .

The centerpiece of every amusement enterprise, towering high over its midway, was the roller coaster. The modern coaster is descended from a gravity ride called the Russian Mountain that was a popular amusement in St. Petersburg as early as the sixteenth century. It was inspired by a more primitive winter amusement built in the form of an ice toboggan slide. Russian Mountains soon appeared in other parts of Europe and in 1817 a more sophisticated ride called the Promenades Aeriennes, running on wheels, was erected in Paris. European enthusiasm for these devices waned, however, and by the middle of the century they had all but disappeared. In the United States, the development of the coaster as an amusement advanced with the appearance of a coal-carrying device built at Mauch Chunk, Pennsylvania, called the Switchback Railway. Erected in 1827, with a back-track added in 1845, it ran along a "gravity road" and it soon became a popular tourist attraction. The success at Mauch Chunk led to the issuing of several patents for a gravity ride operating on the same principle and designed exclusively for the purpose of amusement. The first to actually construct such a device was La Marcus Adna Thompson.

La Marcus Thompson was born on Ohio in 1848. The founder of a successful clothing company in Indiana, he was compelled for reasons of health to sell the business, and subsequently turned his attention to the invention of amusement devices. The Switchback that Thompson introduced at Coney Island in 1884 was the first of its kind ever built. It was composed of two undulating tracks, 600 feet long, with a loading station at either end. Passengers had to disembark and reboard to complete the trip. A description of the device appeared in the *New York Herald* on June 2, 1884.

> It is a sort of summer coasting hill, except the 'hill' is a wooden trough about three feet wide, which forms a circular incline whose circumference is about the extent of two city blocks. Benches on runners fit into a narrow track in this trough, and a half a dozen people are whirled around this track at a frightful rate of speed. This new 'game' only opened at two o'clock in the afternoon, and by six o'clock, at the moderate rate of five cents for a whirl, the proprietor must have realized about $200.

By August, there were four more roller coasters in operation at Coney Island, including Charles Alcoke's Serpentine Railway, which improved upon Thompson's design by linking the tracks at both ends so that they formed a single oval-shaped circuit. A year later, Philip Hinkle intro-duced a vastly improved elliptical coaster that was steeply graded, with forward-facing seats. The new coasters outpaced Thompson's Switch-back and for the moment he chose to retreat from Coney Island. Around the same time another coaster design was introduced, not at Coney Island, but at a roller skating rink in Haverhill, Massachusetts. In 1886, Stephen E. Jackman and Byron Floyd patented a device, the first built with a figure-eight design, called the Roller Toboggan that closely resembled a modern roller coaster. The Sliding Hill at Haverhill was equipped with toboggan sleds that coasted down a track on rollers. Jackman and Floyd soon parted company, with Jackman coming to New York, where he patented a breaking system for coasters that improved their safety. His coasters at Coney Island included a combination water chute and toboggan slide called Shooting the Rapids, the Musical Railroad, Jackman's Thriller, and the Whirlwind coaster.

Various experimental designs for gravity rides were tested in the years that followed. One of the most novel was the Centrifugal Cycle Railway, or Flip-Flap, patented by Lina Beecher and installed at Boyton's Sea Lion Park around 1900. It was reminiscent of a centrifugal device that had been exhibited in Paris a half century earlier. The Flip-Flap coaster had a twenty-five-foot loop at the end of its hill. However, the speed at which the cars entered the loop caused discomfort to its riders and it was short-lived. Edwin Prescott's Loop the Loop coaster, erected on Surf Avenue in 1901, corrected some of the earlier ride's flaws. This coaster had an elliptical loop, allowing riders to enter and exit on a more gradual incline. It was the first truly successful centrifugal ride and some people paid admission just to enter its enclosure and watch others coast through its loop. One observer remarked, "I wouldn't ride that for $50,000." George Francis Meyer's Cannon Coaster, introduced in 1902, was the first attempt at a "leap the gap" coaster. Its cars accelerated as they sped through the bore of a large wooden cannon and were propelled across a gap in the tracks. The ride was tested with sandbags, but was deemed unsafe and its experimental gap was eliminated. One of the most daring and innovative coasters was Christopher Feucht's Drop the Dip, which debuted on Coney Island's Bowery in 1907. It was the first coaster to use steep grades and a track intentionally designed to terrify its riders. It burned to the ground after just two months in operation but was rebuilt by Feucht with additional features. It became the prototype for the high-speed coasters that were to follow.

By 1907 there were more than twenty coasters and scenic railways at Coney Island. There seemed to be no limit to the demand for these devices. Elmer Blaney Harris, who chronicled his visit to the resort in 1908, wrote:

A million rides a day at ten cents per ride is the average record on the mechanical riding devices of Coney Island, when the season is good. People stand in line an hour for a ride that is 'over' in two minutes. They ride before eating to stir up an appetite, they ride after eating to soothe the 'hot dogs,' they ride when exuberant for the fun of riding, they ride when jaded to buck themselves

up. Like any other excitant, the scenic has become a habit.

Eccentric rides such as the Whirlfly appeared and operators of competing attractions sought to entice riders with extravagant claims and blandishments. Jackman's Musical Railroad billed itself as "The Most Exciting Novelty and the Greatest Ride on Earth" but there was no music or scenic effects, only a bar that appeared poised to knock one's head off and a sign that read: "No Kissing Allowed in This Tunnel." Uncle Sam's Cannon Coaster, deprived of its gravity-defying gap, sought to lure male riders with the rhetorical query: "Will she throw her arms around your neck and yell? Well, I guess yes!" Coasters became bigger and also more dangerous. Cars were pitched from the tracks of the Giant Racer and the Rough Rider at Coney Island in horrific accidents that resulted in the loss of life. But rather than repel riders, the element of danger instead enhanced the coasters' allure.

The exposed wooden scaffolds and metal tracks of the roller coasters stripped the architecture of the amusement park bare and reduced its horizon to one of raw motion. It was left to La Marcus Thompson, who returned to Coney Island shortly before the turn of the century, to fuse the energy of the coaster with compelling architectural and scenic motifs. After his departure from Coney Island, Thompson made many changes in the design of his coasters, adopting some of the innovations of his competitors and introducing improvements of his own, such as the articulated train that doubled the number of passengers the cars could carry. Thompson felt

THE LOOP THE LOOP AT CONEY ISLAND. FANCIFUL ARCHITECTURE EMBELLISHED BOTH THE EXTERIOR AND INTERIOR SPACE OF AMUSEMENT PARKS BUT ROLLER COASTERS AND MECHANICAL RIDES GAVE THE PARKS A DISTINCTLY MODERN, AMERICAN CHARACTER. (AUTHOR'S COLLECTION)

that the coaster was best used as a sightseeing device ridden for pleasure and not simply for the thrills it could produce. In 1887, working in Atlantic City in partnership with James J. Griffiths and John Miller, he built the first Scenic Railway. It combined the most advanced features of a roller coaster with scenic effects used in Old Mill water rides, including illuminated tunnels, dioramas, painted scenery, and tableaux. The ride was a great success. Thompson soon terminated his partnership with Griffiths—who be-

came his principal rival—and formed the L. A. Thompson Scenic Railway Company. By 1906, he had six scenic coasters at Coney Island, including the Dragon's Gorge and the Buzzard's Roost at Luna Park, the Sea Shell Scenic Railway at Dreamland, Pike's Peak, and the Oriental Scenic Railway. The Oriental was touted as "A Ride 'Mid the Wonders of the World," while Pike's Peak, looming high over Surf Avenue, ranked among Thompson's most imposing creations. Its track ran over a mile in length, winding its way through mountainous caverns and ascending upward to a height of 138 feet. The ride was 285 feet in diameter at its base and incorporated a water ride called the Whirlpool Rapids. Thompson's Scenic Railway at Brighton Beach Park, created for the St. Louis Exposition in 1904, was the longest of its kind in the world. Each of Thompson's scenic railways had architecturally distinctive terminals equipped with beer gardens, dance halls, soda fountains made to resemble dollhouses, and souvenir kiosks. The terminal at the Oriental Scenic Railway had a central archway that rose to a height of forty feet with a twenty-foot-high cascade. "Many of the evils of society, much of the vice and crime which we deplore," he once said, "come from the degrading nature of amusements entered into. To inveigh against them avails little, but to substitute something better, something clean and wholesome, and persuade men to choose it, is worthy of all endeavor." Thompson was revered at Coney Island as the "father of the gravity ride," but he was not the sole builder of its scenic railways. William Mangels and John Miller collaborated to create the Rocky Road to Dublin while Fred Thompson devised Luna Park's Mountain Torrent. Each of these attractions had decorative facades. Thomas Ryan's Coasting Through Switzerland at Dreamland had a facade created by the stage designer Richard Rummel.

DRAGON'S GORGE AT LUNA PARK. TWO ENORMOUS DRAGONS, EACH WITH A WINGSPAN OF SEVENTY-FIVE FEET, FLANKED THE PROSCENIUM OF THE DRAGON'S GORGE SCENIC RAILROAD. THEIR EYES WERE FORMED BY GLOBES OF GREEN ELECTRIC LIGHTS TWO FEET IN DIAMETER.

The fanciful architecture that embellished the facades of Coney Island's rides and showplaces transported visitors to a faraway realm. The scenic devices and mechanical wizardry within them went a step further, causing audiences to behold things that only existed in their imaginations. Illusions and mechanical-scenic spectacles such as "A Trip to the Moon" and "Creation" exploited the technological innovations introduced at the dawn of the twentieth century to create extraordinary effects. They were multimedia productions that anticipated the virtual reality rides introduced at the close of the same century. Although moving dioramas had existed before, Fred Thompson's "Trip to the Moon" practically invented the illusion ride. Thompson's earlier venture was a cyclorama called "Darkness and Dawn" that evolved over time into a more complex illusion. First presented at the Omaha Exposition in 1898, it was later exhibited on the Bowery, but was destroyed by a fire in 1903. It was revived in 1907 at Luna Park as "Night and Morning." The audience was entombed in a coffin-shaped room covered by a glass lid. After a mock burial, the audience was led through a passageway where they encountered animated skeletons and visited the River Styx, where the souls of the damned—including

HENRY ROLTAIR'S "CREATION." ITS ARCHED PORTAL WAS SUPPORTED BY THE OUTSPREAD WINGS OF AN ANGEL, SCULPTED IN THE FORM OF A FEMALE FIGURE STANDING THIRTY FEET TALL WITH BREASTS BARED.

(BROOKLYN PUBLIC LIBRARY–BROOKLYN COLLECTION)

a faithless janitor strapped to a red-hot radiator and bankers roasting on plates of gold—suffered hellish torments. They eventually arrived at a graveyard where winged souls ascended heavenward. As the tableau dissolved, a woman was shown clinging to a cross of gold bathed by prismatic fountains.

Illusion shows, scenic spectacles, and disaster reeactments were presented at Coney Island by showmen and promoters such as Henry Roltair, William Ellis, A. J. Austen, and Herbert Bradwell. Henry Roltair, who came to the United States from Great Britain, began his career as an illusionist working with famed magician Alexander Herrmann. Roltair was a master of an optical effect called metempsy-chosis, in which transformations were brought about on stage before the eyes of the audience. In "Pharaoh's Daughter," which he presented at Dreamland in 1906, a statue came to life to instruct the daughter of Pharaoh who had come to the Temple of Isis in search of the infant Moses. Roltair was best known as the creator of spectacular shows such as "House Upside Down" and "Creation," which he debuted at the St. Louis exhibition. "Creation" presented the six days of Genesis as a series of dramatic spectacles. "Arabian Nights Up to Date," which Roltair staged at Dreamland in 1907, consisted of seven separate illusions in updated settings of the Arabian Nights tales.

William Ellis was a dominant force at

ARABIAN NIGHTS AT DREAMLAND. ROLTAIR'S "ARABIAN NIGHTS UP TO DATE" WAS ADORNED WITH PLASTER FIGURES REPRESENTING DAYS OF THE WEEK. EACH OF ITS SEVEN CHAMBERS HELD A DIFFERENT ILLUSION. IN ONE, A WOMAN DROVE AN AUTOMOBILE IN MIDAIR AND THEN TURNED THE MACHINE UPSIDE DOWN. IN ANOTHER, ALI BABA BROODED IN HIS CAVE BEFORE A CANDLESTICK IN WHOSE FLAME APPEARED THE VISAGE OF A YOUNG WOMAN. (BROOKLYN PUBLIC LIBRARY–BROOKLYN COLLECTION)

Dreamland whose numerous shows included "Hereafter," "End of the World," "Orient," and "Hell Gate." "Hereafter," presented in an auditorium equal to one-third the size of the park, was an "electric opera" based upon the Faust legend that employed a 200-voice choir. "End of the World" was an elaborate production of Dante's *Divine Comedy*. Adjoining auditoriums were used to stage Doomsday—in which the wicked were clutched by demons and dragged into the pit of the Inferno—and Paradise. They were connected by an underground Purgatory filled with grotesque statuary created by French sculptor Maurice Goudard. A bas-relief of the Angel Gabriel and writhing bodies inspired by Gustave Doré adorned its facade. Ellis's most spectacular creation was called "Orient." Its set piece was Belshazaar's palace at Babylon, its roof supported by pillars of staff resembling massive columns of marble and chalcedony. Arranged about it were various lesser attractions including Herod's Temple, the Hanging Gardens, a Turkish coffeehouse, a geisha house, acrobats from the palace of Gaekwar of Baroda, and whirling dervishes from the Sahara. The gate and great wall enclosing "Orient" was said to be the largest ever constructed of staff. It was over two hundred feet long, and the arch that formed its entrance was almost a hundred feet high with a ninety-foot span. Massive statues of Babylonian deities and winged bulls were at the base of the archway and its dome was illuminated with electric lights. At the conclusion of Belshazzar's Feast a luminous hand appeared to inscribe the words "Mene, Mene, Tekel, Upharsin" in fiery letters on the palace walls, which collapsed during the destruction of the city. "One wonders that the people are not crushed," a observer wrote, "yet all these tricks are scientifically worked out with assurances of safety to both performer and visitor, yet leaving in the mind of the spectator an emotion of keen surprise, wonder, and sometimes awe." The spectacular facade of the Ellis attraction "Hell Gate" was surmounted by a titanic statue of Satan with a sardonic smile and outstretched wings. It featured a boat ride into a maelstrom that continued along an underground channel through caverns depicting the earth's molten interior. The ride was dismantled after six seasons and then recreated in 1911. Workmen were repairing a leak in its spillway when an electrical short-circuit ignited the fire that destroyed Dreamland.

Mechanical disasters and "scenographic reproductions" created by showmen such as A. J. Austen and Herbert Bradwell were presented at independently operated auditoriums along Surf Avenue. The Mount Pelée show re-created the eruption of a volcano on the island of Martinique, while the havoc wreaked by the Galveston Flood was depicted on one of the largest stages in America with the help of trained electricians, scenic artists, and mechanics deploying over a hundred electrical devices, a cyclorama over two hundred feet long, and "more scenery than could be placed on half a dozen Broadway theater stages." A. J. Austen's presentation of the Johnstown Flood was touted as "the greatest electrical scenic production in the world" and was a popular attraction at the Buffalo Pan-American Exposition before coming to Coney Island in 1903. It was followed in 1906 by Bradwell's "Great Deluge," re-creating the events of the biblical Flood. Other scenic spectacles included Austen's "New York to the North Pole," which debuted at the St. Louis Exposition, and the "Great Italian Earthquake." According to the *Brooklyn Eagle,* an important feature in the presentation of the "big shows" at Coney Island was the use of mechanical effects that required a mastery of the latest inventions of electricity, light reflection, and sound-producing devices. Showmen such as Roltair were able to produce effects that were "absolutely new to the public" by employing "artisans of rare skill." The paper noted that "sculptors and scene painters are brought from foreign countries because of the dearth of their peculiar talent and skill in this country."

.    .    .

By the second decade of the twentieth century, the amusement industry in the United States had achieved a creative apogee. In a remarkably short span, two thousand amusement parks were built at seaside resorts, fairgrounds, and trolley parks all across the country. Most were situated near urban centers with a heavy concentration of European immigrants. Cosmopolitan in spirit, they embraced a new American dictum: that one could play as hard as one worked. George Tilyou's Steeplechase Park was so successful he was able to build others like it in San Francisco, St. Louis, Bridgeport, and Atlantic City. La Marcus Thompson opened an amusement park at Rockaway Beach within sight of Coney Island. And while Fred

Thompson was content with one Luna Park, others adopted its format and appropriated its name. Frederick Ingersoll, a designer of figure-eight roller coasters, built Pittsburgh's Luna Park in 1905, and soon many other Luna Parks appeared in cities around the world. Amusement parks such as Cleveland's Euclid Beach, Cincinnati's Coney Island, Chicago's Riverview Park, and Boston's Revere Beach all were indebted to Thompson's formula for manufacturing the carnival spirit.

The forward momentum of the amusement industry slowed somewhat during World War I when materials became scarce but rebounded when the war came to an end. During the 1920s, however, the demand for hand-carved carousels dried up. Charles Looff was dead, and poor health had forced Charles Carmel to close his shop. Stein and Goldstein turned to carving circus and carnival figures and stationary horses displayed outside barbershops. Only M. C. Illions continued to carve carousel horses entirely by hand. The elegant carousel of old had been eclipsed by the roller coaster, which was just entering its golden age. Master builders such as John Miller, Harry C. Baker, and Fred Church would soon create legendary Coney Island coasters such as the Thunderbolt, the Tornado, and the Cyclone.

When the Depression struck, the entire amusement industry went into a tailspin. The coaster's golden age came to an abrupt end and hundreds of parks closed their gates. But by then, Coney Island's extravagant style of amusement architecture was firmly embedded in American popular culture. At Coney the carnival spirit held fast, not perhaps in a form that Fred Thompson might have envisioned, but rather as a vast amusement marketplace. Its ability to enthrall was hardly diminished even when its artistry had waned. An architectural historian who visited it in 1947 wrote:

> No real estate specialist located its emporiums of fun according to the calculated flow of pedestrian traffic: down every noisy alley something yet to be seen beckons the crowd. No architect's hand detailed facades to catch a pedestrian's eye: each entrepreneur of escape painted his own come-on with a spontaneous hand. The plaster is cracking and the paint is peeling, the flashy décor of each concession has no relation to any unified design pattern, nowhere is there harmony or perfection. This in itself makes us feel comfortable. We are certainly not

RIDERS ON THE CHANTICLEER CAROUSEL. THE "FOUR-ABREAST BANTAMS" FIRST APPEARED AT CONEY ISLAND IN 1893. THE CHANTICLEER WAS APPARENTLY BROUGHT BACK TO EUROPE AT A LATER DATE UNTIL BOSTOCK ARRANGED FOR ITS RETURN TO THE UNITED STATES. THE SHIP THAT WAS TRANSPORTING IT SANK IN THE NORTH SEA BUT IT WAS RECOVERED. FROM 1913 UNTIL 1964 IT WAS HOUSED ON THE LAWN AT STEEPLE-CHASE.

(FRIED COLLECTION)

perfect and the imperfection of Coney's setting eliminates any demand upon us to be so. Amusement Park Baroque, as it came to its fullest and most flamboyant development at Coney, became a caricature—always a friendly and hilarious one—not only of reality but of the dream world itself.

# CHAPTER SIX

# HONKY-TONK

CONEY ISLAND's roaring and rambunctious tone set it apart from other American seaside resorts. The Coney of cafes, concert halls, dance dives, and catchpenny pleasures survived fires, blue laws, police raids, and reformers and constituted a characteristic feature of the resort on a par with its amusements and mechanical rides. Coney Island had few American counterparts—its closest kin were the English working-class resorts of Margate and Blackpool. Borrowing freely from many strains of popular entertainment, from English and European music halls; from minstrelsy and the penny pitch sideshow; from the beer gardens, concert saloons, and dime museums of the Lower East Side; and from the bawdy pleasures of the Shantyville midway erected on the outskirts of the Philadelphia Centennial Exhibition, it concocted its own unsurpassed amusement amalgam. To Coney came the huckster and the soubrette. Anything that was deemed unsuitable for the new amusement parks found its place in the populist sideshow that made up Coney Island's Bowery.

Coney Island's honky-tonk heyday from 1890 to about 1915 spanned a quarter of a century that witnessed a transformation in the cultural life of the nation and brought forth a heterogeneous and hybrid popular culture and new forms of mass entertainment. The same cultural landscape that produced Steeplechase and Luna Park gave birth to vaudeville, ragtime and syncopated music, Tin Pan Alley, the nickelodeon, and a social dance revolution. Each enlivened Coney Island in countless venues large and small, contributing to a Bowery by the Sea that especially appealed to young men and women of the immigrant class who sought employment and entertainment in its unbridled atmosphere.

Coney's concert halls and dance dives were successors of the open-air concert pavilions first erected at the old Coney Island Point. By 1888, when as many as a quarter of a million people visited the island on a hot summer day, Coney had seven dancing pavilions, and most who visited could be found "at the bob end of the beach helping to keep the lid of the boiling pot of delirious diversion dancing at its utmost speed." The greatest concentration of dancing establishments and concert halls were located on the Bowery, the resort's rambunctious midway, and on Surf Avenue, its principal artery. When it was first laid out in 1880, Surf Avenue was envisioned as a means of relieving the congestion from pedestrians and horsecars in West Brighton, which spilled out almost to the ocean's edge. But in short order, the plank walkways and narrow alleys leading to and from the beach were occupied by concert halls, storage sheds, and amusement stalls, and Surf Avenue quickly became the transportation hub of the amusement district, linking Ocean Parkway and the Concourse with West Brighton's railway terminals and hotels. Culver Depot, the Sea Beach Palace, and the Gunther Depot all deposited their passengers on Surf Avenue. Along its path were many of the resort's most important venues, including the Elephant Colossus, Feltman's Ocean Pavilion, Henderson's Music Hall, Ravenhall's Coney Island House, the Jumbo Hotel, the Alhambra Concert Garden, and the Albermerle Hotel. Surf Avenue helped delineate the white-hot limits of the amusement zone that composed Coney Island proper. Running roughly a mile in length form West Fifth Street to West Twentieth Street, and extending from Mermaid Avenue to the

SURF AVENUE, CIRCA 1905.

(PHOTO BY ADOLPH WITTEMANN. MUSEUM OF THE CITY OF NEW YORK, THE LEONARD HASSAM BOGART COLLECTION)

ocean, it was, in the words of Julian Ralph, the "most bewildering, noisy approach to bedlam that we know of in America."

Coney Island's honky-tonk heart and soul, the Bowery, ran parallel to Surf Avenue for a few short blocks from Tilyou's Steeplechase to Feltman's Pavilion and was bisected by numerous narrow alleys that led to the ocean. It was originally a boardwalk paved with planks, created in 1882 by Peter and George Tilyou to direct patrons to their Surf Theater. They named it Ocean View Walk, but it was soon more com-

PROMENADING ALONG THE BOWERY, CIRCA 1903.

(LIBRARY OF CONGRESS)

monly called the Bowery. The Surf Theater prospered for a time, presenting vaudeville performers such as Pat Rooney and Sam Bernard, until Peter Tilyou ran afoul of John McKane. But by then, other venues were already lining the Bowery, including Solomon Perry's Glass Pavilion and Louis Stauch's Newark House. The Bowery really took flight with the arrival of Anson Stratton in 1884. With McKane's blessing, Stratton erected several dance palaces and concert halls along its length. By the 1890s, with competing venues such as Koster's Music Hall, Connor's Imperial Theater, Vacca's Theater, Inman's Casino, Wacke's Trocadero, and Paddy Shea's Saint Dennis Hotel, the Bowery was in full swing.

The heady atmosphere of the Coney Island concert halls in the waning years of the nineteenth century mirrored the demographic changes affecting American popular culture, which was steadily becoming more urban in character and ethnically more diverse. Minstrels in burnt cork and wispy songstresses with reed-thin voices continued to share the stage with song-and-dance men such as Pat Rooney and Frank Burns. "The island," wrote one observer, "sounded as madly merry as the old days," with "Sweet Rosie O'Grady" and "She May Have Seen Better Days" sung in concert halls nestled side by side. But now they had to compete with the syncopated rhythms of rag music and the so-called "coon songs" that were becoming enormously popular. Increasingly, the concert hall singers drew inspiration from husky-voiced ballad belters such as May Irwin and Maggie Cline, who could command a stage. Coney soubrettes

delivered "Maggie Murphy's Home" and "Down Went McGinty" outfitted in glaring gowns of red, blues, and yellow, with stockings and hair ribbons to match. Novelty acts were especially popular. "They have a great girl in one of the concert saloons on the Bowery," one newspaper wrote. "She sings 'Murphy Owes Me Rent' and other songs of the Maggie Cline order and sings them in a way that makes the young men wild. But what pleases them most of all is her exits. She generally turns cartwheels going off the stage." The same soubrette charmed John L. Sullivan with a rendition of "It's Irish, You Know." Another singer brought her performance to a close by tossing into the air fistfuls of paper that were transformed into tiny American flags scattering the length of the stage. The band struck up "Hail Columbia" as she took her bows. On the music hall stages, showgirls performed skirt-and-wing dances. At Vacca's Theater, celebrated as the "most notoriously rough place on Coney Island," a troupe of fifteen "beauties" danced nightly in flesh-colored tights and low-cut bodices to the strains of raucous music. At the Glass Pavilion the nightly entertainment included a comic opera company and an all-female orchestra. In addition to the singing waiters at landmarks such as Joe's on the Bowery, concert saloons employed "table girls" who, after turns at singing, joined male customers at their tables to encourage beer drinking. The most celebrated Coney Island "beer huckster" was Fatty Langtry, who weighed well over 250 pounds and earned the moniker Champion Big Man Boxer of the World. For more than twenty summers he regaled customers at Coney cabarets with his

# "MEET ME TONIGHT IN DREAMLAND"

Coney Island provided inspiration to many turn-of-the-century composers and lyricists. Marches, waltzes, rags, and novelty numbers that evoked it were composed by musicians as diverse as John Philip Sousa, Harry Von Tilzer, E. T. Paull, James Thornton, and Henry Frantzen.

The most commercially successful composition was "Meet Me To-night in Dreamland" with its appealing melody and evocative lyrics:

*Meet me to-night in Dreamland,*
*Under the silvery moon,*
*Meet me to-night in Dreamland,*
*Where love's sweet roses bloom.*

*Come with the love light gleaming,*
*In your dear eyes of blue.*
*Meet me in Dreamland,*
*Sweet dreamy Dreamland,*
*There let my dreams come true.*

It sold a phenomenal 5 million copies in sheet music in 1909.

Everything about Coney Island inspired a song: its amusement parks ("Dreamland Waltz," "Down at Steeplechase," "Meet Me Down at Luna, Lena"), its rides ("Bamboo Slide March and Two Step," "Ziz March and Two Step"), its grand hotels ("Manhattan Beach March," "Brighton Beach March"). There were novelty numbers such as "Mariutch (make-a-the-hootcha-ma-kootch) Down at Coney Island" that Mae West included in her repertoire, paeans to summer sweethearts ("Good-bye, My Coney Island Baby," "My Coney Island Girl"), and songs that celebrated a joyous excursion to the seashore ("Gay Coney Island," "Rolling Down to Coney"). Rogers and Hart paid it tribute with the memorable lyric: "We'll go to Coney, / And eat baloney / On a roll" from *Manhattan.* Harry Carroll's classic "By the Beautiful Sea" was composed in 1914 on the terrace of the Brighton Beach Casino looking out over the ocean at Coney Island.

SIDEWALK MUSIC VENDOR AT CONEY ISLAND. HIS SIGN ADVERTISES "ALL THE LATEST SONGS" ON EDISON CYLINDERS.
(MUSEUM OF THE CITY OF NEW YORK, THE BYRON COLLECTION, 93.1.1.3381)

trademark cry, "Who wants the handsome waiter?"

The bawdiness of the concert halls made them a target of reformers. By the turn of the century the Bowery was being described as "that wicked half-mile of boardwalk" and had replaced the Gut as a focus of Brooklyn's vice reform movement.

One of the most startling and pathetic things to be seen at Coney Island is the strange attraction it exercises over young girls. The noise, the jingle, the junketing, the music, the flaring pictures, the loud voices of touts proclaiming wonders to be seen for a dime, the boats, the merry go rounds, the dancing platforms, the museums, the concert halls, the bathers and all the thousand and one 'attractions' make a Vanity Fair at which young girls swarm open eyed, open mouthed, wondering at everything and taking all the tinsel for gold. To their simple minds the place is a fairyland, and it never dawns upon them that there can be any harm where there is so much good humor and laughter. The ugly things which lie below the surface of Coney Island are not seen till it's too late to avoid them. The very corruption of the place glitters and the whirlpool of demoralization has them long before they perceive its existence.

Coney Island's concert halls and drinking establishments were targets of Sunday blue laws enacted in 1895. The blue laws permitted only sacred music concerts on the Sabbath, forbade the wearing of tights and low-cut gowns by concert singers, and ordered barrooms screened from the view of passersby. Most concert houses found ways to skirt the laws, however, and performers on stage made a mockery of the requirement that they dress in more modest "street" clothing. "It has been found," a reporter observed, "that in color and general construction, the street costume can be so changed as to be hardly recognizable as such. While all the stars of the stage wore street costumes, most of them would have looked decidedly queer on the street."

Huge crowds poured into Coney Island that summer in spite of the blue laws. Attendance was increased by the nickel trolley fare that came into effect that season, making Coney accessible to even greater numbers of people. The crowds became so dense at times that some concert saloons were repeatedly obliged to "clear the house," prompting a Brooklyn judge to speak out against enforcement. "Coney is not like the lower part of the city," he explained. "It is a seaside resort; the breathing place for hundreds of thousands who are compelled to work hard all week, and when Sunday comes want, and actually need, a little recreation and pleasure." Nevertheless, new restrictions were imposed the following year when the Raines Law was enacted. The law barred the sale of alcoholic beverages on Sunday in most establishments, but it, too, could be easily circumvented. Reformers warned that Coney Island was becoming "a vast training-school of vice."

The most scandalous of the Coney Island shows were the "cooch dancers" performing in the so-called Oriental theaters. The most famous was Little Egypt, whose performance at the World's Columbian Exposition in Chicago had caused a sensation. Others included the raven-haired Fatima, who had danced at the Pan-American Exposition billed as the Sultan's Favorite, and Princess Rajah, who performed her "muscle dance" with a snake that once bit her. The Streets of Cairo openly flaunted the blue laws. The deputy police commissioner, after witnessing the beautiful Adgy dancing in the den of lions, declared that the "danse du ventre" could no longer be performed on Sunday at Coney Island, but a reporter who visited the resort less than a month later observed: "At the most vicious of the dances on Sunday afternoon six stalwart policemen of the Twenty-fourth precinct in full uniform, with badges resplendent upon their manly breasts, gazed unblushingly upon the performance of the woman said to be the most celebrated of her kind in the world." A concerted campaign to

THE ALGERIAN THEATER ON SURF AVENUE, CIRCA 1897.

(MUSEUM OF THE CITY OF NEW YORK, THE BYRON COLLECTION)

suppress the shows was not undertaken until 1897, when the licenses of some show places were revoked. But even that short-lived crackdown had little lasting effect.

When a fire decimated a large swath of the Bowery in 1899, the buildings commissioner labeled it an act of "Divine Providence." Most of the Bowery escaped destruction, but many buildings were destroyed, including Henderson's concert hall, Stauch's dancing pavilion, Koster's Music Hall, and Feltman's Ocean Pavilion. Reformers urged that the entire Bowery district be swept clean and replaced with a seaside park extending from the Concourse to Sea Gate. Some Coney Island property owners, including George Tilyou, at first responded favorably to the notion of a "grand ocean promenade." The journalist Walter Creedmoor disagreed. "The 'masses' love Coney Island as it is," he wrote, "and although they will probably bear with dumb resignation any attempt to transform it into a region of asphalt walks and patches of scorched 'keep off the grass' sward, they will certainly turn their backs upon it in its new form and seek their recreation elsewhere." By the time the city got around to rejecting the proposed park, the Bowery had rebuilt itself and was back in business.

However, fire struck Coney Island once more, in 1903, gutting the Bowery and taming it a bit. During the 1903 fire a crowd of seventy thousand spectators gathered on Surf Avenue to witness the conflagration. At the concert halls and pavilions beyond the danger zone the dancing and merrymaking continued even as the flames crept closer. Among the crowd were fan-

LITTLE EGYPT. HER REAL NAME WAS FAHREDA MAHZAR AND SHE PERFORMED THE "DANCE OF THE HAREM REVELERS" IN THE STREET OF CAIRO AT THE WORLD'S COLUMBIAN EXHIBITION IN 1893. "WHEN I DANCED, I WAS NEVER NEARLY NUDE," SHE EXPLAINED MANY YEARS LATER. "MY DANCE WAS NEITHER VULGAR NOR SHOCKING." (MUSEUM OF THE CITY OF NEW YORK)

tastically costumed women who had rushed out to gawk at the fire between turns on the stage. At one point a crowd of five hundred people that gathered along the beach to watch the fire's progress became hemmed in between the ocean and the advancing flames. Policemen led the shouting, hysterical crowd on a mad dash to safety. Many who lived in the fire zone fled to the beach, where they dug trenches in the sand in a desperate effort to save some of their possessions. Others escaped in rowboats just ahead of the flames that leapt out along the jetties.

Coney's liberating mix made it a summer proving ground for many young performers. The legendary vaudeville duo Joe Weber and Lew Fields were fourteen-year-olds when they played at Phil Duffy's Saint Nicholas Hotel, one of Coney Island's first concert pavilions. They performed their comic song-and-dance numbers from 10 A.M. until midnight for wages of two dollars a day, plus beer checks, which they sold to the waiters. When Duffy discovered they were secretly performing a skit called "The Market on Saturday Night" at another pavilion he confronted them. They escaped into the ocean dressed in their market women costumes.

Harry Houdini's first Coney Island performance was in 1891, when he appeared in a tent act with strongman Emil Jarrow. In 1894, the Houdini Brothers, Harry and Dash, performed at Vacca's Theater. Their specialty was a box escape called the Metamorphosis. At one point a rival named Risey challenged the brothers, who wagered a hundred dollars that he could not duplicate their stunt. That evening the theater was packed and a sign on the stage

LEVITATION ACT AT A CONEY ISLAND SHOW.

(MUSEUM OF THE CITY OF NEW YORK, THE BYRON COLLECTION, 93.1.1.3425)

announced: "Next: Risey's going into the box." Risey complied, but after five minutes in the box he begged to be let out. While playing at Coney Island, Houdini met Bess Raymond, who performed at the Sea Beach Palace with a song-and-dance team called the Floral Sisters. They fell in love and married less than a month later, honeymooning at Coney Island.

Many performers were exposed to Coney Island at a tender age. Buster Keaton was just six years old when he performed at Steeplechase Park with the Three Keatons in 1901. The Gerry Society, a child welfare organization, hauled his parents before Mayor Robert Van Wyck and denounced them for subjecting the child to the sinful ways of Coney Island. The mayor reminded the society that he bicycled to Coney Island every Sunday. "I never saw any sin," he replied, "only people having a good time. The poor are entitled to entertainment too." George Burns was eight when the Pee Wee Quartette first visited the beach. "We were not a smash hit at Coney Island," he recalled. "We had forgotten that bathing suits don't have pockets. Well, we went from beach to beach singing our hearts out, because people kept applauding. But the hat came back full of nothing but sand and some tokens for the concessions at Steeplechase." Harpo Marx first teamed up with his brothers Groucho and Gummo at Henderson's Music Hall at Coney Island in 1907. Minnie Marx had booked the act as a quartet called the Four Nightingales. She "shanghaied" her stage-shy son, who became the reluctant fourth member. (Lou Levy was a non-Marx part of the act at this point, not Chico.) They sang "Darling Nelly

HARRY HOUDINI PHOTOGRAPHED AT BRIGHTON BEACH WITH THE CELEBRATED CHINESE MAGICIAN CHING LING FOO. (LIBRARY OF CONGRESS)

Gray" and Harpo was too scared to sing a note. "My reaction was instantaneous and overwhelming," he later confessed. "I wet my pants." Years before she headlined at Brighton Beach, Fanny Brice used a clever ruse to pay for her trips Coney Island. She rode on the trolley with a handkerchief stuffed with pebbles and pretended to drop it out the window. Then, bursting into tears, she would swear that her trolley fare was in it. Someone eventually came forward to pay her fare. Mae West enjoyed visiting Bostock's Wild Animal Arena as a child. Her father, "Battlin' Jack" West, was a prizefighter and bouncer at various Coney Island dives where boxing matches were staged. Years later, viewing her wax likeness in the Eden Musee, she quipped, "Keep the exhibits arty, boys." Bud Abbott grew up at Coney Island and once appeared as a Katzenjammer Kid outside a Coney house of mirrors. His father was employed at Dreamland. Other performers worked in obscurity at Coney Island early in their careers. Clara Bow cut hot dog buns at Nathan's before she won fame as the "It Girl." Cary Grant was briefly employed as a stilt walker on the Bowery, where he wore a sandwich board advertising Steeplechase Park.

Jimmy Durante cut his teeth at a Coney Island cabaret called Diamond Tony's, where the song-pluggers included female impersonators and the singing waiters added to their earnings by working as pimps. "You couldn't build a Sunday school out of those night spots," he recalled. "People knew they were tough joints, and if they gave 'em a play, had nobody but themselves to kick if they lost their shirts." The next year Durante teamed up with Eddie Cantor at Carey Walsh's concert saloon. "It was a little fancier," Durante explained. "The bouncer wore a soup-an'-fish suit an' there was a sign in the toilet that says, GENTS, PLEASE BUTTON UP YOUR FLY." Durante spent many more summers performing at Coney Island nightspots such as the College Arms, where he teamed up with Eddie Jackson.

Other notable Coney Island cabarets included Perry's White Seal Café, where Irving Berlin performed as a singing waiter; Scotty Morgan's Palm Garden; George Whiting's College Inn; Maggie White's; and the Harvard Inn. The Harvard Inn was owned by Brooklyn mob boss Frankie Yale, who hired a young thug named Al Capone to work as a bartender and bouncer. While employed at the Harvard Inn in 1917, Capone crossed paths with Frank Galluccio, a small-time hoodlum. In the brawl that ensued, Gallucchio drew his knife and Capone was left with his famous scar. Such incidents were not uncommon at Coney Island. The notorious gang leader known as Kid Twist and a confederate called Cyclone Lewis were gunned down on the Bowery in 1908 by Louis "the Lump" Pioggi, apparently in a fit of jealousy over a concert hall singer. One of the victims fell dead in the doorway of a restaurant decorated to celebrate its opening with a floral wreath in the shape of a horseshoe with the word "Success" spelled out across it.

The concert saloons, hotels, and venues of every description along Surf Avenue and the Bowery offered a bewildering range of entertainment, everything from burlesque shows at the Surf Avenue Opera House to roulette and red-and-black games at the Pocono House. As Coney Island gained a greater measure of respectability, larger venues began presenting bona fide stars of the vaudeville circuit. Fred Henderson's music hall was the first to present comic operas with full stage productions as well as "refined vaudeville." Performers who graced its stage included Al Jolson, Sophie Tucker, Noble Sissle and Hubie Blake, and Bert Williams. Brighton Beach had two first-rate vaudeville houses, the Brighton Beach Music Hall and the larger New Brighton Theater on Ocean Parkway. Even the Manhattan Beach Opera House began to showcase minstrel shows and vaude-

THE BOWERY, CIRCA 1912. THE BOWERY RAN LESS THAN A QUARTER OF A MILE BUT WAS CRAMMED WITH CONCERT HALLS, SHOOTING GALLERIES, CHOP SUEY JOINTS, AMUSEMENT STANDS, AND FOUR ROLLER COASTER RIDES. IT WAS MARVELOUSLY DESCRIBED BY ELMER BLANEY HARRIS, WHO TRAVERSED IT IN 1908. "BANDS, ORCHESTRAS, PIANOS AT WAR WITH GRAMOPHONES, HAND-ORGANS, CALLIOPES; OVERHEAD, A ROAR OF WHEELS IN A DEATHLOCK WITH SHRIEKS AND SCREAMS; WHISTLES, GONGS, RIFLES ALL BUSY; THE SMELL OF CANDY, POPCORN, MEATS, BEER, TOBACCO, BLENDED WITH THE ODOR OF THE CROWD REDOLENT NOW AND THEN OF PATCHOULI; A STREAMING RIVER OF PEOPLE ARCHED OVER BY ELECTRIC SIGNS—THIS IS THE BOWERY AT CONEY ISLAND." (LIBRARY OF CONGRESS)

ville acts. Among the performers who appeared at Brighton Beach were W. C. Fields, Eddie Foy, Irene Franklin, the Four Cohans, Fanny Brice, Ethel Barrymore, Nora Bayes, and golden-haired Eva Tanguay, who strutted across the stage in white tights as she brazenly sang "I Don't Care," and "It's All Been Done Before but Not the Way I Do It."

By the 1890s, Coney Island venues such as the Greater New York Hotel and the Trocadero Hotel on the Bowery were including illustrated songs and moving pictures on their programs.

# SILENT FILM AT CONEY ISLAND

Coney Island was a brash celebration of the human body in motion. Thus it was ideally suited for the new medium of motion pictures, a medium devoted entirely to the moving image. During the film industry's formative period Coney Island was the subject of more short silent films than any other location. Among the earliest cinematic depictions of bodies in motion were of bathers gamboling in its waves, cake-walkers on its beach, and couples tossed about on its mechanical rides. Many of these images were captured by the Edison Manufacturing Company and American Mutoscope and Biograph, which produced over fifty films at Coney Island between 1895 and 1905. These early films, along with countless images captured on post-cards, projected and magnified the fantastic iconography of Coney Island, producing a kind of synergy of popular culture. Films such as *Coney Island at Night* (1905) and *Fire and Flames at Luna Park* (1904) gave audiences that hadn't vis-ited Coney Island their first glimpse at its amusement parks, while *Shooting the Chutes* (1896) and *Around the Flip-Flap Railroad* (1902) offered an experience of its mechanical rides.

Most early films used the camera simply to document Coney Island's attractions. A few, such as *Boarding School Girls* (1905) and *Stagestruck* (1906), constructed a simple, humorous narrative out of a chase through an amusement park. The short film *The Veiled Beauty* (1907) served to remind the audience of the chimerical nature of all things one encountered at Coney Island. A masher pursues a young woman into Dream-land convinced she is a beauty. It is only after she removes her veil that her ugliness is revealed. In *Monday Morning in a Coney Island Police Court* (1908), Coney's topsy-turvy nature is the subject of comic courtroom burlesque. The film is an early example of D. W. Griffith's work at Biograph. Coney's hurly-burly atmosphere lent itself to the physical humor of comic actors such as John Bunny (*Jack Fat & Slim Jim at Coney Island,* c. 1910), Harold Lloyd (*Speedy,* 1928), and Fatty Arbuckle and Buster Keaton. Arbuckle and Keaton were paired in *Fatty at Coney Island* (1917), in which Keaton dresses as a girl and doubles as Fatty's date on a ride on the Shoot the Chutes.

BUSTER KEATON AND ROSCOE "FATTY" ARBUCKLE IN THE FILM *FATTY AT CONEY ISLAND.* (THE MUSEUM OF MODERN ART/FILM STILLS ARCHIVE)

Some Coney Island historians have even asserted that the first commercial exhibition of a motion picture in the United States took place at the Trocadero Hotel in 1893. Practically overnight, rows of Edison Kinetoscope machines and penny-a-peek moving picture boxes began appearing outside Bowery concert halls. Racy titles such as "Tenderloin Secrets" and "Scenes in a Massage Parlor" ensured their popularity. In 1895, moving pictures were shown under a tent on Surf Avenue and by the late 1890s there were numerous motion picture parlors equipped with Mutoscope machines. Patrons sat at tables and drank while they watched the films. By one count there were upward of 450 moving picture shows playing at Coney Island in 1908.

Few attractions were more popular than Coney Island's dancing pavilions, where the music seemed to play on endlessly. During the 1890s, new forms of dance such as the two-step and the syncopated rhythms of ragtime brought about enormous changes in social dancing in the United States. Coney Island, already a hotbed of motion, was soon caught up in the whirl of the dance revolution. Young dancers known as "pivoters" who flocked to the pavilions included "thousands of girls who are seized with such madness for dancing that they spend every night in the dance halls." One of the earliest of the dance fads was a form of rag dancing called the cakewalk, which gained popularity through the stage performances of the comic song-and-dance team of George Walker and Bert Williams. Both were African Americans. Cakewalking enjoyed enormous popularity. A cakewalk contest at Steeplechase Park in 1902 was described in great detail by the *Brooklyn Eagle*. Every contestant was "a real negro" recruited from the "sporting element of the colored population."

Among the men there were frock coats and silk hats of all colors and descriptions. There were collars that reached far above the ears and others whose spreading wings swept over the shoulders of the wearers and half way down their backs. . . . The men were gay, gayer than ever would be permitted in real life, but compared with their partners they were as modest house flies to the grandest of butterflies. These partners, the 'ladies of color,' who stepped for the prizes, wore dresses of every conceivable color and every conceivable texture, from heavy black silk to the flimsiest and thinnest golden and silver gauze. Some of them simply glistened.

At Manhattan Beach, Arthur Pryor, the self-styled "Paganini of the trombone," scored cakewalking and rag arrangements for John Philip Sousa's band.

The atmosphere in the dancing pavilions varied greatly, attracting patrons of different classes and races, further distinguished by contrasting styles of dress as well as differences in social norms. At Dreamland's elegant ballroom the orchestra performed under a giant seashell at the ocean end of the pier and its vast white expanse was illuminated with ten thousand incandescent lights. At Stauch's flag-bedecked pavilion, three thousand couples at a time

DANCERS AT STEEPLECHASE PARK.

(FRIED COLLECTION)

danced to the ragtime rhythms of Al Ferguson's orchestra, while others dined in the balconies overlooking the dance floor. An investigator from the Women's Municipal League found that "in the most fashionable there is a good deal of promiscuous intercourse, flirting and picking up of acquaintances, but the dancing itself is usually proper and conventional; in the most Bohemian, behavior is free and pronouncedly bad forms of dancing are seen." Unattached working girls were considered most at risk.

Many young women gravitated to the dance houses on the Bowery, well aware of the reputation of some of the pavilions there. While reformers looked askance, those who found delight on the dance floor in an atmosphere of freedom, far removed from the workaday world, saw matters quite differently. One young woman explained, "I have heard some of the high people with whom I am living say that Coney Island is not tony. The trouble is these high people don't know how to dance." By 1910 rag-inspired dances such as the Turkey Trot and Grizzly Bear gave couples more freedom to improvise and the term "dance craze" was coined to describe the revolution taking place on the dance floors of New York City. Big crowds packed Coney Island dance palaces such as the Pabst Loop Hotel and the Kaiser Garden. With success came order. Every respectable dance hall had its own dancing masters. In 1914, the dance team of Vernon and Irene Castle, the reigning royalty of ballroom dancing, unveiled their Venetian-style Castle Summer House at Luna Park and Djuna Barnes was already bemoaning the passing of the old Coney Island, "the Coney which a few years ago tolerated nearly any kind of dance and which now tolerates nothing that borders on the sensational."

The unconventional character of Coney Island made it naturally attractive to the avant-garde writers and artists who congregated in

MARDI GRAS PARADE, CIRCA 1904, REVIEWED BY ITS KING AND QUEEN. THE ROYAL PAIR'S ARRIVAL WAS DELAYED TWENTY MINUTES WHEN IT WAS DISCOVERED THAT THE KING'S CROWN JEWELS AND TIGHTS HAD BEEN STOLEN. "SOMEBODY'S PINCHED THE ROYAL PANTS!" A COURTIER SHOUTED. THE QUEEN BRAVELY WENT FORTH ALONE IN HER LANDAU, BUT A BURST OF FIREWORKS CAUSED THE HORSES TO BOLT. THE QUEEN SHRIEKED, THE ROYAL COACHMAN TUGGED AT THE REINS, AND OFF THEY WENT, PURSUED BY ROUGH RIDERS, INDIANS, AND BEDOUIN ARABS, WHO BROUGHT THE CARRIAGE TO A STOP AFTER IT HAD RACED THREE-QUARTERS OF A MILE TOWARD THE BROOKLYN MAINLAND. (AUTHOR'S COLLECTION)

New York in the years leading up to World War I —figures such as Djuna Barnes, Alfred Stieglitz, Marcel Duchamp, Francis Picabia, and Man Ray. Duchamp and Picabia joined Beatrice Wood for a ride on a Coney Island roller coaster and posed together in a photo studio there. Stieglitz, Paul Strand, and Georgia O'Keeffe ventured out to Coney Island on Memorial Day in 1916. "It was a great party and a great day," O'Keeffe later wrote. Allen Norton published a magazine for the literati called *Coney Island Splash*, and Joseph Stella captured Coney Island's dyanmism in a painting entitled *Battle of Lights, Mardi Gras, Coney Island*.

The purest expression of Coney Island honky-tonk was the annual Mardi Gras held each September. Initiated in 1903 as a charitable event for the Coney Island Rescue House, it very quickly grew into an extravagant six-day carnival that prolonged the resort's season and brought it to a spectacular climax. The Mardi Gras transformed the entire amusement zone

MARDI GRAS FLOAT. THE FLOATS WERE FRETTED WITH INCANDESCENT ELECTRIC LIGHTS LINKED BY ROPES AND PULLEYS TO THE TROLLEY LINES THAT RAN ALONG SURF AVENUE. WHEN THE PARADE ARRIVED AT SURF AVENUE, THE GARLANDS OF ELECTRIC LIGHTS THAT LINED IT WERE EXTINGUISHED AND THE LIGHTS ON THE FLOATS FLASHED ON. (AUTHOR'S COLLECTION)

into a glorified version of the Bowery. There were carnival balls, a Mardi Gras king and queen, and nightly parades with noisy brass bands, costumed marchers capped with ten-foot-high human heads, and spectacular floats. The parade route along Surf Avenue was illuminated with millions of electric globes attached to streamers that crisscrossed the trolley lines.

In 1906, the parade was dubbed a Carnival of Plenty. A float bearing the Prince of Plenty and Queen Prospera led the parade through a flambeaux of red sparks and white incandescents. It was followed by a procession of resplendent floats arrayed with fantastic figures, giant flasks of wine, flanks of mutton, and a twenty-five-foot-long lobster, borne on a succession of flatbeds that read "Plenty of Wine," "Plenty of Meat," "Plenty of Money," and "Plenty of Laughter." Floats at other Mardi Gras parades depicted "Roosevelt in Africa" and "Old Newspaper Friends" and were accompanied by sausage wagons that pretended to grind live dogs into frankfurters. In 1921, Coney Island staged an Anti–Blue Law Mardi Gras with placards that blared, "Russia went dry in 1919, went mad in 1921."

Mardi Gras merrymaking began in earnest at the conclusion of each nightly parade. The crowd, armed with bags of confetti and brandishing slapsticks, wooden rattles, cowbells, tin horns, and every manner of noise-making device, created a frightful din. "It seemed as though everybody on Coney Island wanted to get on

the Bowery at the same time," one newspaper wrote. "Every place along the Bowery was jammed and it was a most difficult thing for the waiters to serve drinks. The soubrettes were bombarded with confetti and the orchestras were drowned by the unearthly shrieks and clang of the horn and cowbell." An endless stream of paper rained down upon the merrymakers until Surf Avenue and all of the surrounding byways were several inches deep in it. Women sometimes donned bathing caps to protect themselves from the confetti, which became entangled in their hair.

Enormous crowds attended the Mardi Gras celebrations. In 1908, more than a half million came on most nights, with as many as 3 million attending over the course of six days. Many establishments ran out of food and drink well before midnight.

Coney Island's season officially came to a close on the Monday following Mardi Gras, when the parks shut their gates for the winter. Then Luna Park's bandmaster and his men paraded down Surf Avenue at the head of a crowd that numbered five thousand diehards. The first stop was the police station on West Eighth Street, then came the firehouse, and in turn every familiar amusement establishment was visited. They played "We Won't Go Home 'Till Morning," and "We'll Be with You When the Roses Bloom Again," and then bid each one a fond farewell for the duration of Coney's long, cold hiatus.

# CHAPTER SEVEN

# THE NICKEL EMPIRE

As the second decade of the twentieth century drew to a close, Coney Island was undergoing a transformation as dramatic as any that had come before. The paramount agent of change, as swift and as unyielding as the cataclysmic fires that periodically swept across the resort, was the surging crowd; the instrument that delivered the crowd to its ocean terminus was the five-cent subway line, which reached Coney Island in 1920. Five cents sufficed to pay the fare, and when the crowd arrived at Coney it was five-cent amusements that they craved. The changes wrought by the crowd soon reduced to memory the great hotels raised by railroad barons a generation earlier, and eventually eclipsed even the amusement citadels sculpted by Coney Island's most visionary showmen. A nickel became the currency of the new epoch, and for five cents Coney was rechristened. It became the Nickel Empire.

By the time the subway extension reached Coney Island, the resort had already undergone dramatic changes that had greatly reconfigured its landscape. The amusement zone that once spread from Norton's Point to the precincts of Manhattan Beach experienced a period of retrenchment. The western end of the island had effectively seceded from the rest of Coney Island to become an exclusive community called Sea Gate, home of the Atlantic Yacht Club and of many celebrities, including Sarah Bernhardt. The Victorian opulence that set Manhattan Beach apart from the rest of Coney Island had faded into memory. The hotels created by Austin Corbin had operated in tandem with Coney Island's racetracks. When anti-betting laws closed the tracks in 1909, the Manhattan Beach company began selling off lots along Sheepshead Bay. The Manhattan Beach Hotel was razed in 1911; the Oriental Hotel was demolished five years later. Brighton Beach fell victim to a fire in 1919 that consumed the bathhouse, the giant coaster, and many of the attractions that lined the Pike. The venerable Brighton Beach Hotel lingered a few more years; then it, too, was razed. Through it all, however, the amusement industry was able to prosper. The 1917 season proved to be the most successful on record, and the outbreak of the war only briefly interrupted the climate of prosperity. Ratification of the Eighteenth Amendment initiating Prohibition in 1919 dampened Coney's spirits a bit, but in spite of the lack of beer great crowds poured onto a beach hard-pressed to accommodate such enormous numbers.

Coney Island's beach had become a narrow strip, eroded by the tides and carved up by commercial bathing concessions. Access to the beach was impeded by jetties, fences, and other obstacles that restricted public use. Bathing areas, controlled by so-called "bathhouse barons," were terribly congested, and many who wished to use them could not afford the fees imposed by the bathing establishments. The city sought to alleviate some of the worst conditions by erecting the Municipal Bathhouse in 1911. The following year the West End Improvement League proposed the construction of a much-needed boardwalk at Coney Island that would ensure access to the beach. A lengthy legal battle ensued, and in 1915 the State Supreme Court affirmed public ownership of Coney Island's beach. Steeplechase Park and other bathing establishments were ordered to remove any structures that prevented access to bathing areas. When some of the bathing concessions resisted, the city dispatched gangs of workmen with axes to dismantle them. Brooklyn Borough President Edward Riegelmann personally posed with an axe for newspaper photographers at Steeplechase Park. The historic decision upholding public access to the beach removed a major obstacle to construction of a boardwalk. A Brooklyn alderman emphatically declared, "There is no reason why the city should not do something to give the people of this city full enjoyment of the rights they have been awarded by the courts." Proponents demanded "a boardwalk stretching from one end of the beach to the other." But little immediate headway was made, and shortly thereafter the country found itself in the midst of a world war.

Then, in 1920, the subway extension reached Coney Island. The completion of the subway line greatly hastened the creation of Coney Island's boardwalk. Express trains from Times Square were now able to reach the Stillwell Avenue subway station in about forty-five minutes, and in just thirty-five minutes from Lower Manhattan. As many as a million people poured in during a single day. To accommodate the enormous crowds, a boardwalk eighty feet wide and not quite two miles long was erected at a cost of about 4 million dollars. Some 3.6 million feet of timber was used in its construction, and about 1.7 million cubic feet of sand were added to the beach. The opening of the boardwalk in 1923 was celebrated with several days of festivities, including parades, costume pageants, and a dinner at the Shelbourne Hotel with Governor Alfred E. Smith, who summered at Sea Gate, as the guest of honor. The boardwalk immediately became one of Coney Island's most recognizable landmarks.

The crowd that surged onto Coney Island's beach reflected the demographic changes that had transformed New York City. Some 23 million immigrants had entered the United States between 1881 and 1920. About 40 percent of the city's population was foreign-born, and an even

PROMENADING ON THE CONEY ISLAND BOARDWALK.

greater number, over four and a quarter million, were of foreign parentage, representing the enormous influx of eastern and southern Europeans. Coney Island's own demographics reflected these extraordinary changes. The resort's year-round population rose from less than twelve hundred in 1880 to more than seventy-five thousand by the 1920s. Italians, Greeks, Jews from Poland and Russia, and a host of other nationalities established homes in the neighborhoods that bordered the amusement zone. During the summer months, the masses from the city's teeming ethnic enclaves poured into Coney Island, and visitors to the resort marveled at what they saw. Whereas four decades earlier visitors from abroad such as José Martí had marveled at the diversity of the *classes* of people that mingled at Coney Island, they now marveled at the diversity of *nationalities* and *cultures* spread out before them. They wondered aloud whether such a place of leisure had ever before existed on earth. "To understand the crowd, one must go to Coney Island," remarked the French prime minister, Edouard Herriot, who visited in 1924. "The inexhaustible human river flows along the streets, past the Italian or Greek rotisseries, which turn out an uninterrupted sausage called hot dogs, past the naively pretentious astrologers' booths, the tattoo artists and the hideous four-legged woman. One is carried along into the torrent with all the languages and all the races of the globe." About Coney's grand new boardwalk, the French visitor commented: "Around this city of cheap pleasure for cheap people, New York has built a magnificent promenade, three kilometers long and swept by the air of the sea. Families which cannot go to the rich watering places come in hordes on Sunday to enjoy the municipal beach. It is like the Promenade des Anglais at Nice turned over to the proletariat."

Other visitors were less delighted with the great masses of humanity that spilled out over the beach. The poet Federico García Lorca, who visited Coney Island in 1929 during his sojourn in New York City, wrote of finding himself adrift amid its "vomiting multitudes." An English visitor who came that same season found very little at the resort to recommend to readers of the *London Daily Mail* and much that was appalling. "Coney Island is slum New York transported to the sea front by underground trains that function like a machine gun," wrote Sir Percival Philips. "For five cents the East Side worker is whirled by tunnel under a river and city to the free beach." Arriving at his destination, the writer found the three-mile-long beach overrun by "sweltering humanity in bathing costumes, packed sardine-fashion on a foreshore of burning sand." Visitors to Coney Island, he wrote, were assailed on all sides by "incessant noise," oppressed by a "confusion of tongues," and suffered from "thirst, insatiable and insistent."

To Giuseppe Cautela, Coney Island presented an entirely different face, one that swept away for a brief few hours the degradations visited upon the immigrant class and the working poor. "When you bathe at Coney Island you bathe in the American Jordon," he wrote in *The American Mercury* in 1925.

It is holy water. Nowhere else in the United

CROWDS AT CONEY ISLAND BEACH DURING THE 1930S.
(BROOKLYN PUBLIC LIBRARY—BROOKLYN COLLECTION)

States will you see so many races mingle in a common purpose for a common good. Democracy meets here and has its first interview skin to skin. The garments of Puritanism are given a kick that sends them flying before the winds. Here you find the real interpretation of the Declaration of Independence. The most good for the greatest number. Tolerance. Freedom in the sense that everyone minds his business. In no place have I seen so many lovers as on this beach. On no beach so many wonderful children. Muscles that develop from labor, and beauty that sweats in factories meet here.

As an Italian American, Cautela was troubled by the recent immigration laws that imposed severe restrictions on the entrance of Italians into the United States. Many of his countrymen might never have the opportunity to visit Coney Island, a place where one could stand with one's

THE RIEGELMANN BOARDWALK, CIRCA 1929. IT COST FIFTY CENTS TO RENT ONE OF THE OCEAN ROLLER CHAIR COMPANY'S WICKER ROLLING CHAIRS.        *(NEW YORK POST*/REX USA LTD.)

soul bared, where "man in shackles breaks his bounds," and where one could "climb to dizzy heights and touch the gods with your finger."

.     .     .

Coney Island had indeed been transformed into what one writer called a "paradise of the proletariat." More than 24 million nickel fares were collected at the Stillwell Avenue subway terminal in 1928 alone. The presence of such enormous numbers of people brought about a virtual transformation of Coney Island's topography. The boardwalk, now in place, would soon have to be repositioned and further extended, and the beach itself expanded with great amounts of new sand added. Streets, including Surf Avenue and the Bowery, would have to be realigned and widened to accommodate the crush of both pedestrian and vehicular traffic, with many of the changes coming at the expense of the Bowery amusement zone, which was carved into a smaller grid. At the same time, new landmarks were constantly being added to the resort's already eclectic skyline. The most imposing new attraction was a Ferris wheel erected by Herman J. Garms. Dubbed the Wonder Wheel, it stood 150 feet tall and was notable for its unique double ring of cars, which carried 169 passengers. Eight of its twenty-four cars were suspended from the wheel's outer frame like those on a traditional Ferris wheel. The other sixteen cars were suspended from its spokes and swung back and forth on tracks as the giant wheel rotated. The Wonder Wheel had its debut on Memorial Day in 1920. It dominated the skyline near West Twelfth Street. An equally impressive landmark was added to the boardwalk when the Half Moon Hotel was erected in 1927. Equipped with 400 rooms, it was Coney Island's grandest hotel. Its twin wings, each eleven stories high, flanked a central court and a sixteen-story central tower capped by an illuminated dome. The Spanish Colonial architecture included decorative urns and finials, and the interior incorporated nautical motifs. Built at a cost of 3 million dollars far from the congested center of the amusement district, it was touted as New York City's "only hotel on the Atlantic Ocean." Separated by a distance of about one mile, these two imposing landmarks stood out like contrasting bookends.

This was a prosperous period at Coney Island. Handsomely dressed couples came to promenade on the fashionable new boardwalk or to ride one of the wicker roller chairs. They dined at the new Child's Restaurant on the boardwalk, dubbed "The Rendezvous of the Elite," where bands played nightly and there was rooftop dancing under the stars. They stopped at the elegant Galleon Grille at the Half Moon Hotel, or followed the crowds to Stauch's or Joe's Restaurant on the Bowery. Along the way they might pass Mary Pickford and Douglas Fairbanks surveying the beach, or encounter nineteen-year-old Greta Garbo riding the roller coaster on her first American visit, or perhaps wave hello to Charlie Chaplin, who was recuperating at Brighton Beach following the premiere of his new film, *The Gold Rush*. The range of amusements was quite remarkable. There was Chinese theater on the boardwalk, marathon dances at Stauch's, kissing marathons at Luna Park, Modern Venus swimsuit contests at Steeplechase, six-day bicycle races at the Veledrome, and boxing and wrestling bouts and even bullfighting with Mexican matadors and picadors at Coney Island Stadium. The heady atmosphere was reflected in the crowds in record numbers patronizing Feltman's Coney Island pavilion, which declared itself "caterers to the millions." Year after year, Charles Feltman had been enlarging his showplace, which now included a bowered Deutscher Garten, restaurants, a dancing pavilion, the fabulous Feltman Carousel, the Ziz roller coaster, and an open-air movie theater. Scattered throughout the pavilion were seven hot-dog grills, but by then Feltman's was far more renowned for its deluxe shore dinner prepared by a "company of cooks" and served by a "regiment of waiters." When Feltman died in 1910, his sons Charles and

Alfred took charge of the Coney Island landmark and during the 1920s, twelve hundred people were employed there. In 1923, the year that the boardwalk opened, Feltman's Coney Island served more than 5 million customers.

Of the countless small businesses that thrived at Coney Island in the heyday of the Nickel Empire none was more successful than Nathan's, which stood directly across from the Stillwell Avenue subway station. Nathan Handwerker came to Coney Island in 1915 and worked for a single season slicing hot dog rolls at Feltman's. While employed there he became acquainted with Eddie Cantor and Jimmy Durante, who encouraged him to open his own concession. The following year he set up a hot dog stand near the corner of Stillwell Avenue and Surf Avenue on property that he leased from Edward Tilyou. It was a modest beginning. Nathan charged five cents for a hot dog that cost a dime at Feltman's and he threw in a free glass of root beer and a pickle. Business was slow at first and Nathan almost went bust. Murray Handwerker swears that his father didn't even bother putting up a sign until 1925, when the name Nathan's Famous was established. By

PARTICIPANTS AT THE MODERN VENUS CONTEST AT STEEPLECHASE PARK.

(FRIED COLLECTION)

that time the subway had arrived and the crowds pouring out of the nearby Stillwell subway station were greeted with a billboard with a pointing finger that blared, "Follow the Crowd to Nathan's." The crowds grew so thick that fights occasionally broke out for a place at the counter. Nathan's became synonymous with the Nickel Empire, selling something like seventy-five thousand hot dogs each weekend and proclaiming: "From a Hot Dog to a National Habit."

. . . .

With the arrival of the five-cent subway, Coney's showmen confronted the task of cater-ing to far greater numbers of people who had considerably less money in their pockets. The men who invented Coney Island's amusement parks and devised many of its seminal attractions were now deceased. George C. Tilyou died in 1914. Fred Thompson and La Marcus Thompson both succumbed in 1919.

Edward Tilyou was eighteen years old at the time of his father's death. The park he took charge of advertised "25 big attractions for 25¢" where "25,000 people laugh at one time." The younger Tilyou was not inclined to tinker with a formula that had proved so successful. He understood how and why it worked so well. "Those of us who run amusement parks see

EATING SWEET CORN ON THE BOARDWALK, CIRCA 1925.

(BROWN BROTHERS)

FELTMAN'S RESTAURANT, CIRCA 1933. THE OPEN-AIR MAPLE GARDEN IS FILLED WITH MARDI GRAS CELE-
BRANTS.

human nature with the brakes off, day after day, from May to September," he explained. "People out for a good time forget all about the dress parade of business and social life. They cut loose from repressions and restrictions, and act pretty much as they feel like acting—since everyone else is doing the same thing."

Fred Thompson's death had a more lasting impact on the resort even though in later years he had been less active as a showman at Coney Island. With his partner, Skip Dundy, Thomp-

son in 1905 had erected the Hippodrome, the largest showplace in Manhattan. There they staged spectacular productions such as "A Yankee Circus on Mars," which incorporated many of the clever effects that had worked so successfully at Luna Park. However, the cost of the productions proved too great a burden and Thompson and Dundy were forced to cede control of the Hippodrome to the Shubert organization after just two seasons. Dundy succumbed to pneumonia in 1907 and Thompson, who had wed the actress Mabel Taliaferro a few months earlier, thereafter devoted most of his time to theatrical productions. But Thompson's marriage and his entertainment empire soon collapsed into disarray. By 1912 he was $600,000 in debt and unable to satisfy his creditors. A consortium headed by the advertising magnate Barron Collier took control of Luna Park. The new owners added ten additional acres to the park and installed new attractions. "The Fall of Adrianople," produced in 1913, was a spectacular re-creation of the siege of a Turkish city by Bulgarians during Balkan War. "Great Sea Divers," staged in an enormous tank filled with water, reenacted the sinking of a ship that was later salvaged by deep-sea divers. Mechanical-scenic productions such as "Aerial Night Attack," which depicted a German zeppelin raid on a miniature French city, and "Over There" re-created dramatic incidents of the war in Europe. Arthur Jarvis was hired as Luna Park's manager in 1924 and many additional changes were made. The park with its forty-eight acres of attractions was now being promoted as Greater Luna, touted as "a monument that has gradually arisen Phoenix-like from the Luna Park of old." New attractions included Jarvis's own Mile Sky Chaser, a saltwater pool called the Aquadrome, a funhouse called The Pit, and many new mechanical amusements. Jarvis also installed a mechanical cyclorama called "The Battle of Château-Thierry" in the building that once housed Thompson's "Trip to the Moon." Luna's new manager boasted that the park employed fifteen hundred people and that its attendance the previous season was equal to that of "any International Exposition ever held in this country." But even the new attractions could not hide the fact that the park lacked the inspired vision that Fred Thompson's genius once provided.

The deaths of Fred Thompson and George C. Tilyou secured Sam Gumpertz's position as Coney Island's preeminent showman. Gumpertz was born in Washington, D.C., in 1868. Prior to his tenure at Dreamland, he had had a remarkable career, having worked as child acrobat at age nine, performed as a member of the Congress of Rough Riders in Buffalo Bill's Wild West Show, worked as a theatrical promoter and as a publicist who advanced the careers of Houdini and Sandow the Strong Man, and managed four Midwestern amusement parks. Gumpertz came to Coney Island in 1904 at the request of Senator William Reynolds to produce Dreamland's Midget City. The following year the indefatigable showman imported two hundred Bantoc tribesmen from the Philippines for presentation at Dreamland's Igorot Village. Eventually, Reynolds hired him as the park's general manager. Gumpertz's approach to the amusement business was straightforward and direct. "Novelty, that's the answer," he declared. "None of these park amusements is lasting. Few people try one more than a half dozen times in a visit and almost nobody wants the same thing the next season. The only way to make an old show go is to hang out a new sign—and that won't work more than one time with the audience." To secure novel attractions for his shows, Gumpertz circled the globe six times and brought back authentic "wild men" from Borneo, Berbers from Algeria, Somali warriors, "plate-lipped" Ubangi women from the Congo, and "giraffe-necked" women from Burma. During twenty-eight years as a Coney showman, he established his place as the amusement industry's premier exhibitor of indigenous peoples as sideshow attractions, while at the same time displaying an attitude of paternalism that was typical in his day toward those he exhibited. "The primitive tribes and savage peoples have a fascination for me," he explained. "We are in sympathy, as the Latins say."

Gumpertz did not personally conceive the idea for a permanent sideshow at Coney Island. It was apparently suggested to him by a former Barnum hand who managed the Loop the Loop coaster adjacent to Dreamland. The result was Dreamland's Big Circus Sideshow, where Gumpertz presented his Congress of the World's Greatest Living Curiosities. When Dreamland burned to the ground in 1911, Grumpetz erected a tent for his show on the smoldering remains of the park. After it became clear that Dreamland would not be rebuilt, the showman created the Dreamland Circus Sideshow as a permanent venue for his Congress of Curious People and Living Wonders of the World. To manage the concession, Gumpertz enlisted famed sideshow spieler Omar Sami, who had come to Dreamland to promote a show called "The Sacrifice." (Sami was among the many employees asleep in the park when the fire erupted, and he would have perished had he not been awakened by Wang Fang, a player in his show.) Dreamland Circus Sideshow served as a showcase for the unusual human specimens Gumpertz secured during his many trips abroad, and which he

leased to carnivals, dime museums, sideshows, and circuses throughout the United States. For many sideshow performers who traveled during the winter months it became a summer residence. The roster of those who appeared there included Baron Paucci, who stood twenty-four inches tall and was touted as the world's "Smallest Perfect Man"; the diminutive Lady Little, whom Gumpertz adopted as his daughter; Eli Bowen the "legless wonder"; and the legendary Zip the What-Is-It. During the 1920s the sideshow was attracting as many as thirty thousand visitors a day.

In 1915, Gumpertz took possession of the Eden Musee in New York City and brought its celebrated wax figures to Coney Island. A venerable Manhattan showplace, the Eden Musee was renowned for its lifelike wax tableaux and its famous Chamber of Horrors. When the museum went bankrupt, its entire contents were auctioned off and Gumpertz was able to acquire setpieces such as "Too Late for the Opera," and "The Electrocution of the Four Gunmen" for a modest sum. He also secured exclusive use of the name. The collection, with the addition of new figures, was housed in a building on Surf Avenue adjacent to the Dreamland Circus Sidehow. Gumpertz later added an annex called Underground Chinatown, complete with an opium den and a wax tableaux called "Killing the Missionaries by Chinese Boxers," which elicited howls of protest from the Chinese consulate. In 1928, a fire engulfed the Eden Musee, destroying the entire collection. Newspapers provided a detailed account of the conflagration. The *New York Herald Tribune* reported that

"Marat slumped in his bathtub and Charlotte Corday, dropping her knife, melted at his feet. Ex-President Taft dwindled within his clothes and ran out over his shoetops. The sprucely erect policeman caved in at his knees, buckled at the waist and collapsed within his blue uniform. Leopold and Loeb mingled in common wax with Gerald Chapman, the garroter, and the rest of the Chamber of Horrors and ran out through a crack in the floor." Undeterred by the fire, Gumpertz rebuilt the museum and supplied it with new wax figures. By then Gumpertz had become something of an amusement czar at the Coney Island. He was president of

the Coney Island Board of Trade, headed the Brighton-by-the-Sea Development Company, and was manager of the resort's largest bathhouse. In 1932, while his friend of forty years, John Ringling, was recuperating at the Half Moon Hotel, Gumpertz secretly engineered a coup that enabled him to gain control of the Ringling Brothers and Barnum & Bailey Circus, assuming the position of senior vice president and general manager.

The success of the Dreamland Circus Sideshow and the Eden Musee led to a proliferation of similar attractions at Coney Island, and with Sam Gumpertz's departure, Professor Sam Wag-

EDEN MUSEE WAX MUSEUM.

(AUTHOR'S COLLECTION)

ner assumed the mantle as Coney's premier showman. Wagner's World Circus Side Show on Surf Avenue presented many of Coney Island's most famous attractions including Jolly Irene, Myrtle Corbin the four-legged woman, Zippo and Pippo, and strongman Warren Lincoln Travis. Wagner faced competition from showmen such as David Rosen, proprietor of the Wonderland Circus Sideshow, whose roster of human curiosities included Albert-Alberta "the double-bodied marvel," and Charlotte the Two-Headed Girl. Venues such as the Strand Museum, Hubert's Museum, and the Olympia Circus Sideshow similarly advertised the "greatest variety of sensational and living wonders from all parts of the world."

.     .     .

Mechanical amusements continued to hold a prominent place at Coney's amusement venues as showmen were forced to compete for the patronage of crowds demanding greater thrills at cheaper prices. Attractions such as the Gyroplane and the Scenic Spiral Wheel whirled riders about at Luna Park. Bumper cars such as the Dodgem and Skooter made their appearance at the resort. Luna Park installed the Tumblebug and the Scrambler, while Steeplechase added the Caterpiller and the Frolic. There were mechanical funhouses and mechanical slides, such as Jack and Jill, on which passengers rode a conveyor to the top of a tower, then slid down a spiral slide reminiscent of Luna Park's Helter Skelter. Newer and faster roller coasters were constantly being unveiled. Harry Baker installed the Big Dipper on Surf Avenue in 1921, just in sight of the Giant Racer. Steeplechase Park added two gravity rides, the Zip and the Limit, built by coaster wunderkind John Miller. In 1924, Luna Park unveiled Arthur Jarvis's Mile Sky Chaser, calling it Coney Island's "speediest, steepest, and safest ride ever built." Constructed at a cost of $140,000, it incorporated elements of the Chase Through the Clouds coaster that Jarvis had created some years earlier at Brighton Beach. Boasting a 110-foot steep drop, the coaster attracted 7,428 riders its first day and a million during its first season in operation.

It was soon eclipsed, however, by a trio of classic, high-speed coasters, built at Coney Island during a period that many regard as the Golden Age of the roller coaster. The first was the Thunderbolt, erected by John Miller on the Bowery in 1925 at the site of the old Red Devil Rider, and incorporating into its foundation a portion of the former Kensington Hotel. Although plagued by accidents during its first two seasons, it drew enthusiastic crowds. A year later, the Tornado debuted on the Bowery at Stillwell Avenue. Designed by Fred Church and originally called the Bobs coaster, it was built on an extremely narrow track with steep hills and tight spiral turns. A concession called the New Amusement Department Store occupied the space below the coaster and housed a carousel, a wax museum, and sideshow. Rising above it was a one-hundred-foot-high bejeweled tower. When the Tornado debuted on Memorial Day in 1926 it was proclaimed the most thrilling gravity ride yet devised. Its reign lasted just one year, until the following season, when the

Cyclone Racer was unveiled. The new coaster, which replaced the Giant Racer, was erected by Jack and Irving Rosenthal, two brothers whose ambition was to own the fastest roller coaster ever built. Vernon Keenan, chief engineer of the Harry Baker Company, was hired to design it. Its construction required 233,000 feet of lumber and 240 tons of steel. It had a 3,000 feet of track

## THE "TEN-IN-ONE" SHOW

Sideshow performers were a staple at Coney Island as early as 1880 when the first tent show appeared on the beach. The "ten-in-one" shows were for a time confined to the margins of the resort until Sam Gumpertz created a permanent sideshow at Dreamland. Gumpertz convinced

SPIELER AT CONEY ISLAND SIDESHOW.
(AUTHOR'S COLLECTION)

with steep spiral dips, the highest measuring 83 feet. The ride took one minute and forty seconds to complete its course, with cars attaining a speed that exceeded a mile a minute. To attract a crowd, an enormous sign spelling out the word "Cyclone" in letters ten feet high was affixed to the coaster's wooden frame and outlined with some five hundred electric lights. "It's one grand

many sideshow attractions that a seaside residence was preferable to life on the carnival circuit. Coney thereafter became a summer home for numerous sideshow performers who had various reasons for settling there. Some, when they grew older, concluded their careers at Coney Island. Their ranks included Amanda Siebert, known as Jolly Irene, who weighed well over six hundred pounds, and rated as one of Coney Island's most beloved figures, and Jane Barnell, the bearded Lady Olga who toured for almost fifty years and appeared in the Tod Browning classic movie *Freaks* (1932). She claimed that Coney's salt air suited her asthma.

The most famous Coney Island sideshow attraction was William Henry Johnson, whose career as Zip the What-Is-It spanned more than sixty years. An African American born in New Jersey, Johnson suffered from a condition called microcephely, which produces an abnormally small head and brain. Dressed in a suit of hair, his head shorn except for a small tuft at the top to accentuate its unique shape, Johnson spent the early stages of his career exhibited by Barnum as the Missing Link. According to legend, Charles Dickens viewed him at Barnum's American Museum and cried out "What is it?" Late in his career he adopted a comic persona, playing the violin with the ballyhoo band while dressed in a billowy white tunic and occasionally engaging in mock boxing contests with other performers. After he retired from the Rin-

gling Brothers Circus, Johnson and his manager, Captain O. K. White, took up residence at Dreamland Circus Sideshow, where he performed for the last fourteen years of his life. Johnson's affable nature endeared him to colleagues as well as the public and stories about his exploits are plentiful. He was once credited with saving the life of a child who had nearly drowned. A birthday banquet held in his honor in 1914 and attended by his many friends was touted as a "feast of freaks." He died in 1926 at the age of eighty-three.

Zip's many successors included a pair of microcephelics from Georgia named Elvira and Clayton Snow who performed as Pippo and Zippo. They first appeared at Professor Sam Wagner's World Circus Side Show in 1928 billed as the Pinhead Peaches from Georgia and became Coney's most popular sideshow attractions. They were among the scores of sideshow performers whose careers were guided by Sam Wagner. Others included Albert-Alberta the double-bodied European Enigma, Major Mite, and Harry Bulson the Spider Boy. Crowds at Coney Island ten-in-ones and pit shows were often abusive and sometimes they were quite cruel. Nevertheless, many sideshow performers whose physical characteristics placed them at the margins of society elsewhere found a measure of confraternity there. "If the truth was known," Lady Olga once observed, "we're all freaks together."

THE TORNADO ROLLER COASTER WITH ITS BEJEWELED TOWER. A WRITER, SURVEYING CONEY ISLAND'S SKY-LINE DURING THE 1930S, DESCRIBED ITS "ROLLER COASTER TRACKS COILED AND CONTORTED LIKE SNAKES TRAPPED IN A BONFIRE."

thing after another in Coney," the amusement trade publication *Billboard* wrote shortly after the coaster opened for business on June 26, 1927. "The latest ride sensation that has swept the island is the Cyclone. It lives up to its title, and has already established an enviable reputation as a thriller. It is accumulating the shekels abundantly." The Rosenthals charged twenty-five cents admission a ride; within a few weeks they had entirely recouped their investment. But even Keenan had to concede that coaster builders were being tested to their limits. "We've gone about as far as we can getting thrills out of gravity coasters. To hold our patrons we'll have to do the impossible," he complained. "People nowadays like to wave to their friends and show off. They want to believe the rides are dangerous. If they think they're in peril every moment, they call the ride 'grand' and come back for more. Our trick is to get the kick without the danger."

.    .    .

In spite of the immense popularity of the roller coasters, sideshows, and mechanical rides, it was becoming increasingly difficult for the amusement industry to remain profitable in the face of a shifting social environment. As demographic and societal changes took hold, the shows not only became cheaper, they grew predictably more human in scale. Crowds that fifteen years earlier might have flocked to the Ellis shows at Dreamland now stood in line for a glimpse of Rubberneck Joe Cramer or Al Flosso's magic act at Wolff's Freak Show. Steeplechase

Park continued to draw large crowds, but Luna Park had begun to stumble precipitously. The Durbar of Delhi with its parade of sixty regally appointed pachyderms had been replaced by Adele Nelson's baby elephants performing the Charleston. The cycloramas produced with modest success by Arthur Jarvis could hardly compete with motion pictures, while automobiles gave many the mobility to visit the natural wonders depicted at Coney's scenic railways. As more of the large-scale shows and mechanical-scenic productions closed their doors, they were replaced by sideshows and "ceroplastic" exhibits such as Slums of Paris, where patrons toured a Parisian underworld populated by wax figures. The Bowery perhaps best reflected the changes that swept across Coney Island during this period. Coney's irreverent midway had faced another crackdown on its concert dives in 1910 that left it a bit tamer but largely intact. Prohibition, however, virtually doomed it. Deprived of the sale of beer, which was practically the life-blood of the resort, the Bowery's honky-tonk era all but came to an end.

The Nickel Empire reached its zenith midway during the 1920s, and then gradually fell into decline as economic pressures began to mount. Coney showmen had grown overly confident that the resort was depression-proof. It had weathered previous economic downturns with little adverse effect, but this did not hold true after 1929. "The nickel was first a symbol of a new order," observed one writer, surveying Coney's landscape after the Depression had taken hold; "it became in time a reality. The mass market slowly forced Coney Island's time-honored price scales downward. The fifty-cent rides became a quarter. The quarter rides became fifteen cents. The ten-cent rides became a nickel. . . . But until the Depression of the 1930s the abundance of the nickels was unaffected by war or panic or depression." The same forces that played such a critical role in the development of Coney Island now seemed to be working to its disadvantage. Coney's history, up to this point, had followed a trajectory of accommodation and consumption. During the 1870s, capitalists had attempted with marginal success to create a seaside resort for the rich. Three decades later, clever showmen built enclosed amusement playgrounds for the enjoyment of the middle class. But of no less importance was the role the resort served as a "safety valve" for the city's teeming populace. At Coney Island, where accommodation of extraordinary numbers of people became a hallmark, the consumption of leisure as a commodity for the masses took on a new meaning. This relationship fell out of balance during the 1930s when the number of people the resort could accommodate reached its maximum limit and the ability of the crowd to consume was at an all-time low. The vast crowds arriving at Coney by subway and trolley lines did little to bolster declining rev-

CHILDREN AT A CONEY ISLAND KIDDIE PARK IN 1924.

(AUTHOR'S COLLECTION)

BATHERS AT STEEPLECHASE PARK.

(FRIED COLLECTION)

enues at the resort. Indeed, many concessionaires complained that their revenues plummeted as the numbers that poured in increased because those who came were poorer and could afford to spend less. "The people come, all right," said one showman, "but they come in such tremendous crowds that they get in one another's way. They come to walk on the boardwalk and crowd the beach, but they don't spend their money on good clean fun like they used to." For many, Coney was literally the only place to which they could go to escape the sweltering tenements during the dreadful summer months. Poor families arrived with their own food. They bypassed the sideshows, shooting galleries, and hot dog stands and paid their fifteen cents to queue up for hours outside the Municipal Bath; or they avoided the bathhouses altogether by changing under the boardwalk or by wearing bathrobes or kimonos over their bathing suits. In the evening, thousands, including entire families, slept on the beach undisturbed by the police.

Coney Island felt the full force of the

STEEPLECHASE RIDERS AT THE PAVILION OF FUN.

(FRIED COLLECTION)

widening Depression. The season of 1932 was one of the most disastrous ever, even though crowds that year were record-breaking. Carousel operators at times were forced to reduce fares to a penny. Sideshow barkers tore ten-cent tickets in half and sold both halves for a nickel, but even then the audiences they attracted were smaller in size than in seasons past. Even the storied Cyclone coaster had to cut its prices. The only concessions that remained profitable were food stands that sold custard, French-fried potatoes, and watery lemonade for a fraction of their former prices. Coney's beleaguered showmen predicted that unless things turned around, in five years there wouldn't be a single ride or game left at the resort. Said one, "Why, hell, there used to be a time you could set up a bottle game, cost you maybe one, two hundred bucks, an' clear that in a week, three balls for ten cents. Now you're lucky if you take that much in a season." Said another, "Nowadays you have to half kill 'em to get a dime."

Among those who tried to soldier on through the lean years of the Depression was Dr. Martin Couney, who had exhibited his Infant Incubators at Coney Island for four decades. Couney developed his incubator for premature infants as an intern at a Paris hospital during the 1890s and from then on he supported his work through public exhibitions. He accepted only infants from poor families, without charging any fee, and during his long career he was credited with saving the lives of 7,500 premature babies. Couney's incubator building at Dreamland was destroyed by the fire that decimated the park in 1911. During the 1930s, the incubators were housed in a building on the boardwalk that resembled a small hospital. Like other Coney Island showmen, Couney was forced to reduce his prices during the Depression. "Thirty-five years ago I could do more business with 60,000 visitors than I can do with 500,000 now," he complained. "Coney is so degraded now—even the hot dogs cost only a nickel—that people bargain to see my babies." In 1932 the incubator building survived yet another devastating fire that destroyed a thousand-foot-long stretch of the boardwalk. Several square blocks filled with bathhouses, bungalows, and summer cottages were leveled. Silver's Baths, the Streets of Bagdad, and many other showplaces went up in flames. Two thousand people were left homeless and thousands more lost their possessions in the burned-out bathhouses. Couney bundled his infant charges into baby carriages to escape the blaze, but the wind shifted, sparing his incubators. The boardwalk was quickly rebuilt, but Couney bemoaned the changes that had overwhelmed the resort in the years since he had first arrived. "Once upon a time Coney Island was the greatest amusement resort in the world," he recalled. "What do people see when they come to Coney Island today? Fascination, Sensation, Custard, Hot Dogs and Bingo! . . . The old colorful Coney Island is gone."

Coney's showmen had been counting on the repeal of the Eighteenth Amendment to restore a measure of prosperity to the resort. When beer flowed once again in 1933, all of Coney Island celebrated in grand style. Four hundred thousand people were on hand and the showmen exulted. "We've taken it on the chin for a long time," said one. "We've been waiting thirteen long years for beer to bring back some money to Coney Island. Now we have it, and we're going to make the most of it." Steeplechase Park dispensed free beer to all its adult customers. At the Hotel Eleanor, at Feltman's, and at countless small venues where the price of beer ranged from five cents to twenty cents a glass, the crowds were thick. Moreover, the revelers did not confine their spending to the beer gardens. The amusement venues and the side-shows did a respectable business as well. Still, the economic downturn continued to take its toll. Bankruptcy delayed the opening of Luna Park at the start of the season in 1933, and when the park finally opened its gates it was forced to operate in receivership. Whatever aspirations the Half Moon Hotel harbored of establishing an upscale resort at Coney Island faded overnight. Other longtime landmarks stumbled as well. Even the venerable Feltman's had to cut its payroll from twelve hundred to less than four

COUPLE AT LUNA PARK PHOTOGRAPHED BY WALKER EVANS, CIRCA 1929.

hundred. The Depression ultimately cost Coney at least half its attractions and changed it forever. Dubbed the "Poor Man's Riviera," it became synonymous with the cheapest forms of amusement and with enormously large crowds, images that would define it for generations to come. Fallen from the ranks of the premier seaside resorts, it nevertheless remained a playground for the masses, undiminished in the eyes of those who unabashedly claimed it as their own.

# CHAPTER EIGHT

# EMPIRE OF THE BODY

Coney Island emerged from the Depression with its amusement zone largely intact but with its prodigious resources considerably eroded. No longer a laboratory of the mass culture or engine of the amusement industry, it became instead the resort of last resort for those who could afford little more than the nickel it took to get there on the subway. Coney's beach was now its premier attraction and the crowds that swarmed over it supplied its signature image. Coney had become an empire of the body, celebrating the human form in all its diversity in such vast numbers so as to astound one's comprehension: bodies arrayed in various states of dress and undress, bodies intertwined and in motion that were tossed by the tides and upended, bodies of every class and description. Coney celebrated them all—the freaks and bathing beauties, the contortionists and high-wire performers, the modern Venuses and subway Adonises. The human body was indeed the defining element at Coney Island that connected all of its seemingly disparate parts from era to era. A generation earlier, Coney Island had unleashed the human body in ways that were previously unimagined. Its bathing pavilions and dance palaces beckoned to the multitudes and seized hold of them. Its machinery of amusement sent them reeling and catapulted them through space. Motion drove Coney Island, motion in its roiling and heaving waves that devoured and consumed the shore and deposited it elsewhere, motion in its revolving wheels and manic coasters, motion in its dancers and the bathers on its beach, a pulling and tugging whirlpool of excited motion. When Coney no longer had the capacity to astound and amaze the masses, the crowd itself became a heaving canvas, a kind of populist performance piece.

In much the same way that Manhattan's Bowery served as the common boulevard for the denizens of the city's Lower East Side, so Coney Island was a summer gathering ground for this cacophonous multitude. "To understand the Boardwalk of Coney Island you must know the sidewalks of New York," the *New York Times* wrote. "Just as Park Avenue ends at Bailey's Beach, so Hester Street, Mulberry Bend, Harlem and Brownsville end at Coney, the playground of the tenements." From the moment one disembarked at the BMT platform at Stillwell Avenue, one heard the languages and dialects of every nation of Europe. "The parents shout out instructions to the children in Yiddish, German, Italian, Polish, or Czech," a writer observed; "the children respond in the dialect of the east side." What made it all the more extraordinary was that few of those who visited Coney Island had ever ventured into the ocean in their native countries. At Coney, where

European immigrants far outnumbered native-born Americans and where English was at best a second language, they were persuaded to do so. Picnics were the most common form of recreation for countless immigrants who came to the city from rural communities. On Coney's beach they were able to re-create the communal picnic on a greatly enlarged scale. Coney's beach was thus transformed during the period between the two world wars into a multi-ethnic canvas.

Covering about fifty-seven acres and extending a little more than two and a half miles,

CONEY ISLAND, JULY 4, 1938.

(© BETTMANN/CORBIS)

# PHOTOGRAPHING AT CONEY ISLAND

Ever since the days when the Camera Obscura enabled visitors at West Brighton to gaze upon the perambulations of bathers on the beach, photographers have been drawn to Coney Island. As early as 1892 a writer, struck by the pernicious relationship between the camera and the bathing suit, warned that the human body clothed in "flimsy flannel" could too easily succumb to the "magic touch of the man with the gelatine film." Early images of Coney Island were obtained by George B. Brainerd during the 1880s and by Robert Brocklow during the 1890s. Some very fine images were produced by Joseph Byron between 1895 and 1905. Scores of

CONEY ISLAND BEACH IN 1938 PHOTOGRAPHED BY REGINALD MARSH. REGINALD MARSH HAS BEEN CALLED THE ARTIST LAUREATE OF CONEY ISLAND. MARSH FIRST CAME TO THE BEACH IN THE EARLY 1920S AS A SKETCH ARTIST FOR *VANITY FAIR* AND THEREAFTER RETURNED EVERY SUMMER, OFTEN FOUR TIMES A WEEK, TO PHOTOGRAPH AND SKETCH ITS CAROUSEL RIDES, SIDESHOWS, AND THE CROWD THAT SPREAD OUT "IN ALL DIRECTIONS, IN ALL POSITIONS, WITHOUT CLOTHING, MOVING LIKE THE GREAT COMPOSITIONS OF MICHELANGELO AND RUBENS." HE CREATED HUNDREDS OF BLACK-AND-WHITE PRINTS AND TEMPERA PAINTINGS IN THE COURSE OF TWO AND A HALF DECADES DEVOTED TO CONEY ISLAND.     (MUSEUM OF THE CITY OF NEW YORK, GIFT OF MRS. REGINALD MARSH, 90.36.1.178).

photographs of Coney Island were created for stereoscopes produced by Alfred Campbell, Detroit Photo Company, and Underhill and Underhill.

Photographers who wanted to capture the vitality of New York's street life and document its iconography gravitated to Coney Island in much the same way that they haunted Times Square and Fourteenth Street. Walker Evans's early work includes photographs of Luna Park and the Wonder Wheel taken during the 1920s. Henri Cartier-Bresson photographed Coney's beach for *Harper's Bazaar* and Margaret Bourke-White did so for *Life* magazine. Harold Roth, Arthur Leipzig, Sid Grossman, and Ben Ross produced remarkable photographs at Coney Island during the 1940s and 1950s, as did Robert Frank, Lisette Model, Elliott Erwitt, and Bruce Davidson ("The Gang"). Others who worked there included Diane Arbus and Bruce Gilden and, more recently, Joseph Stashkevetch and Mary Ellen Mark ("American Odyssey"). Among the most memorable photographs of Coney Island are those created by Arthur Fellig, known more commonly as Weegee. His most famous image is a photograph of the beach taken in 1940 in which thousands of bathers packed together stare directly into the camera. A half-century later, Kim Iacono produced a photograph called "After Weegee's Beach" that was both a homage and a sly wink at the famous image. Taken from the identical camera angle, it records the footprints left behind in the sand by the crowd at day's end.

COUPLE AT CONEY ISLAND PHOTOGRAPHED BY HENRI CARTIER-BRESSON IN 1947.
(HENRI CARTIER-BRESSON/MAGNUM PHOTOS)

CONEY ISLAND BEACH IN 1946, PHOTO-GRAPHED BY MORRIS ENGEL.    (CULVER PICTURES)

Coney Island's beach was divided into twenty-two beach divisions called bays. The bays functioned as informal extensions of the city's neighborhoods. Each community, whether Nor- wegians from Bay Ridge or Italians from East Harlem, gravitated to a portion of the beach where they were the dominant group. Italians congregated between Steeplechase Park and

## CUSTARD, TAFFY, AND RED HOTS

From the time when the clam was king and sausages first became Coney "red hots," food has been devoured in vast quantities at Coney Island. Dining at Coney Island was as combustible as its fastest rides. Coney's palate was as rich and varied as New York's immigrant stream, but its offerings were undeniably American. Saltwater taffy was an early staple at the beach along with the ice cream cone, which was first manufactured there in 1905 by the man who claimed to have introduced it the previous year at the St. Louis Exposition. Around the same time, a peddler known as John the Greek made his mark selling waffles filled with ice cream at a stand near the Helter Skelter. Pizza pie was first sampled at Coney Island at Totono's Pizzeria in 1924. Frozen custard was introduced in 1927. Turkish Taffy had its debut during the 1940s. It was invented by Victor Bonomo, whose father had had a candy factory at Coney Island since 1897. Coney had three hundred food and drink concessions selling frozen custard, corned beef and cabbage, shish kebab skewered on a grill, bagels

and lox, little neck clams, waffles, and ears of corn roasted and buttered for ten cents. There were Romanian tearooms, oysters at the Assembly Chop House, chop suey at Canton Low, knishes at Shatzkin's, hamburger with gardenia onions at Feltman's, and roast beef, fried potatoes, and frankfurters at Nathan's Famous and at Nedick's. A hundred million hot dogs were consumed at Coney Island each year and the undisputed hot dog–eating king was Babe Ruth, who devoured two dozen at one time and washed them down with a gallon of lemonade.

FOOD STAND AT CONEY ISLAND, CIRCA 1939.
(BROOKLYN PUBLIC LIBRARY—BROOKLYN COLLECTION)

Stillwell Avenue, Jews gathered in the vicinity of Hahn's Roosevelt Baths, Scandinavians and Irish were the dominant groups at McLochlin Baths, and African Americans were concentrated near the Municipal Baths. Food, music, and language varied from bay to bay. Coney's crowd was variegated. Its colors, smells, and sounds did not blend or meld together, they collided and recompounded. Brooklyn's neighborhoods did not dissolve onto the beach, they proudly planted their flags in the bays, they bathed happily in their ethnicity and their pride of turf, and they glistened in their native sweat, drop by drop.

.    .    .

Ultimately all of the distinct groups that spilled onto Coney Island's beach were linked by virtue of being participants in the crowd. The crowd with its immense numbers assumed an identity that, in the end, trumped ethnicity or neighborhood loyalty by imposing a common identity more closely linked to class. Each group staked its claim to a small portion of the beach as an expression of parochial solidarity; but once its members became part of the crowd this parochial identity was subsumed into a kind of crowd ethos in solidarity with all others. Participation in the crowd at Coney Island conferred a measure of privilege and entitlement on those whose lives were anything but privileged. Unashamed, they celebrated themselves in the vastness of the crowd with an air of joyful triumphalism. Viewed from without, every aspect of the crowd might seem objec-

tionable: the cramped sweaty hordes on the subway cars pouring out onto Stillwell Avenue, the claustrophobic, writhing masses on the beach, each person occupying a space no larger than a coffin, the noise and jangle of the mechanical amusements—all could appear crass and mind-numbing. And yet, the sign at Stauch's Pavilion that cried out "Go Where the Crowds Go" could well have served as a rallying cry for the masses who seemed drawn to the crowd for the pure pleasure of being part of it. "We loved the crowd," a visitor to Coney Island recalled recently. "People didn't mind the contact. It was hot all week long at home in the tenements and so you looked forward to Coney Island at the end of the week. That was the treat. You couldn't wait to get there." Said a woman who went each summer on holiday with her parents and siblings, "I remember all the smells of Coney Island. The chutes. That's what we called the roller coasters. The freak shows. The Cyclone that seemed like it was going to dive right into the ocean. Going to Coney Island, that was the best thing of all." Bathing shoulder to shoulder at Coney Island was both satisfying and ennobling in ways that sharply contrasted with other forms of recreation. It was bigger than any parade, more inclusive than any political rally, and more democratic than any spectator sport. It was like the Fourth of July and every other patriotic outpouring rolled into one. When as many as a million people visited on a single day, Coney became the sixth largest city in the United States.

By the 1930s, as many as 35 million people were visiting Coney Island each summer. Most came on the subway, and with the arrival of the first subway cars in the predawn hours, the crowd began to surge forth from the suffocating confines of the BMT terminal. "Humanity flows over Coney seeking relief from the heat of the city," the Federal Writers' Project guidebook explained. "Italians, Jews, Greeks . . . feeble ancients, mothers with squirming children, fathers with bundles, push and collide as they rush, laughing, scolding, sweating, for a spot on the sand." A portion of the vast crowd headed first for one of the bathhouses. There were more than thirty bathing establishments to select from. Large bathhouses such as Steeplechase Baths, Ward's, and Washington Baths charged about fifty cents for a locker and provided amenities such as a pool, handball court, punching bags, and a sunbathing deck. Raven Hall, one of the oldest, had a picnic grove and dance pavilion. Silver's Baths and Stauch's were known for their steam baths, which were popular with Russian and Jewish patrons. Less prestigious establishments with fewer amenities charged as little as fifteen cents. Bathhouses were one more link to the city's poorer neighborhoods, where public baths were familiar institutions. Communal solidarity was transferred to many of Coney Island's bathing establishments, which gained a loyal following among a particular neighborhood group. By the late 1930s, however, despite

CONEY ISLAND BOARDWALK, CIRCA 1940.

(© LUCIEN AIGNER/CORBIS)

prohibitions against the wearing of bathing suits on public streets, less than a quarter of those arriving at the beach patronized a bathing establishment. Many who could not afford the price of a bathhouse visited "bedroom bathhouses" in private dwellings that charged ten cents and accommodated as many as ten couples in single bedroom. Many wore swimsuits under their clothing and bypassed the bathhouses entirely. They were known in Coney Island parlance as "drippers."

The multitude arrived at the beach resembling an army with all its provisions in tow: entire families, including aunts and uncles, arms laden with bedsheets and army surplus blankets, beach chairs rented for a dollar, gunny sacks and small battered suitcases, picnic baskets filled with salami sandwiches, beer and pop bottles, pickle jars, suntan lotion, and bath towels. Larger siblings dragged smaller ones by the arm. Elderly grandparents paused to daub their foreheads with handkerchiefs. Each was determined to carve out a place on the scant fifty-seven acres of sand. Bodies on checkerboard blankets and bedsheets of every imaginable color were everywhere pressed close together, leaving barely a trace of coarse red sand exposed. Legs and limbs were everywhere entwined. Backs, necks, and torsos tanned olive brown and café crème commingled. Adolescent girls in Garbo makeup and taffy-colored hair sunbathed beside matronly aunts in caftans. Grandmothers in pajama pants and floppy hats with their bathhouse keys worn around their necks peeled the shells off hard-boiled eggs, flanked by players of klabash and canasta. Old

Jewish gentlemen playing pinochle and elderly Italians playing scopa shaded themselves under newspapers and Panama hats. Countless children in tiny white sailor hats devoured pickles and frankfurters, and countless adults devoured thick crusts of Italian bread, bologna sandwiches, tomatoes, and chopped liver, along with knishes and Eskimo pies purchased from peddlers in white suits, and washed them down with beer or soda pop bought from small food concessions under boardwalk. And all about was the sound of guitar and mandolin players; the percussive chorus of the waves that mixed with the drumbeat of boys pounding on tomtoms; a distant Hungarian Gypsy tune that mingled with "Bie Mir Bist du Shoen" and turned into "Torna a Surriento"; a trumpet playing a tinny and unwelcome reveille; the yowls of girls plagued by brothers and of boys grieving for collapsed castles of sand; and the wounded cries of a hundred hands stepped upon. All of these merged into a single "sharp, uneven falsetto roar" created by a million voices that "drowned out the surge of the sea." All the sounds and smells of Coney Island seemed to multiply and mingle. The sun that neither rose nor set over the ocean at Coney Island while relentlessly beating down upon so many backs produced what one writer called Coney's perfume: a "mingled fragrance of hot bodies, and hot dogs, horses, paint, peanuts and sideshows . . . as distinctive as the odor of an orphanage or a circus."

The crowd, densest at the midpoint between the boardwalk and the surf, seemed to spill right into the ocean. Here were the builders of human pyramids and gymnasts, the "swarthy sheiks" playing leapfrog, the ballplayers and those shaking an angry fist at ballplayers. Here were the hand-holding lovers oblivious to a million eyes and the entwined lovers in the sand. Here were the plump matrons with linked arms that the lifeguards called "dunkers," the enormous woman in the polka-dot sundress and latex stockinets with the waves washing over her, and the gentleman with skin pale as sour cream in the rented number 14 bathing suit that dangled almost to his ankles. A bit farther out were the wave-jumpers and riders of sea horses and air mattresses, fat uncles on inner tubes, and half-hysterical children straining on water wings. Farther still were the long-distance swimmers and exhibitionists who tested the patience of the lifeguards, and those who perched like ravens on the jetties draped with discarded clothing that fluttered like so many flags. Every so often a knot of onlookers would gather about a child that had become separated from its family. Three thousand lost children were collected

LOST CHILD, CIRCA 1941. CONEY'S CROWDED BEACH WAS PATROLLED BY 106 LIFEGUARDS, 13 PLAIN-CLOTHES POLICEMEN, AND 5 POLICEWOMEN. ON AN AVERAGE DAY THE CROWD GENERATED 127 LOST CHILDREN AND PRODUCED A TRAINLOAD—ROUGHLY FIVE HUNDRED CUBIC YARDS—OF GARBAGE.

(AUTHOR'S COLLECTION)

by the police and lifeguards in a single season. They were kept in wire cages under the boardwalk until claimed by their parents. Each year, on August 15, the beach acquired a distinctly Old World flavor when the devout gathered at Coney Island for "Cure Day" in the belief that those who bathed in the ocean on the Feast of the Assumption of the Blessed Virgin would be relieved of all physical defects. Initiated by Irish Catholics, the custom was adopted by newcomers, including Italians, who practiced their own devotion to La Madonna Assunta. On that date thousands gathered at the Municipal Baths, hours before it opened, awaiting their turn to plunge into the ocean. Many disabled persons, aided by family members, discarded their crutches and bathed or knelt in prayer in hope of obtaining a cure.

. . .

As the numbers spilling onto the beach

*LITTLE FUGITIVE* (1953). MORRIS ENGEL'S FILM MASTERFULLY CONVEYED THE EARTHINESS OF CONEY ISLAND DURING THE 1950S. INDEPENDENTLY PRODUCED AND SHOT WITH A HAND-HELD CAMERA AND A CAST COMPOSED ALMOST ENTIRELY OF NON-ACTORS, IT FOLLOWS THE ADVENTURES OF A BOY WHO FLEES TO CONEY ISLAND AFTER HE IS DECEIVED INTO BELIEVING HE HAS ACCIDENTALLY SLAIN HIS OLDER BROTHER.

(THE MUSEUM OF MODERN ART/FILM STILLS ARCHIVE)

increased, efforts were made to exert greater control over the behavior of the crowd. Magistrates enforced a variety of beach ordinances, including those barring certain forms of bathing attire. In 1910, eight young men were arrested for wearing tight-fitting "Parisian"-style swimsuits. A decade later, women caught without stockings were escorted from the beach and "one-piece swimsuits" with less than five inches of skirt were deemed immoral. During the mid-1930s, fines of up to fifty dollars and sentences of up to ten days in jail were meted out to men with "topless bathing costumes" and those caught with the shoulder straps of their swimsuits turned down. The wearing of swimsuits on the boardwalk was frowned upon, and a three-dollar fine could be imposed for changing under it. Peddlers and ballplayers were also fined. Generally speaking, however, the crowd was well behaved and required little policing.

In 1938, jurisdiction over Coney Island was transferred to New York City Parks Commissioner Robert Moses. Moses was New York's most visionary and most controversial master builder. He was almost single-handedly responsible for many of the Empire State's most recognizable landmarks, including bridges, highways, parks, and cultural institutions. In 1929 he created Jones Beach in Nassau County, which was regarded as a model of public recreation planning. Installed as New York's parks commissioner five years later, Moses declared Coney Island "cheapened and commercialized to death." Moses outlined his plan for Coney's revitalization in a report submitted to Mayor Fiorello La Guardia in 1937. "There is no use bemoaning the end of the old Coney Island fabled in song and story," he wrote. "There must be a new and very different resort established in its place." Echoing reform-minded public officials who a half-century earlier sought to create a seaside park, Moses proposed to sweep aside Coney's catchpenny devices and mechanical amusements, which he deplored as noisy and unhealthy, and replace them with expanded facilities for bathing and outdoor recreation. Calling it a mecca for "people of smallest means," he decried the appalling conditions at Coney Island's beach, where every bather was afforded about sixteen square feet of space, roughly the size of a coffin. "A community which calls itself civilized might do a little more by way of recreation for its citizens between the tight spaces of the cradle and the grave," he declared. "Certainly there is no reason to perpetuate out-of-doors the overcrowding of our tenements." He called for more land in public ownership, stricter enforcement of ordinances, fewer mechanical noise-making and amusement devices, and a more orderly growth of year-round residents. Under Moses's stewardship, thirty additional acres were added to the beach in 1940 by repositioning a portion of the boardwalk and moving it back 300 feet. The boardwalk was then extended across Brighton Beach and white sand replaced the reddish brown sand that had been pumped in when Coney's boardwalk was first built. The improvements let stand Coney Island's amusement zone with its sideshows and mechanical rides in spite of Moses's contention that the public was losing interest in them.

The amusement district Robert Moses took charge of extended from Surf Avenue to the boardwalk for a distance of about two miles and was crowded with seven hundred independent concessions. It included Luna Park and Steeplechase Park, eleven roller coasters, thirteen carousels, five sideshows, twenty shooting galleries, and scores of game stands, rides, and arcades. Moses acted quickly to impose his vision on Coney Island, enacting new ordinances governing behavior on the beach. The wide-ranging list of injunctions included fines for tumbling and human-pyramid building, speechmaking, the playing of phonographs, and the use of newspapers as beach blankets. Ordinances that prohibited the sale of food on the beach were more stringently enforced and knish peddlers would sometimes try to evade the police by wading out into the ocean with their baskets in tow. Under Moses's regime, eating peanuts and disposing of their shells on the beach could lead to a fine of two dollars for littering. However, Coney's sideshows suffered most from the sanctions imposed by Moses and License Commissioner Paul Moss. Efforts to rein in the sideshows had begun almost a decade earlier, urged on by Sam Gumpertz, who contended that sideshow "ballyhoo" had

RIDERS ON THE COMET COASTER IN 1945.

(EILEEN DARBY/TIMEPIX)

become a public nuisance. An ordinance prohibiting free outside exhibitions by sideshow barkers was reinstated by Commissioner Moss and the managers of numerous establishments, including Sam Wagner and Dave Rosen, were arrested. The Coney Island Chamber of Commerce protested to Mayor La Guardia in a telegram decrying the ordinances as a "body punch to our business life."

.    .    .

In spite of the new ordinances, Coney Island's amusement zone carried on much as it had in the past. Its heady heart and soul was still the Bowery, which one writer described as the "concentrated distillate of all the midways of all the carnivals in America." Its "dancing dolls" and "penny heart" games may have been cleaned up a bit by Commissioner Moss, and the sideshow banners may have been toned down a notch, but the Bowery was as noisy and frenetic as ever. If Coney's beach mirrored the diversity

## DEATH AT THE HALF MOON

Coney Island was a haunt of New York underworld figures and gangsters since the time of Monk Eastman and Shang Draper. By the 1930s, the rising star of New York's criminal underworld was Charlie "Lucky" Luciano. Luciano was a protégé of "Joe the Boss" Masseria, but was also courted by Masseria'a rival, Salvatore Maranzano. In April 1931, Masseria and Luciano dined together at the Nouvo Villa Tammaro at Coney Island. After dinner the two men played a game of cards. When Luciano briefly stepped away from the table, several accomplices including Bugsy Siegel and Albert Anastasia rushed in and assassinated Masseria, who was found with the ace of diamonds clutched between his fingers. Maranzano briefly took command of the Unione Sicilione but was murdered less than five months later by Luciano and his confederates.

Albert Anastasia, who played an important part in Masseria's death, was a key figure in Murder Incorporated, a gang of underworld

enforcers led by Louis "Lepke" Buchalter and Abe "Kid Twist" Reles. In 1937 Lepke was indicted, but rather than face prison he went into hiding. He spent several months in 1938 concealed by Anastasia in a flat above the Oriental Palace dance hall at Coney Island. After two years in hiding, Lepke—now America's Public Enemy Number One—finally surrendered. He was convicted of murder and died in the electric chair at Sing-Sing. Rather than face the same fate, Abe Reles turned against his associates in Murder Incorporated, implicating Anastasia and Bugsy Seigel in a pair of killings. To insure his safety the underworld "songbird" was held at the Half Moon Hotel in Coney Island under constant police watch. On November 12, 1941, Reles fell to his death from his hotel window. Luciano later boasted that the police assigned to protect Reles had been paid to stage the murder. One newspaper writer quipped, "He could sing, but he couldn't fly."

and divisions of the city's neighborhoods, the Bowery with its arcades and eclectic brew of amusements was a place where all nationalities and races could commingle. They were carried along on a torrent of smells and sounds: the voices of barkers and countermen and of women selling sweet corn; the incessant clatter of penny slot machines, pinball games, and fortune-telling devices that were ancient relics of the Nickel Empire; the staccato of Speedway motor cars and shooting galleries; the odor of peanut-roasting machines; and the overhead pulse of the Tornado and the Thunderbolt that sounded like the rattle of bones and convulsed into a single metallic roar. The sideshows appeared a bit more degraded and the wax museums seemed even more lurid than before. Sam Wagner's World Circus Sidehow, by then in operation almost two decades, drew half as many patrons to gawk at Pippo and Zippo and Sealo the Seal Boy. Freaks of nature cast in wax and ceroplastic re-creations of sensational events such as the "Electrocution of Hauptmann" were the attraction at the World in Wax Musee. A vestige of the old Bowery survived at Lane's and the Shamrock Irish House, whose singing waiters defied competition from flashy new arcade games such as Syd Kahn's Fascination and recent attractions such as the Rocket and the Boomerang. There were as well along the Bowery and about the boardwalk a curious array of one-man acts that recalled the performing artists who plied their talents on the beach during an earlier era: strongmen such as the Mighty Atom, vocabulary men and human automatons, phrenologists such as James Bostwick ("The Man You Will

Eventually Ask"), and "guess-your-weight" artists, such as Selig Hochheicer, who with high hat, tuxedo, monocle, and spats stood outsides Joe's Restaurant for thirty years.

The owners of Coney's amusement parks and concessions had postponed the acquisition of new rides during the worst years of the Depression and many older attractions, especially Luna Park, had fallen into disrepair. There was hopeful anticipation that the World's Fair held in New York in 1939–1940 would enhance Coney's fortunes. The Fair was a disappointment, however, and when it closed many of its attractions were brought to the resort. Steeplechase Park acquired the Parachute Jump, the Bobsled Ride replaced Stauch's dance hall, and Luna Park gobbled up a dozen smaller attractions, dubbing itself Luna Fair.

Ironically, it was the outbreak of World War II that gave Coney its biggest boost since the heady days of the 1920s. Caught unprepared, Coney's attractions first had to conform with wartime "dim-out" and "blackout" regulations. Steeplechase Park, which had been ablaze with sixty thousand bright lights, installed two thousand shaded bulbs, while Luna Park was fretted with a comparable number of blue ones. Game stands were obliged to cover their electric lights with blankets at night in order to comply, although interior lights were allowed. Dim-outs darkened the boardwalk at night and most of its concessions were deserted after dusk, giving a gloomy aura even to the roller coasters that roared through the shadows. Still, Coney Island threw itself into the war effort in its own fashion. Many concessions adopted war-related

THE CONEY ISLAND CYCLONE, CIRCA 1939. "A RIDE ON THE CYCLONE IS A GREATER THRILL THAN FLYING AN AIRPLANE AT TOP SPEED," CHARLES LINDBERGH ONCE REMARKED. A COASTER RIDE IN 1948 CURED EMILIO FRANCO, WHO WAS AFFLICTED WITH A HYSTERICAL MALADY THAT RENDERED HIM SPEECHLESS. THE FIRST WORDS HE UTTERED WERE "I FEEL SICK."                                (FRIED COLLECTION)

themes. Pop-'Em-In games became Hit-the-Axis pan games. Ball-toss stands had caricatures of Hitler and Hirohito superimposed on the hindquarters of horses for servicemen to hurl baseballs at. A shortage of ammunition forced many shooting galleries to shut down, however, and Luna Park had to cancel its Most Beautiful Red-Head contest because so many young women were occupied with the war effort. The

Bowery had an "Axis Atrocities" show, and wax museums added General Douglas MacArthur and Chiang Kai-shek to their rosters. "Back the Attack" was the theme of the Mardi Gras carnival held in 1943, which promoted the war bond drive. Since Surf Avenue was dimmed out, floodlights were used to illuminate floats that portrayed the Allied Nations.

A visit to Coney Island by servicemen on

leave became the home-front equivalent of D-Day. Coney ranked with the Statue of Liberty and the Empire State Building as the most popular attraction for men and women in uniform and many insisted upon visiting the boardwalk even during the winter months. Sailors on shore leave danced the jitterbug with their sweethearts at the Atlantis Club and at the Hi-Ho Casino in Brighton Beach where big bands performed; they whirled about on the Caterpillar ride and clung to each other in the Tunnel of Fun. Most rides cost just twenty-five cents during wartime and Coast Guard officials insisted that Coney photo studios charge a reduced rate for servicemen. Ironically, the rationing of gasoline proved to be an enormous benefit to Coney Island. Families that might have ventured to other resorts came to Coney Island instead. The season of 1943 was the most successful since 1925, with a record 46 million visitors counted. The beach was jammed, but the crowd was more subdued with so many young men overseas.

Luna Park, sadly, did not survive the war years. The park had slipped in and out of bankruptcy during the Depression. In 1935 it changed hands again and the new owners sought to restore some of its lost luster. The Streets of Paris cabaret was installed in the Willow Grove and Billy Jackson's Midget Village was added as well as some minor attractions. But after three rather dismal seasons the park again succumbed to bankruptcy. A new consortium took control in 1940 and its new manager declared bluntly that it needed to be torn down and rebuilt. The aging Chutes and the Dragon's Gorge scenic railway were refurbished and fifteen new attrac-

tions from the New York World's Fair, including the Boomerang Ride, were installed. Old, outdated attractions were replaced with new ones such as the Flying Wasps and Swooper, and new acts such as the Aqua Girls were added to Luna's popular free circus. A wartime motif was given to the Opera House where "Hitler at the End of a Rope" was presented. However, in August 1944, a fire that erupted in the Dragon's Gorge coaster leveled half the park. It destroyed twenty attractions including the Mile Sky Chaser, the Chutes, the circus arena, and the Mirror Maze, as well as Luna's landmark Kaleidoscope Tower, which had been leased as an advertising platform to Coca-Cola. The ballroom, Wonderland, and a dozen rides and smaller concessions survived the blaze. The park briefly reopened with its fire-ravaged ruins roped off, but it ceased operation at the close of the season.

With the demise of Luna Park, Steeplechase Park stood alone as the last of Coney's three great amusement parks. Over the years, the park made only minor changes to its roster of attractions. The ancient Steeplechase racecourse still encircled the cavernous Pavilion of Fun. From its huge glass facade, the park's madly grinning Funny Face logo glared maniacally, enticing the crowd to visit "Steeplechase—The Funny Place." Most visitors entered the pavilion through the revolving Barrel of Love. Within the pavilion were the classic amusement devices introduced a half-century earlier by George C. Tilyou, including the Whirlpool, the Hoop-La, and the Human Pool Table. At one end stood the Blow Hole Theater. Riders exiting from the

Steeplechase racecourse were unsuspectingly led to the stage of the Blow Hole Theater, where they encountered a dwarf dressed as a clown, a farmer who swung through the air on a cable, and a cowboy, and were subjected to a series of pratfalls. As they attempted to cross the stage, gusts of air from blow holes under the floor whooshed up the young women's skirts while the dwarf prodded the young men with a tiny electric rod. The audience, composed almost entirely of previous riders, roared with laughter. At the center of the pavilion stood the splendid El Dorado carousel, whch had been acquired by George Tilyou after it survived the Dreamland fire. The carousel's ornate facade served as an entrance to the park on Surf Avenue. Within the pavilion were also two restaurants and a large ballroom. The park's exterior grounds included the world's largest swimming pool, Tilyou's ancient Ferris wheel, the Chanticleer carousel, an elegant boardwalk carousel created by Mangels, a Flying Turns coaster, and a second smaller roller coaster. A fire on the board-walk in 1939 destroyed the Flying Turns coaster,

SAILORS IN THE BARREL OF FUN AT STEEPLECHASE PARK.

(BROOKLYN PUBLIC LIBRARY–BROOKLYN COLLECTION)

the Barrel of Fun, and several other Steeplechase attractions, but spared the pavilion. Two years later the park acquired the Parachute Jump from the World's Fair and installed it on the site where the fire had taken place. Steeplechase was able to weather the Depression by steadfastly adhering to its policy of providing "family-style" amusements at a relatively modest price. The famous Steeplechase combination ticket cost fifty cents during the 1930s for admission to the park's thirty-one rides and attractions. The park was always well maintained and its attendants, who wore bright red racing steward's jackets and Kelly green racing caps, excluded rowdies from the grounds.

· · · ·

In the aftermath of the Second World War, Coney got a much-needed facelift. The arcades and amusement facades along Surf Avenue and the Bowery received new coats of paint after years of neglect due to wartime shortages, and new rides such as the Gyro Globe, Cuddle Up, and Flying Dips appeared. Coney's Chamber of Commerce estimated that 36 million people visited the resort during the season of 1946, and Steeplechase Park began the 1947 season by admitting the 20 millionth paying customer to the park's Pavilion of Fun. On July 3, 1947, Coney Island hosted a crowd estimated at two and a half million people that was described as the largest ever assembled in the nation's history. They had gathered to witness a military air show and pyrotechnic exhibition presented by the Army Air Corps. The crowd completely

THE BLOW HOLE THEATER AT STEEPLECHASE PARK.
(FRIED COLLECTION)

filled the beach and boardwalk for a distance of almost three miles from Brighton Beach to the Half Moon Hotel. Hundreds of fully dressed spectators surged into the surf to glimpse the extraordinary spectacle that transformed the evening sky over Coney Island into a simulated war zone.

Coney, even without Luna Park, could still be touted as New York's "Baghdad on the BMT." Business was steady at the popular Clam Bar Restaurant on Surf Avenue and crowds were thick on the boardwalk as they passed by the giant Chesterfield advertising sign. There were plenty of patrons at the Lido Pool and long lines formed at the Cyclone. Not all of Coney's landmarks fared so well, however. The Half Moon Hotel was converted into a geriatric hospital in

NATHAN'S FAMOUS AT CONEY ISLAND, CIRCA 1939. A LANDMARK SINCE 1916, IT WAS FOUNDED BY NATHAN HANDWERKER, WHO INTRODUCED THE FIVE-CENT HOT DOG. BY THE 1950S IT WAS SELLING 6 MILLION ANNU-ALLY, WITH A RECORD 54,000 SOLD DURING A SINGLE DAY IN 1954. NELSON ROCKEFELLER, WHILE CAM-PAIGNING THERE FOR GOVERNOR, REMARKED, "NO ONE CAN GET ELECTED IN THIS STATE WITHOUT BEING PHOTOGRAPHED EATING A HOT DOG AT NATHAN'S FAMOUS."

(PHOTO BY ANDREW HERMAN. MUSEUM OF THE CITY OF NEW YORK, FEDERAL ARTS PROJECT)

1949 and Feltman's Restaurant, which never recovered from the Depression, went out of business in 1954. Scores of arcade and game stands prospered, but many concessionaires complained that the subway straphangers had to be coaxed into parting with a dime, and others swore their survival depended upon the patronage of a great number of people who came to Coney Island on excursion buses from as far away as Maryland. Still, the crowds continued to swell. On July 4, 1955, Coney Island's beach recorded what was perhaps its greatest single-day throng ever, estimated at well over one and a half million people. Two days later,

Nathan's served its one hundred millionth hot dog.

.    .    .

Coney Island's stability and much of its unique flavor can be attributed to the neighborhoods contiguous with the amusement district, which housed Irish and Greek immigrants, Hungarians, Jews from Eastern Europe and Russia, Italians, and African Americans. A thriving Italian neighborhood extended from Stillwell Avenue to about West Twenty-third Street with landmarks such as Our Lady of Solace Church and Gargiuolo's Restaurant. Beyond it lay a Jewish neighborhood that extended to West Thirty-seventh Street, where it bordered the enclosed community of Sea Gate. The year-round residents of these adjoining working-class neighborhoods lived in two-story multifamily dwellings concentrated along Mermaid and Neptune Avenues. Interspersed were hundreds of summer bungalows whose occupants doubled the island's population during the summer months. African Americans, who made up less than 2 percent of Coney Island's population prior to 1950, were concentrated between West Eighth Street and Ocean Parkway. East of Ocean Parkway lay Brighton Beach, which by then had been transformed into a crowded neighborhood that drew much of its population from the Lower East Side and the city's other immigrant enclaves. Most of its inhabitants resided in six-story apartments that lined Brighton Beach Avenue, extending all the way to the boardwalk. Brighton Beach was home to a large Jewish immigrant population, whose presence led to the conversion of the Brighton Music Hall into a Yiddish theater. Brighton's mainstay was the Brighton Baths, which occupied the site of the former Brighton Beach Park. Open to members only, it had a semi-public beach, a pool, handball courts, dining facilities, a bandstand, and facilities for nude sunbathing. Farther to the east lay the more prosperous Manhattan Beach, where single-family dwellings had replaced the manicured lawns of the Oriental Hotel. Far removed from Coney's amusement zone, Manhattan Beach had its own boardwalk Esplanade as well as the Manhattan Beach Casino and bandshell where big bands performed. During the war years the eastern tip of Manhattan Beach housed a merchant marine training center.

Joseph Heller, who grew up in Coney Island's Jewish neighborhood during the Depression, confessed later that he had no idea that he was living in what some considered an economically distressed community. He had not felt deprived. "It was a blessing of our childhood to be oblivious of our low economic state and how others might regard us," he wrote. "We had our beach and our boardwalk, our safe streets, the food and clothing we needed, and I don't believe the circumstance of moderate poverty was too upsetting to our parents either. Nearly all were immigrants and living on a roughly equal level. This was the nature of life; they had learned that in Europe." Like many others, Heller reminisced about riding the Cyclone and visiting Steeplechase Park hoping to obtain an intact combination ticket from well-dressed patrons exiting the park. Other writers such as Isaac

Bashevis Singer and playwright Neil Simon drew upon their firsthand experiences of Coney Island's neighborhoods to inform their work. Singer lived in Sea Gate when he first came to the United States and Coney Island provided the setting for several of his books, all of which were written in Yiddish. While Isaac Singer's journey to Coney Island began in his native Poland, the migration of Woody Guthrie to Coney Island began in America's heartland. Guthrie came to live at Coney Island in 1944 after a stint in the merchant marine. The poet of America's downtrodden felt quite at home in the largely immigrant and politically left-leaning community that existed at Coney Island. Guthrie's landlady, who called him "Voody," operated a bookstore on Mermaid Avenue and complained that he seldom paid the rent. Woody's son Arlo was born at Coney Island and his daughter Cathy died there, tragically, in a fire.

Despite its ethnic mixture, Coney Island was by no means exempt from the racism and prejudice so endemic in American culture. Austin Corbin excluded Jews from Manhattan Beach and for a time they were barred from Sea Gate. Jews residing in Coney Island were sometimes taunted by visitors who came to bathe on the beaches in their neighborhood, and Jewish and Italian youths sometimes clashed. Game stands during the first decades of the century had "Hit the Nigger" ball-toss games and bla-

## "A DAY IN CONEY ISLAND"

"I had been in America for eighteen months, but Coney Island still surprised me. The sun poured down like fire. From the beach came a roar even louder than the ocean. On the boardwalk, an Italian watermelon vender pounded on a sheet of tin with his knife and called for customers in a wild voice. Everyone bellowed in his own way: sellers of popcorn and hot dogs, ice cream and peanuts, cotton candy and corn on the cob. I passed a sideshow displaying a creature that was half woman, half fish; a wax museum with figures of Marie Antoinette, Buffalo Bill, and John Wilkes Booth; a store where a turbanned astrologer sat in the dark surrounded by maps and globes of the heavenly constellations, casting horoscopes. Pygmies danced in front of a little circus, their black faces painted white, all of them loosely bound with a long rope. A mechanical ape puffed its belly like a bellows and laughed with raucous laughter. Negro boys aimed guns at metal ducklings. A half-naked man with a black beard and hair to his shoulders hawked potions that strengthened the muscles, beautified the skin, and brought back lost potency. He tore heavy chains with his hands and bent coins between his fingers."

ISAAC BASHEVIS SINGER

tantly racist "coon songs" were common in the Bowery concert halls. Although Steeplechase Park actively encouraged African Americans to patronize the park, they were denied use of its pool. A form of de facto segregation excluded African Americans from at least some of Coney Island's beaches. Nevertheless, it would be impossible to imagine Coney Island emerging as it did without the extraordinary confluence of races and cultures present there. Coney much more resembled a mercurial cauldron than a melting pot. Its neighborhoods with their admixture of ethnicity brought a measure of much-needed stability to its potent amusement zone.

.     .     .

By the 1950s, however, much of the housing stock in the neighborhoods bordering Coney's amusement zone was substandard. Robert Moses seized upon this to advance his efforts to reduce Coney's amusement zone and replace it with recreational facilities and year-round residential units. He again declared that the public was losing interest in Coney's rides and sideshows and disclosed a plan to obtain the majority of the property along the boardwalk through a series of foreclosures. His intention was to create an amusement ghetto that would gradually shrink to extinction. The demise of Luna Park enabled him to convert the site it once occupied to residential use. A subsequent attempt to rezone virtually the entire amusement zone, excluding Steeplechase Park, was rejected, however, when Coney's Chamber of Commerce protested. In 1957, Moses brought the New York City Aquarium to the site formerly occupied by Dreamland. The site had long served as a municipal parking facility serving the Municipal Baths. A year later he presided at the groundbreaking of Luna Park Houses on the former park site, and declared that it marked the end of the old Coney Island, "romantic only at night and in midsummer, rotting inside and out in spite of nostalgic fables." Indeed, some Coney Islanders trace the decline of the resort to the completion of these residential towers in 1961. They contend that Moses turned a blind eye to the deterioration of the amusement zone in the years that followed. "He put a kibosh on us," said one longtime resident. By then, Moses and those with whom he was aligned had gained a free hand to proceed with the public housing he had championed in other parts of the city, which critics have decried as a policy of "class separating." The city began to replace Coney's old, dilapidated housing with upscale high-rises and cooperatives. Most of the land lying between Ocean Parkway and West Eighth Street was placed in the hands of private developers such as Fred Trump, who built a dozen residential towers on the site. It had formerly housed Coney's minority population, which was forced to relocate to other quarters in the West End, where the housing authority had already begun "dumping" displaced families from other parts of the city. When that area suffered further deterioration, it was targeted for urban renewal. Mermaid Avenue, the principal thoroughfare traversing Coney's neighborhoods, and many surrounding blocks were leveled to make way

STEEPLECHASE RIDER.

for public housing, much of which was never built. The density and squalor of the city had thus been transported almost to the ocean's doorstep by city planners who seemed unconcerned that Coney Island was not simply an amusement quarter, but rather a series of discrete neighborhoods to which the amusement zone was anchored. Coney had once more been transformed. At one end of Surf Avenue, the high-rise towers of Trump Village held an almost exclusively white, middle-class population that was often in conflict with Coney Island's old guard and the honky-tonk atmosphere of its amusement zone. To the west, living side by side with the dwindling remnants of Coney Island's Jewish and Italian communities, was an impoverished minority population hemmed in by urban renewal and beset by the crime that spilled out onto the boardwalk and the arcades.

Somehow the amusement zone held on, with Steeplechase Park serving as its anchor. The park had become somewhat rudderless with the death of Edward Tilyou in 1944. Surviving members of the Tilyou family were often at odds over the direction the park should take. Few new attractions were added during the 1950s and its Pavilion of Fun had grown antiquated. But it continued to draw crowds, and eventually some of the older rides were retired and replaced. Around the same time, Dewey

Albert and Herman Rapps, who had acquired the Feltman property, began to develop an amusement concession called Astroland Park. They introduced new attractions such as the Sky Ride and the 230-foot-high Astro Tower, which replaced the classic Feltman Carousel in 1964. That season proved disastrous, however. Racial disturbances erupted in July in Harlem and Brooklyn's Bedford-Stuyvesant neighborhood, and while no serious confrontation occurred at Coney Island, the racially charged atmosphere, poor weather, and competition from the World's Fair in Flushing, Queens, all combined to produce the worst season in more than a quarter of a century. At the end of the season Steeplechase Park closed its gates forever. A ceremony to mark the park's passing was held on September 20, 1964. There were farewell speeches and "Auf Wiedersehen" and "Auld Lang Syne" played on the public address system. As the music concluded, the park's closing bell slowly began to ring out, tolling once for each year it had operated. With every stroke, a bank of lights within the Pavilion of Fun was extinguished by the park's electrician, until at the last stroke the pavilion was completely dark. For one brief moment it blazed brightly again. Then it went dark forever. To many, it seemed that Coney Island itself had simply ceased to exist.

# CHAPTER NINE

# THE MERMAID PARADE

ON SEPTEMBER 21, 1966, Fred Trump held a party at Coney Island. The occasion was the demolition of Steeplechase Park's Pavilion of Fun. Two years had passed since Steeplechase Park had closed its gates and more than a year had elapsed since Trump had acquired the property. Attempts to find a new operator for the amusement park had proved unsuccessful. Trump intended to erect a string of high-rise apartments on the site, even though the property was not zoned for housing. He acted before the city could consider an application for landmark status for the structure. There were champagne toasts, and bathing beauties clad in bikinis were on hand to take part in the festivities. Jimmy Onorato, the park's manager for thirty-seven years, recalled that Trump handed out bricks to throw at the pavilion's windows.

Coney Island spiraled downward in the wake of Steeplechase's closing. The park had employed some four hundred people each season and had anchored the western end of the amusement zone, generating business for nearby attractions along West Sixteenth Street,

including the Thunderbolt roller coaster. Its absence was calamitous. "I've seen good times and I've seen bad times," said one concessionaire. "Now they're bad. And they're getting worse." The demise of Steeplechase left a gaping hole in Coney Island's beleaguered amusement zone. Raven Hall Baths, which lay directly west of Steeplechase Park, and two blocks that surrounded it had burned to the ground the previous year. The area farther to the west was filled with boarded-up concessions and others that were barely holding on. The amusement zone's expansion to the east had long been blocked by the Aquarium and the Brightwater apartment complex in Brighton Beach. Along Surf Avenue, from West Eighth Street to Ocean Parkway, its progress was halted by row after row of high-rise apartments whose drab architecture was the antithesis of Luna Park's towers and minarets.

Bit by bit, the amusement landmarks of Coney's fabled past were being dismantled or sold for parts. The Feltman Carousel, considered by some the finest of its kind ever constructed in the United States, was removed in

1964 to make room for Astroland's new tower. It was resurrected a few months later and installed at the New York World's Fair at Flushing Meadows, refitted with pieces salvaged from another Coney Island carousel. The grandest of all carousels, the El Dorado, was removed when Steeplechase closed in 1965. The hand-carved carousel, created in Leipzig, Germany, once delighted half a million riders in a single season. Its riders had included Teddy Roosevelt and Enrico Caruso. After it was dismantled, the carousel was placed in storage; it was later acquired by a Japanese amusement park. The other Steeplechase attractions were also dismantled and sold to amusement operators around the country. The sixteen horses sheathed in black fiberglass that raced in rows of four around the park's mechanical track were acquired by a Florida amusement park.

Throughout the 1970s Coney Island remained embattled. By 1975, funding for urban renewal programs had been frozen and large

FIREWORKS DISPLAY AT ASTROLAND IN 1964.

(CITY OF NEW YORK DEPARTMENT OF PARKS AND RECREATION, PHOTO ARCHIVE)

swaths of the resort were reduced to some of the worst slum conditions in the city. Crime increased dramatically. Coney's neighborhoods were crumbling and the adverse effects further eroded the amusement district. Fred Trump's plan to erect housing on the Steeplechase Park property had been blocked by the City Planning Commission, which took possession of the land with the intention of creating a public park. The park never materialized and the site languished. A concessionaire who leased the property from Trump set up a string of small rides and amusement stalls along Surf Avenue, while the land facing the boardwalk remained littered with abandoned cars, trailers, and other debris. Left standing was the rusted hulk of the Parachute Jump, dubbed the "Eiffel Tower of Brooklyn" by its admirers. A proposal to grant it landmark status was rejected by the Parks Department, which threatened to tear it down. It loomed over the boardwalk "like a funeral obelisk," wrote Joseph Heller.

Although Coney still drew sizeable crowds it no longer rated as a "popular resort." American mass culture had passed it by. Its appeal was more populist than popular. It suffered in comparison with the new generation of themed amusement parks and with gambling and entertainment resorts such as Las Vegas and Atlantic City. "Coney Island is like an old courtesan, her hair frazzled, teeth cracked and too much rouge on her cheeks," a reporter wrote. "She is gutsy

SUNBATHERS AT CONEY ISLAND IN 1967 PHOTOGRAPHED BY BRUCE GILDEN.

(BRUCE GILDEN/MAGNUM PHOTOS)

RIDERS ATOP THE CYCLONE.

(*NEW YORK POST*/REX USA LTD.)

and earthy and past caring about the formal niceties of her trade. And she is comfortable within her circle of old-timers." Mario Puzo, who had spent an afternoon with Heller at Steeplechase Park in 1961 and who revisited two decades later, lamented the fate that had befallen Coney Island. "There was a time when every child in New York loved Coney Island," he wrote, "and so it breaks your heart to see what a slothful, bedraggled harridan it has become, endangered by the violence of its poor and hopeless people, as well as by the city planners who would improve it out of existence. If I were a wizard with one last magic trick in my bag, I would bring back the old Coney Island."

The resort reached a low point when the city threatened to demolish the Cyclone coaster. The city had acquired the fabled roller coaster in 1971 when it was in dire need of repair. When the city was unable to find an operator willing to make the necessary repairs, it offered the ride to the New York Aquarium. The aquarium wanted to demolish the coaster in order to expand its facilities. A "Save the Cyclone" campaign was launched by the coaster's supporters from around the world. Eventually Dewey

## CONEY ISLAND
## AT THE MOVIES

In the opening moments of *Annie Hall* (1977), Alvy Singer, the character created by Woody Allen, offhandedly confides: "I was brought up under the roller coaster in the Coney Island section of Brooklyn. Maybe that accounts for my personality." The film prompted a rejoinder from Mae Timpano, who actually lived under the Thunderbolt. "It wasn't as bad as the movie makes it seem," she said. Films produced during the 1920s such as *The Girl from Coney Island* (1926), *It* (1927), and *The Crowd* (1928) made Coney Island a setting for scenes of courtship. During the 1930s and 1940s it was the ideal location for Jimmy Stewart to woo Margaret Sullavan (*Shopworn Angel*, 1938) and for William Powell to court Myrna Loy (*Manhattan Melodrama*, 1934), and a perfect match for the comic misadventures of Jean Arthur and Charles Coburn in *The Devil and Miss Jones* (1941). Later films such as Neil Simon's nostalgic *Brighton Beach Memoirs* (1986) and *Enemies: A Love Story* (1989) were set in a Coney Island long past. While early silent films presented Coney Island as a glittering realm of escape, more recent films such as Spike Lee's *He Got Game* (1998) and the bleak *Requiem for a Dream* (2001) portray it as a desolate landscape. For Spike Lee, who attended high school at Coney Island, it is a landscape defined by housing projects and basketball courts rather than arcades—a far cry from the dazzling images captured on film a century earlier by American Mutoscope and Biograph.

Albert, owner of Astroland Park, agreed to take over its operation. He leased it from the city for $54,000 and spent another $60,000 making extensive repairs. The coaster reopened on July 3, 1975, and people stood in line for up to three hours awaiting a turn to ride. The Cyclone celebrated its fiftieth anniversary two years later, on June 26, 1977, with champagne toasts and a birthday cake. The coaster's cars were repainted for the occasion and the ten-foot-high letters that adorned it were relit.

That same year, however, a fire leveled another Coney Island landmark, the Tornado roller coaster. By 1983 there was once more talk of tearing down the Parachute Jump, and that year another Coney landmark, the Thunderbolt roller coaster, ceased operating. The Thunderbolt survived only a year after the death of its owner, Fred Moran, whose father, George Moran, had built it. For more than fifty years, Moran lived in a small gray house with faded blue trim that was under the coaster and was once a bordello called the Kensington Hotel. The elder Moran built the coaster directly over the hotel and lived there with his family. The coaster's stanchions were anchored to the house and when it rumbled overhead the walls shook, the dishes swayed, and the pictures hung askew. "Freddy always used to say, 'That's my cash register ringing,'" recalled Mae Timpano, who lived in the house with Moran for many years and continued to reside there after he died.

More ups and downs followed. For a time the crack epidemic and an uptick in crime cast a pall over the resort, contributing to its decline and spurring visitors to question whether

Coney's amusement zone would disappear entirely. Eventually, not a single ride remained west of Stillwell Avenue. At the same time, the construction of hundreds of new single-family dwellings between Mermaid and Neptune Avenues brought a bit more stability to Coney's older neighborhoods, whose diverse populations now included Hispanic, African American, Asian, Italian, West Indian, and Middle Eastern residents. The Brighton Beach section of Coney Island had, in the meantime, undergone an extraordinary transformation. By the 1970s the Jewish community in Brighton Beach was composed primarily of elderly residents who had grown increasingly poor. Around 1978, however, the Soviet Union began to relax its migration policies and thousands of new immigrants began streaming into Brighton Beach. The majority were Soviet Jews from the Ukraine, and when they poured in, the neighborhood was dubbed Little Odessa after the port city and resort on the Black Sea. Brighton Beach Avenue, the main thoroughfare running under the elevated tracks of the subway and lined for more than a generation with kosher butcher shops and small markets, was overnight reborn. Today it is crowded with Russian nightclubs and restaurants specializing in borscht and blini with black caviar, with markets stocking delicacies from Riga and Kiev and boutiques that advertise their fashions behind windows painted over with Cyrillic lettering, with bookshops and newsstands where pensioners pause to buy the Russian-language daily *Novoye Russkoye Slovo*, and with countless sidewalk stalls. More than half the shops are owned by émigrés from the former Soviet republics. About forty thousand live there, a greater number than anywhere else in the world, making it a magnet for other Russian-speaking immigrants residing in New York City, who come to Brighton Beach to dine at restaurants such as the Odessa and the National, to shop at its markets, and to frequent its nightspots. Brighton's transformation stood in sharp contrast with Coney's faded honky-tonk.

Despite numerous setbacks, Coney Island held its ground. In 1980, Coney Island USA was formed by Dick D. Zigun and several colleagues to breathe new life into Coney's amusement zone. A nonprofit organization partially funded by the city's Department of Cultural Affairs, Coney Island USA sought to revitalize and reinvent the sideshow tradition and hurly-burly spirit that once thrived at Coney, a tradition that Zigun calls "Americana bizarro." A Yale Drama School graduate, Zigun was born in Bridgeport, Connecticut, the birthplace of P. T. Barnum, and just a short distance from the Shakespeare Festival in Stratford. "I grew up with Barnum and Shakespeare," he recalls. "There was nobody to tell me that you can't put them together." Zigun was preternaturally drawn to Coney Island. "Coney Island in a blue-collar way is very bohemian," he explains. He first came in 1979 intending to refurbish a building to use as a theater. The building burned down but his troupe was able to stage a few productions at Lily Santangelo's World in Wax museum. The group's first permanent home, until it lost its lease in 1995, was a former arcade on the boardwalk. Today it resides in a historic building erected in 1917 that originally housed Child's Restaurant.

During the 1950s the building was home to Dave Rosen's Wonderland Circus Sideshow. Its upper floor holds the Coney Island Museum, Zigun's eclectic collection of sideshow and amusement park artifacts, which include a wicker boardwalk rolling chair and one of the original Steeplechase horses. In 1983, Coney Island USA staged the first of its annual Mermaid Parades, a campy homage to the Mardi Gras parades that had been discontinued three decades earlier. Two years later it launched Sideshows by the Seashore, a traditional ten-in-one show whose attractions over the years have included Michael Wilson, Combustible Kiva the fire-eater, Melvin Burkhart the Anatomical Wonder, and assorted snake charmers, glass walkers, and sword swallowers. It also sponsors an annual tattoo and motorcycle festival, eclectic concerts including a legendary pairing of John Cage and Sun Ra on the boardwalk, and a film festival.

Efforts to resuscitate Coney's amusement district over the years had proved fruitless. The former Steeplechase property remained undeveloped for more than three decades. After its sale to Fred Trump, a proposal surfaced to enclose a large swath of the amusement district, including the Wonder Wheel, in a 160-foot-high, climate-controlled glass pleasure dome. The plan, which would have enabled Trump to erect high-rise towers along the boardwalk, was rejected. The city then acquired the land from Trump, but its plan to create a seaside park on the twelve-acre site stalled as city agencies debated whether it would be more fruitful to retain the area as an amusement center. Proposals to erect a theme park and a Tivoli Gardens

were considered, but the city failed to act. In the meantime, the city became embroiled in a lawsuit with amusement operator Norman Kaufman, who had leased the property, first from Trump and later from the Parks Department. Kaufman, who installed a string of carnival rides along Surf Avenue, had acquired nine of the original Steeplechase horses in the failed hope of resurrecting the ride. In 1985 Horace Bullard, a Harlem-born entrepreneur, signed an agreement with the city to build and operate a new amusement park at Steeplechase and the adjoining property. Bullard's plan envisioned a reconstructed Parachute Jump, a four-horse Steeplechase ride, a water chute, and forty other attractions on twenty acres of land that included the Thunderbolt, which he hoped to refurbish. Bullard's plan collapsed when, after ten years, he was unable to acquire adequate financing and the city withdrew its support. In 1997, spurred by the successful revitalization of Times Square, developer Bruce Ratner unveiled a plan for a virtual reality amusement park to be built in tandem with an amateur sports arena that was already being considered for the site. When sufficient support for the Sportsplex failed to materialize, the city again changed course. KeySpan Stadium, home of the Brooklyn Cyclones minor league baseball team, was erected on the site. The city also committed $30 million for boardwalk improvements, bathhouse facilities, and a much-needed overhaul of the Stillwell Avenue subway terminal. The stadium was unveiled in the spring of 2001, more than three decades after Steeplechase Park closed its gates. The Parachute Jump, which stands beyond the right-field fence, was repainted in time for opening day and a quarter of a million spectators welcomed the return of baseball to Brooklyn during the course of the Cyclones' inaugural season.

Today, Coney Island's amusement zone is confined to a small portion of the Bowery from West Tenth Street to Stillwell Avenue, but the place is as noisy and frenetic as ever. Astroland Park, in operation for about three decades, has anchored the amusement zone ever since Steeplechase closed. The park occupies a narrow strip running from the boardwalk to Surf Avenue and its two dozen rides practically collide with one another. Its most famous attraction, the Cyclone roller coaster, was declared a historic landmark in 1988. In 1997 it celebrated its seventieth anniversary. The festivities marking the occasion included a women-only coaster riding marathon, and a member of the Flying Wallenda family performed a headstand on a high-wire extended between the coaster's two highest points.

Adjacent to Astroland is Deno's Wonder Wheel Park. It is named after Denos Vouderis, a Greek immigrant who peddled hot dogs at Coney Island until he saved enough money to open a restaurant on the boardwalk. When it burned down he rebuilt it and eventually acquired a kiddie park near the Wonder Wheel. Vouderis evidently proposed to his wife on the Wonder Wheel and vowed that he would one day own it. He acquired it from Fred Garms in 1993. The Wonder Wheel was awarded landmark status in 1989. It claims the distinction of being the oldest operating ride at Coney Island

and attracts as many as two hundred thousand riders a year.

Other independent rides and amusements line the Bowery and a portion of Stillwell Avenue. A small sideshow advertises the "World's Smallest Women" and another exhorts the crowd to view "Alien Bodies, direct from Roswell." Teenage girls snake in and out of Faber's Fascination and the El Dorado Arcade. Others pause on their way to the boardwalk to consider a ride on the Zipper and the Saturn 6. At McCullough's kiddie park on the Bowery children stand impatiently in line. The McCulloughs are descendents of George C. Tilyou and the family has been in the amusement business for more than a century. Like his father who worked as a carousel operator, James McCullough, who is seventy-three years old, personally keeps his machines up and running, often with the help of his four daughters. As always, the amusement ride operators keep an eye toward the sky. Their livelihood, now as ever, depends upon the weather.

On the ballyhoo stage outside Sideshows by the Seashore at West Twelfth Street, Eek the Geek, his head swathed in a black mask, attempts to entice the crowd to enter. The building's walls are decorated with painted canvas banners depicting the live acts within that include Koko the Killer Clown and Serpintina the snake charmer. Many of the banners are the work of the group's artist-in-residence, Marie Roberts, a native of Coney Island who is steeped in its traditions. Her grandfather led the fire crews that tried in vain to extinguish the Dreamland fire. Two of her uncles were electricians working at the park when the fire broke out. Another uncle, Lester A. Roberts, was the "outside talker" at Sam Gumpertz's Dreamland Circus Sideshow. She grew up with sideshow luminaries such as Baron Paucci and Violetta the armless-legless wonder as houseguests. Of her relationship with Coney Island USA she observes, "It was like finding family again."

Coney's old hands look around and consider carefully the changes on the horizon. Change comes hard these days to Coney Island where the past and present seem to be more closely interwoven than in most other places. Coney has its traditions that are embodied both in its amusement monuments as well as in the individuals who tend them. Just as Coney was preparing to embrace the return of baseball to Brooklyn it lost the Thunderbolt roller coaster. The coaster carried its last rider in 1983 and had been owned by Horace Bullard since 1985. Over the years it acquired a thick canopy of foliage that transformed its appearance from one season to the next. After visiting the site, city inspectors declared it unsafe and called for its demolition unless immediate repairs were made. Appeals from preservationists and roller coaster aficionados went unheeded and a city work crew came to the site and bulldozed the coaster along with the house beneath it. Those who witnessed its destruction included a tearful

ASTROLAND PARK.

(*NEW YORK POST*/REX USA LTD.)

Mae Timpano. The day the Thunderbolt came down Phil Jacobs died. Phil was the gruff bartender at his brother Ruby's bar. The brothers grew up dirt poor at Coney Island during the Depression and made a living selling hot dogs and knishes on the boardwalk. Ruby Jacobs eventually acquired a number of bathhouses including Cook's Baths and Stauch's. When the last one closed he held on to the bar that bears his name and serves as a lively outpost for old as well as new visitors to Coney Island. Ruby died a few months before Phil. They were buried side by side. Inscribed on Ruby's headstone are the words: "Coney Island the Elixir of Life." There were other changes. The venerable Still-

well Avenue subway terminal, which handles over 5 million riders each summer, was finally getting a facelift, but Philip's Candies, a landmark at the terminal for more than half a century, had departed. Then Mike Saltzstein died. Saltzstein had co-owned and operated the B & B Carousel. Built in 1919 at William Mangels's Coney Island factory, the B & B carousel has horses carved by Charles Carmel and is one of fewer then twenty carousels still operating with a brass ring machine. The last of Coney Island's carousels, for years it has delighted riders in the shadows of the seedy flea markets that line one side of Surf Avenue. Saltzstein kept the carousel running year round. With a willingness to

ALIEN BODIES SIDESHOW.

(JOHN MATTURRI)

CONEY ISLAND BEACH, CIRCA 1994.

(DAN CRONIN)

embrace some if not all of the changes that were coming, the mood of Coney Islanders was one of cautious optimism. "I've been through the worst and best of times and I'm very excited about the future," said Ron Guerrero, owner of the Saturn 6 and the last to operate the Thunderbolt roller coaster. He calls Coney a "jewel in the rough." Dick Zigun of Coney Island USA was also optimistic, but like others involved in Coney Island's revitalization he insists that any plan to revive it must include rides and amusements that reflect Coney's honky-tonk spirit. "It has to be consistent with the historic use of the property," he states. "Coney's always been a release valve for New York. We've always had diversity."

. . .

On the boardwalk, salsa bands perform for writhing dancers, their bodies tattooed with beads of sweat, while hundreds of fishermen cast lines from the Steeplechase Pier. An elderly couple strolls past slowly on a visit to Coney Island for the first time in many years. The gentleman gazes in the direction of the forlorn facade of Child's Restaurant and gestures as if to say, "And over there was old Washington Baths." His wife nods her head as though concurring and they stare into the distance, conjuring up the past in their minds. The boardwalk crowds are often thickest outside Ruby's Bar, which remains a repository of Coney Island traditions, a throwback to the time when the boardwalk was lined with bathhouses. It is a familiar retreat for diehard Coney Islanders,

including members of the Polar Bear Club, who enjoy a midwinter bath in the ocean, and their rivals, the Ice Breakers. More recently, when New York's Islamic Society organized a celebration of the Id al-Adha feast, thousands of Muslims assembled for prayers near the rusted frame of the Thunderbolt roller coaster, then rode the Break Dancer and Bumper Cars at Astroland Park, which had been rented for the celebration. The park's vendors sold especially prepared foods and Arabic music played on its sound system. Seemingly unaffected by the changes around it, Nathan's, just a few blocks away, remains something of a mecca for what old Coney Islanders call "finger foods." It is open year round, and each Fourth of July it holds a hot dog–eating contest. In 2001 Takeru Kobayashi from Japan shattered all records by consuming fifty hot dogs in twelve minutes.

Coney's cachet as an amusement center may have declined considerably, but in other respects it remains unchanged. For a century and a half it has mirrored the demographic trends that have characterized New York City and it continues to do so. Roughly 40 percent of the city's 8 million current inhabitants are foreign born, a greater percentage than at any other time since 1910. But unlike then, when migration brought millions of eastern and southern Europeans to New York and the languages spoken were Yiddish, Italian, and Greek, today's visitor to Coney Island's beach is likely to hear Spanish, French, or Urdu, reflecting current patterns of migration from South America, the Caribbean, and Asia. Long stretches of Coney's beach resemble a Caribbean *playa*. Old Mexican

HASSIDIC JEWS AT ASTROLAND PARK.

(*NEW YORK POST*/REX USA LTD.)

before them, have not yet fully integrated into the American mainstream. The atmosphere of the beach reveals little of the outward display of entitlement present at many other resorts. Coney's poor pleasures suffice. Its four-square-block amusement district with its ancient rides and kiddie parks has the feel of a carnival one might visit in a small village, but on a grander scale. But this was always true of Coney Island. That is what made it so easy for generations of immigrants to embrace it a century ago, and what makes it so familiar and appealing to today's newcomers, who recognize beneath Coney's peeled paint the benign visage of the carnival of their homeland.

Coney's honky-tonk past and its eclectic present are exquisitely joined during the annual costumed bacchanalia called the Mermaid Parade. The Mermaid Parade is held each year on the first Saturday after the summer solstice. It is described as "part Mardi Gras, part art parade" and celebrates the symbolic "opening" of the Atlantic Ocean by King Neptune, convincingly plump and paunchy in a loincloth, his body painted blue and his head crowned with long golden locks. As many as 750,000 people visit Coney Island on the day of the parade. The hundreds of costumed participants include high-heeled and spike-heeled and big-haired mermaids, some resembling Carmen Miranda, Buffy the Vampire Slayer, and the Spice Girls. There are jackbooted mermaid consorts and others that resemble Roman gladiators, Valkyries, a draggy Ethel Mermaid, Busby Berkeley Mermaids, and a mermaid that floats in a cocktail glass with Styrofoam ice cubes. There are star-

women sell sugary strips of *churro* and salty *chicharone* to their countrymen. A woman from Equador slices open fresh mangoes. A Guatemalan boy parades past with large bags of cotton candy bundled on a pole. A pair of Islamic women bathe fully clothed with heads covered within sight of a man whose tattoo of a crucified Christ covers his entire back. There are Pakistanis from Coney Island Avenue in Brooklyn, Dominicans from Washington Heights, and Koreans from Flushing, Queens. Farther to the east, at Brighton Beach, thousands of blond and fair-skinned Russians crowd the beach. The newcomers, like the countless others who came

CONEY ISLAND BOARDWALK.

CONEY ISLAND PHOTO BOOTH.

B & B CAROUSEL, TICKET BOOTH.

CONEY ISLAND MERMAIDS.

ARCADES.

ATOP THE WONDER WHEEL.

CONEY ISLAND BEACH.

spangled and glittery mermaids and mermaids in G-strings, myriad sea serpents and naiads, angelfish and blowfish, tentacled creatures and umbrella-headed jellyfish, some blowing conch shells, some with breasts bared or with sand-dollar bustiers, some carrying blue umbrellas from which tiny mermaids dangle. The parade includes many costumed contingents with riders in antique cars or on flatbed floats. One contingent accompanies the funeral bier of a departed mermaid while playing a somber dirge. Other costumed participants sprout red Velcro fins. The members of the Mermaid Liberation Front parade beneath a billowy blue wavescape held aloft by tridents. In 2001 the parade assembled at the newly inaugurated KeySpan Stadium on the former site of Steeplechase Park, where the first Mermaid Parade had been held in 1983. "That first year we had more costumed participants than spectators," recalls Dick Zigun, who presides over the parade in his guise as the mayor of Coney Island, wearing an antique wool bathing suit and derby.

.      .      .

Today's Coney Island bears little resemblance to the vast amusement enterprises and theme parks that now dominate America's leisure landscape. In the end, Robert Moses

CONEY ISLAND MERMAIDS.

(JOHN MATTURRI)

succeeded in reining in Coney Island's amusement zone without entirely eradicating it. His disdain for its mechanical amusements was shortsighted, however. The expansion of the entertainment industry, the proliferation of theme parks, virtual reality rides, giant coasters, and water parks are part of Coney Island's legacy. Most dramatic is the transformation of Las Vegas during the past decade. A comparison can be made between Coney's Island's reinvention at the beginning of the past century and the remaking of Las Vegas at its close. Both sought to transform themselves by banishing less savory honky-tonk attractions in favor of family-friendly resorts. Coney's Canals of Venice, Durbar of Delhi, and submarine rides were precursors of the theme-driven hotel-casinos that heralded the new Las Vegas. Its Globe Tower, an architectural wonder, anticipated the Las Vegas Stratosphere capped with a revolving restaurant and a roller coaster a hundred stories above the ground. If built, the tower would have dwarfed anything conceived of in its day, but it would seem right at home amid the mega-architecture of Las Vegas—a virtual Coney Island—to remind us of the imaginative powers unleashed there a century earlier as it anticipated America's future.

Coney Islanders talk of having "sand in their shoes." One such Coney hand is Bobby

CONEY ISLAND BOARDWALK.

(JOHN MATTURRI)

Reynolds. Reynolds began his career as an "out-side talker" at Huber's Museum in New York before coming to Coney Island during the 1950s to work at Dave Rosen's sideshow when the live acts included Fat Alice from Dallas and Kokomo the Mule-Faced Boy. Years later he operated the International Circus Museum on West Twelfth Street. Now he travels the carnival circuit, but each year around the Fourth of July he sets up a show called "Reynold's Believe It You're Nuts Hysterical Museum" under a tent at Coney Island. The tent's canvas banners advertise the Iron Foot Maiden, Incredible Spidora, and other wonders of nature, but displayed within the museum are sideshow artifacts and memorabilia rather than the "living wonders" the banners depict. Reynolds charges a dollar admission, and if many who visit his museum are disappointed at not finding live acts, few complain. "Why do I come back each season?" he asks rhetorically. "The truth is, I feel comfortable here. I suppose I come to reconnect." He pauses in mid-sentence to demonstrate a magic trick, a smooth sleight-of-hand with a coin he performs in homage to magician Al Flosso, who taught it to him. "Coney Island," he resumes, "is the poor man's Six Flags." He worries that the city will try to sanitize it and predicts that "ten years from now it will be like Forty-second Street. Bland, without the flavor that made Coney great."

Today, Coney represents a kind of anti-Disneyland. And while New Yorkers may accept the Disneyfication of Times Square, they are wary of the same fate befalling Coney Island. New Yorkers have a fondness for Coney just as it is, devoid of the sanitized facades of contemporary theme parks. If it is to be rebuilt, they don't want it transformed into a Disney World on the boardwalk. It has its own cachet and a past that must be respected. It still draws crowds to Nathan's Famous and the Wonder Wheel, and among them are a reverent few who pause at the sites where amusement parks once stood, like visitors to the hallowed ground of a Civil War battlefield. Even during Coney's darkest days, Lou Reed sang "Coney Island Baby" to a new generation that was just discovering Coney Island on it own. A much-faded Baghdad by the Boardwalk, Coney is true to its past. It remains a repository of our cultural memory evoking times past, an entire century when our nation matured and gained its footing, but in the process lost much of its innocence. In its day it was as potent as the movies. More so, perhaps, because its auditors were also participants; its action was live. One can still experience there, in the absence and wreckage of its past splendor, the lingering charge of Coney's kinetic carnival. Too potent to be dismissed simply as an amusement mausoleum, it remains to this day America's populist frontier.

# NOTES

## INTRODUCTION

3 *laboratory,* John F. Kasson, *Amusing the Million: Coney Island at the Turn of the Century* (New York: Hill & Wang, 1978), 6.

3 *"only thing."* Freud reportedly made this remark to a London newspaper years after visiting Coney Island. The quotation may very possibly be apocryphal; however, it is consistent with Freud's view of America.

4 *"valve of pleasure,"* José Martí, "Coney Island," *La Pluma,* December 3, 1881.

4 *"dumping-ground,"* James Gibbons Huneker, *New Cosmopolis: A Book of Images* (New York: Charles Scribner's Sons, 1915), 158.

6 *middle ground,* Robert E. Snow and David E. Wright, "Coney Island: A Case Study in Popular Culture and Technical Change," *Journal of Popular Culture* 9 (Spring 1976): 962, 968–970.

7 *"most enchanting,"* early Steeplechase advertisements and souvenir programs.

8 *"great compositions,"* Reginald Marsh, *Magazine of Art,* December 1944.

8 *Disneyland,* Judith A. Adams, *The Great Amusement Park Industry: A History of Technology and Thrills* (Boston: Twayne, 1991), 99, 143.

## 1. CONEY

12 *"tooth,"* Scribner's Magazine, July 1896.

13 *"debilitating effects,"* Long Island Star, June 30, 1825, cited in Stephen Weinstein, "The Nickel Empire: Coney Island and the Creation of Urban Seaside Resorts in the United States" (Ph.D. diss., Columbia University, 1984), 38.

14 *"natural advantages,"* 1845 advertising trade card (fig. 5).

14 *"unfrequented shore,"* Complete Writings of Walt Whitman, ed. Richard Maurice Bucke, 10 vols. (New York: G. P. Putnam, 1902), 4:16.

14 *"wild charm,"* Fredrika Bremer, *The Homes of the New World: Impressions of America* (London, 1853), 159.

14 *"Church Street,"* George Templeton Strong, *The Diary of George Templeton Strong,* ed. Allan Nevins and Milton Halsey Thomas, 4 vols. (New York: Macmillian, 1952), 1:61.

15 *"pure atmosphere,"* NY Times, July 14, 1873.

15 *"blackened shells,"* NY Times, July 21, 1868.

15 *"gently shelving beach,"* NY Times, July 10, 1866.

16 *"sweltered in our streets,"* NY Times, July 10, 1866.

16 *"There are thousands,"* NY Times, July 16, 1866.

16 *"A poor, jaded specimen,"* Brooklyn Eagle, August 2, 1869.

16 *"Old Ocean,"* NY Times, July 21, 1868.

16 *"great democratic resort,"* Appleton's Handbook (New York, 1869).

16 A "panel-girl" was a prostitute who worked in a "panel-house," or brothel, with sliding panels in the rooms that allowed a confederate to sneak in and rob patrons while they were distracted by the "panel-girls."

16 *"Chow-Chow Man,"* Brooklyn Argus article, quoted in Edo McCullough, *Good Old Coney Island: A Sentimental Journey into the Past* (New York: Charles Scribner's Sons, 1957), 35.

19 *"little time is wasted,"* NY Times, July 14, 1873.

## 2. THE AMERICAN BRIGHTON

20 *"a stone's throw,"* NY Times, May 6, 1877.

20 *"safe from the glaring sun,"* NY Times, May 5, 1877.

22  "dainty palace," *Scribner's Magazine,* July 1880.

23  "the best," quoted in Oliver Pilat and Jo Ranson, *Sodom by the Sea: An Affectionate History of Coney Island* (Garden City, N.Y.: Doubleday, 1941).

26  "sheltered and luxurious," *Percy's Pocket Dictionary of Coney Island* (New York, 1880).

27  "What changes," *NY Times,* May 28, 1880.

27  "plebeian intrusion," *Brooklyn Union,* July 2, 1883.

27  "class of people," *NY Herald,* July 22, 1879.

28  "rises out of the sea," *Leslie's Illustrated Newspaper,* August 16, 1879.

28  "golden promise," *Leslie's Illustrated Newspaper,* August 24, 1878.

29  "people's watering place," *NY Times,* May 1, 1878.

29  "Summer city," *NY Times,* July 18, 1880.

29  "'Chow-Chow man,'" *NY Times,* May 6, 1877.

29  "half and half," *NY Times,* August 20, 1877.

29  "Centennial of pleasure," William H. Bishop, "To Coney Island," *Scribner's Magazine,* July 1880.

29  "The amazing thing," José Martí, "Coney Island," *La Pluma,* December 13, 1881.

30  "in miniature," "A Sunday at Coney Island," *Temple Bar,* June 1882.

31  "natural classification," *NY Times,* July 18, 1880.

31  "diversions," *Percy's Pocket Dictionary of Coney Island* (New York, 1880).

31  "Mulligan's Guards," *NY Times,* August 20, 1877.

31  "damsel," *Coney Island: An Illustrated Guide to the Sea* (Brooklyn, 1883).

32  "machines of great size," *Coney Island* (Iron Steamboat Company, 1883).

32  "miniatures are so distinct," *Percy's Pocket Dictionary of Coney Island* (New York,1880).

32  "summer gardens," *Brooklyn Union,* July 2, 1883.

34  "Japanese zoology," *Leslie's Illustrated Newspaper,* August 6, 1881.

35  "No form of amusement," *Brooklyn Eagle,* August 7, 1883.

36  "Bedlam," *NY Times,* July 18, 1880.

36  "Arion mind," *Brooklyn Union,* August 1, 1879; *Leslie's Illustrated Newspaper,* August 16, 1879.

37  "such spectacles," Bishop, "To Coney Island."

37  "colossal clusters," Martí, "Coney Island."

37  "toilers," *Harper's Weekly,* July 29, 1882.

## 3. THE ELEPHANT COLOSSUS

38  "architectural wonder," *Leslie's Illustrated Newspaper,* July 25, 1885.

38  "Colossal Elephant," *Scientific American,* July 11, 1885.

39  "summer coasting hill," *NY Herald,* June 2, 1884.

40  "beasts of the earth," *Brooklyn Union,* May 18, 1885.

41  "dizzy aerial voyages," *Leslie's Illustrated Newspaper,* July 25, 1885.

41  "Coney Island roller coaster," *Leslie's Illustrated Newspaper,* July 24, 1886.

41  "a motley throng," *Harper's Weekly,* September 14, 1889.

42  "weird-looking sausages…freckled and sun-burned," *Brooklyn Union,* May 18, 1885.

42  "Beer," *NY Sun,* July 18, 1886.

44  "space thus occupied," *NY Sun,* August 15, 1884.

44  "home of all amusements," *Brooklyn Eagle,* July 7, 1892.

45  "Modern civilized men," Frederick Law Olmsted, Sixth Annual Report of the Commissioners of Prospect Park, 1866.

45  mechanical pleasures, Robert E. Snow and David E. Wright, "Coney Island: A Case Study in Popular Culture and Technical Change," *Journal of Popular Culture* 9 (Spring 1976): 962; Stephen Weinstein, "The Nickel Empire: Coney Island and the Creation of Urban Seaside Resorts in the United States" (Ph.D. diss., Columbia University, 1984), 187–188, 193.

46  "aristocracy of commerce," David Graham Philips, "The Delusion of the Race Track," *The Cosmopolitan,* January 1905.

47  "greatest match," *NY Tribune,* June 26, 1890.

47  "How Salvator Won," *Spirit of the Times,* July 12, 1890.

48  seaside city, quoted in Oliver Pilat and Jo Ranson, *Sodom by the Sea: An Affectionate History of Coney Island* (Garden City, N.Y.: Doubleday, 1941), 41.

48  "houses of prostitution," quoted in Edo McCullough, *Good Old Coney Island: A Sentimental Journey into the Past* (New York: Charles Scribner's Sons, 1957), 71.

48  "seamy side," *NY Times,* July 13, 1885; *Brooklyn Union,* August 24, 1885.

48  "I don't suppose," *Brooklyn Eagle,* August 29, 1890.

49  "the law literally," *Brooklyn Eagle,* July 2, 1887.

50  "Paris," quoted in McCullough, *Good Old Coney Island,* 291.

50  "All we ask," *Brooklyn Eagle,* August 17, 1893.

50  "Injunctions," *Brooklyn Eagle,* September 6, 1899.

51  Aqua Aerial Shuttle, *Scientific American,* August 10, 1895.

51  "sea sickness," *Brooklyn Eagle,* June 28, 1892.

52  "homeopathic sanitarium," Julian Ralph, "Coney Island," *Scribner's Magazine,* July 1896, 325.

53  "Bowery must go," *NY Times,* May 11, 1894.

53  "fake Oriental dance-houses," *NY World,* August 2, 1896; *Brooklyn Eagle,* August 18, 1897.

56  "Centrifugal force," *NY Tribune,* August 4, 1901.

57 *"A ride on the horses,"* Harlan C. Pearson, *Tilyou's Steeple-chase & Amusement Exposition* (Concord, N.H.: Rumford Company, 1900).

## 4. BAGHAD BY THE SEA

60 *"mantle of light,"* Brooklyn Eagle, May 17, 1903.

61 *"cemetery of fire,"* James Gibbons Huneker, *New Cosmopolis,* 166.

62 *"delirium,"* Brooklyn Union, May 16, 1903.

63 *"four monster monoliths,"* NY Times, May 17, 1903.

64 *Midway Day,* Woody Register, *The Kid of Coney Island: Fred Thompson and the Rise of American Amusements* (New York: Oxford University Press, 2001), 83.

65 *stupendous carnival,* see John F. Kasson, *Amusing the Million: Coney Island at the Turn of the Century* (New York: Hill & Wang, 1978), 65.

66 *"definite architectural plan,"* NY Times, May 6, 1906.

69 *"grown folks,"* NY Times, May 8, 1904.

70 *"giant collection,"* Brooklyn Eagle, May 8, 1904.

71 *"Verily,"* Barr Ferree, "The New Popular Resort Architecture," *Architects' and Builders' Magazine* 5, no. 11, August 1904.

71 *"Joseph's coat,"* NY Times, May 8, 1904.

71 *"realm of the electric king,"* Brooklyn Eagle, May 15, 1904.

73 *"regenerated,"* NY Times, May 15, 1904.

74 *"anomaly,"* NY Times, May 6, 1906.

76 *"The very name 'Luna,'"* Brooklyn Eagle, May 19, 1907.

76 *"horizon of towers,"* Albert Bigelow Paine, "The New Coney Island," *Century Magazine* 68, August 1904.

77 *"the advent of night,"* Maxim Gorki, "Boredom," *The Independent,* August 8, 1907.

77 *"We are scorched,"* Brooklyn Eagle, August 7, 1907.

77 *"Laughter,"* NY World, September 15, 1907.

78 *"We Americans,"* quoted in Reginald Wright Kauffmann, "Why Is Coney?" *Hampton's Magazine,* August 1909.

79 *"grown tall,"* Frederic Thompson, "Amusing the Million," *Everybody's Magazine* 19, September 1908.

79 *"illuminated palaces of staff,"* Edwin E. Slosson, "The Amusement Industry," *The Independent,* July 21, 1904.

79 *"It expresses joyousness,"* Rollin Lynde Hartt, "The Amusement Park," *Atlantic Monthly,* May 1907.

79 *"glorified city of flame,"* James Gibbons Huneker, *New Cosmopolis: A Book of Images* (New York: Charles Scribner's Sons, 1915), 162.

79 *"every misbegotten fancy,"* Richard Le Gallienne, "Human Need of Coney Island," *Cosmopolitan,* July 1905.

79 *"rushing to the ocean-side,"* Hartt, "The Amusement Park."

79 *"seething mixing bowl,"* Robert Wilson Neal, "New York's City of Play," *World Today,* July 1906.

79 *"The City,"* Gorki, "Boredom."

81 *"Speed,"* Thompson, "Amusing the Million."

81 *"magnified Prater,"* Freud's description in a telegram sent to his family from America.

81 *"Earl's Court,"* NY Times, May 17, 1909.

82 *"over-sea,"* NY World, March 12, 1911.

82 *"Thousands of electric lights,"* Brooklyn Union, May 27, 1906.

83 *"disabled elevator,"* Brooklyn Union, May 27, 1911. For other accounts of the fire, see *NY Times,* May 27, 1911; Brooklyn Eagle, May 27, 1911.

84–85 *"splendid torch,"* NY Times, May 28, 1911; *"canvasses,"* ibid., May 29, 1911.

86 *"hot ruins,"* Brooklyn Eagle, May 27, 1911.

## 5. SEASIDE BAROQUE

87 *"Chinatown,"* Julian Ralph, "Coney Island," *Scribner's Magazine,* July 1896.

87 *"An architect,"* Frederic Thompson, "Amusement Architecture," *Architectural Review* 16, no. 7, July 1909.

88 *"Coney Island style."* For a more complete history of Coney Island carousels and carvers, see Fredrick Fried, *A Pictorial History of the Carousel* (New York: A. S. Barnes and Company, 1964); Roland Summit, *Carousels of Coney Island* (Rolling Hills, Calif.: Roland Summit, 1970); Fred Fried and Mary Fried, *America's Forgotten Folk Arts* (New York: Pantheon Books, 1978); Geoff Weedon and Richard Ward, *Fairground Art* (New York: Abbeville Press, 1981); Charlotte Dinger, *Art of the Carousel* (Green Village, N.J.: Carousel Art, 1983); and Tobin Fraley, *The Great American Carousel: A Century of Master Craftsmanship* (San Francisco: Chronicle Books, 1994).

89 *"highest German conception of naturalness"* . . . *"solid county merchants,"* NY Sun, August 17, 1884.

89 *"menagerie,"* Brooklyn Eagle, June 28, 1892.

95 *"will need barrels,"* William F. Mangels, *The Outdoor Amusement Industry* (New York: Vantage Press, 1952), 139.

95 *"gravity road."* For a history of roller coasters and the evolution of the amusement industry at Coney Island, see William F. Mangels, *The Outdoor Amusement Industry* (New York: Vantage Press, 1952); Robert Cartmell, *The Incredible Scream Machine: A History of the*

*Roller Coaster* (Fairview, Ohio: Amusement Park Books; Bowling Green, Ohio: Bowling Green State University Press, 1987); and Mike Schafer and Scott Rutherford, *Roller Coasters* (Osceola, Wisc.: MBI Publishing, 1998).

96 *"summer coasting hill,"* NY Herald, June 2, 1884.

97 *"for $50,000,"* NY Tribune, April 4, 1901.

97 *"A million rides,"* Elmer Blaney Harris, "The Day of Rest at Coney Island," *Everybody's Magazine* 19, July 1908, 33.

99 *"Many of the evils of society,"* quoted in Cartmell, *The Incredible Scream Machine*, 49.

102 *"One wonders,"* Brooklyn Eagle, May 19, 1907.

102 *"more scenery,"* Brooklyn Eagle, June 14, 1904.

103 *"big shows,"* Brooklyn Eagle, May 19, 1907.

104 *"No real estate specialist,"* "Coney Island: Its Architecture Is the Stuff That People's Dreams Are Made Of," *The Architectural Forum*, August 1947.

## 6. HONKY-TONK

106 *"at the bob end of the beach,"* NY Sun, July 18, 1886.

108 *"most bewildering,"* Julian Ralph, "Coney Island," *Scribner's Magazine*, July 1896.

109 *"madly merry,"* NY Times, August 19, 1897.

109 *"a great girl,"* Brooklyn Eagle, June 29, 1892.

111 *"wicked half-mile,"* Harper's Magazine, May 4, 1901.

111 *"startling and pathetic things,"* Brooklyn Eagle, September 7, 1890.

111 *"street costume,"* Brooklyn Eagle, July 8, 1895.

111 *"seaside resort,"* Brooklyn Eagle, June 10, 1895.

111 *"vast training-school,"* NY World, August 2, 1896.

112 *"At the most vicious,"* NY Tribune, June 30, 1896.

113 *"Divine Providence,"* Brooklyn Eagle, May 27, 1899.

113 *"'masses' love Coney Island,"* Walter Creedmoor, "The Real Coney Island," *Munsey's Magazine* 21, August 1899.

113 *"When I danced,"* NY Herald-Tribune, April 6, 1937.

115 *"into the box,"* William Lindsey Grisham, *Houdini, The Man Who Walked Through Walls* (New York: Holt, 1959), 25.

115 *"I never saw any sin,"* quoted in Rudi Blesh, *Keaton* (New York: Macmillan, 1966), 55.

115 *"not a smash hit,"* George Burns, *I Love Her, That's Why!: An Autobiography* (New York: Simon and Schuster, 1955).

115 *"shanghaied,"* Harpo Marx with Rowland Barber, *Harpo Speaks* (New York: Bernard Geis Associates, 1961), 93.

116 *"Keep the exhibits arty,"* quoted in Oliver Pilat and Jo Ranson, *Sodom by the Sea: An Affectionate History of Coney Island* (Garden City, N.Y.: Doubleday, 1941), 201.

116 *"Sunday school,"* quoted in Pilat and Ranson, *Sodom by the Sea*, 111.

116 *"soup-an'-fish suit,"* Jhan Robbins, *Inka Dinka Doo: The Life of Jimmy Durante* (New York: Paragon House, 1991), 25.

117 *"Bands, orchestras, pianos,"* Elmer Blaney Harris, "The Day of Rest at Coney Island," *Everyman's* 19, July 1908.

118 *Boarding School Girls,* see Lauren Rabinovitz, *For the Love of Pleasure: Women, Culture, and Movies in Turn-of-the-Century Chicago* (New Brunswick, N.J.: Rutgers University Press, 1998), 160–166.

119 *450 moving pictures,* Scientific American, August 15, 1908.

119 *"thousands of girls,"* Julian Ralph, "Coney Island," *Scribner's Magazine*, July 1896.

119 *"real negro,"* Brooklyn Eagle, July 20, 1902.

120 *"most fashionable,"* Beatrice L. Stevenson, "Working Girl's Life at Coney Island," *Yearbook of the Women's Municipal League*, November 1911, 19.

120 *"I have heard,"* Agnes M, "The True Life Story of a Nurse Girl," in *Workers Speak: Self Portraits*, ed. Leon Stein and Philip Taft (New York: Arno, 1971), 104.

121 *"tolerated,"* Djuna Barnes, "The Tingling, Tangling, Tango as 'Tis Tripped at Coney Isle," *Brooklyn Eagle*, August 31, 1913.

121 *"royal pants,"* NY Times, September 23, 1904.

122 *"great day,"* Benita Eisler, *O'Keeffe and Stieglitz: An American Romance* (New York: Nan A. Talese, Doubleday, 1991), 142.

123 *"Plenty of Wine,"* Brooklyn Eagle, September 18, 1906.

123 *"everybody on Coney Island,"* Brooklyn Eagle, September 11, 1909.

123 *"We Won't Go Home 'Till Morning,"* NY Times, September 21, 1908.

## 7. THE NICKEL EMPIRE

125 *"no reason,"* Brooklyn Eagle, January 24, 1915.

127 *"To understand the crowd,"* quoted in Oliver Pilat and Jo Ranson, *Sodom by the Sea: An Affectionate History of Coney Island* (Garden City, N.Y.: Doubleday, 1941), 316.

127 *"vomiting multitudes,"* Federico Garcia Lorca, "Landscape of the Vomiting Multitudes (Coney Island Dusk)," in *Poet in New York* (New York: Grove Press, 1955), 39.

127 *"slum New York,"* Sir Percival Philips, "Coney Island the Incredible," [London] *Daily Mail*, August 19, 1929; cited in Stephanie McGowan, "The Coney Island Experience: A Case Study in Popular Culture and Social Change" (Master's thesis, University of Bremen, 1994), 50.

127 *"bathe in the American Jordan,"* Giuseppe Cautela, "Coney," *The American Mercury,* November 1925.

129 *"paradise of the proletariat,"* NY Times, August 13, 1922.

129 *24 million fares,* Stephen Weinstein, "The Nickel Empire: Coney Island and the Creation of Urban Seaside Resorts in the United States" (Ph.D. diss., Columbia University, 1984), 286.

133 *"human nature,"* Edward F. Tilyou, "Why the School-ma'am Walked into the Sea," *The American Magazine,* July 1922.

134 *"Novelty,"* Reginald Wright Kauffmann, "Why Is Coney?" *Hampton's Magazine,* August 1909.

135 *"primitive tribes,"* quoted in Robert Bogdan, *Freak Show: Presenting Human Oddities for Amusement and Profit* (Chicago: University of Chicago Press, 1988), 198.

136 *"Marat,"* NY Herald-Tribune, March 11, 1928.

139 *"If the truth be known,"* Joseph Mitchell, "Lady Olga," in *McSorley's Wonderful Saloon* (New York: Duell, Sloan, and Pearce, 1943), 103.

140 *"roller coaster tracks coiled,"* "To Heaven by Subway," *Fortune* magazine, August 1938.

140 *"one grand thing,"* Billboard, July 9, 1927.

141 *"gone about as far,"* Elwell Crissey, "New Thrillers Defy Gravity," *Popular Science Monthly,* August 1927.

141 *"nickel was first a symbol,"* "To Heaven by Subway," *Fortune* magazine, August 1938.

143 *"The people come,"* NY Times, August 30, 1936.

144 *"there used to be a time,"* "To Heaven by Subway."

145 *"Thirty-five years ago,"* quoted in Pilat and Ranson, *Sodom by the Sea,* 199.

145 *"We've taken it on the chin,"* NY Times, April 10, 1933.

## 8. EMPIRE OF THE BODY

148 *"To understand the Boardwalk,"* NY Times, August 22, 1937.

149 *"parents shout,"* NY Times, June 3, 1928.

150 *"magic touch,"* The Illustrated American, August 20, 1892.

150 *"Rubens,"* Reginald Marsh, *Magazine of Art,* December 1944.

153 *"We loved the crowd,"* . . . *"I remember all the smells,"* interviews with author.

154 *"Humanity,"* Federal Writers' Project, *The WPA Guide to New York City* (New York: Random House, 1939).

155 *"falsetto roar,"* Brooklyn Eagle, August 10, 1931.

155 *"mingled fragrance,"* NY Times, August 14, 1932.

157 *"Cure Day,"* NY Times, August 16, 1915.

158 *"topless bathing costumes,"* NY Times, June 28, 1933.

158 *"cheapened and commercialized,"* NY Times, March 11, 1934.

158 *"A community which calls itself civilized,"* NY Times, August 21, 1939.

160 *"body punch,"* NY Times, May 31, 1939.

160 *"concentrated distillate,"* "To Heaven by Subway," *Fortune* magazine, August 1938.

161 *"dim-out" regulations,* NY Times Magazine, July 4, 1943.

165 *military air show,* NY Daily Mirror, July 4, 1947.

166 *"No one can get elected,"* Nelson Rockefeller, NY Times, August 3, 1966.

167 *"blessing,"* Joseph Heller, *Now and Then: From Coney Island to Here* (New York: Alfred A. Knopf, 1998), 38.

168 *"Voody,"* Myrna Katz Frommer and Harvey Frommer, *It Happened in Brooklyn* (New York: Harcourt Brace, 1993), 126–127.

168 *"still surprised,"* Isaac Bashevis Singer, "A Day in Coney Island," from *A Crown of Feathers and Other Stories* (New York: Farrar, Straus and Giroux, 1973), 34.

169 *African Americans denied use of Steeplechase pool,* Michael Paul Onorato, "Another Time, Another World: Coney Island Memories" (California State University, Fullerton, Oral History Program, 1988), vii.

169 *Coney's rides and sideshows,* NY Times, October 6, 1949.

169 *"romantic only at night,"* NY Times, July 12, 1958.

169 *"kibosh,"* Onorato, "Another Time, Another World," 9, 13.

169 *"class separating,"* Robert A. Caro, *The Power Broker: Robert Moses and the Fall of New York* (New York: Alfred A. Knopf, 1989), 687.

169 *minority population,* Stephen Weinstein, "The Nickel Empire: Coney Island and the Creation of Urban Seaside Resorts in the United States" (Ph.D. diss., Columbia University, 1984), 291–292.

171 *"Auld Lang Syne,"* Onorato, "Another Time, Another World," xi. The description was provided by his father, Jimmy Onorato, who was Steeplechase's manager for almost four decades.

## 9. THE MERMAID PARADE

172 *Trump handed out bricks,* Michael Paul Onorato, "Another Time, Another World: Coney Island Memories" (California State University, Fullerton, Oral History Program, 1988), 39, 60.

172 *"bad times,"* NY Times, July 5, 1965.

174 *"Eiffel Tower,"* NY Times, October 21, 1977.

174 *"funeral obelisk,"* Joseph Heller, *Now and Then: From Coney Island to Here* (New York: Alfred A. Knopf, 1998), 60.

174 *"old courtesan,"* NY Times, August 9, 1976.

175 *"slothful, bedraggled harridan,"* Mario Puzo, "Meet Me Tonight in Dreamland," *New York Magazine,* September 3, 1979.

175  *"Save the Cyclone,"* Robert Cartmell, *The Incredible Scream Machine: A History of the Roller Coaster* (Fairview, Ohio: Amusement Park Books; Bowling Green, Ohio: Bowling Green State University Press, 1987), 189, 190.

176  *"cash register,"* *NY Times,* August 20, 1983.

177  *"Barnum,"* *NY Times,* July 24, 1995.

183  *"worst and best of times,"* Ron Guerrero, interview with author.

183  *"has to be consistent,"* Dick Zigun, interview with author.

185  *"costumed participants,"* Dick Zigun, interview with author.

187  *"Why do I come back?"* Bobby Reynolds, interview with author.

# INDEX

*Page numbers in italics indicate illustrations or captions.*

**ABOUT THE AUTHOR**

Michael Immerso is a writer, cultural historian, publicist, and social activist.
A native of Newark, New Jersey, he has worked in collaboration
with many of New Jersey's leading cultural and educational institutions
as a curator and designer of cultural programs.
He is the author of *Newark's Little Italy: The Vanished First Ward,*
published by Rutgers University Press, and co-producer
of a documentary film based upon the book.
Throughout the 1980s, he was active both locally and nationally
as a leader of the nuclear freeze movement.
He occasionally serves as a media consultant
for nonprofit organizations.